*Coniugi dilectae Iaquelinae opusculum hoc memetque redd. red. red.*

D

# Electronic Business

**Books are to be returned on or before
the last date below.**

## The British Computer Society

BCS is the leading professional body for the IT industry. With members in over 100 countries, the BCS is the professional and learned Society in the field of computers and information systems.

The BCS is responsible for setting standards for the IT profession. It is also leading the change in public perception and appreciation of the economic and social importance of professionally managed IT projects and programmes. In this capacity, the Society advises, informs and persuades industry and government on successful IT implementation.

IT is affecting every part of our lives and that is why the BCS is determined to promote IT as the profession of the 21st century.

### *Joining BCS*

BCS qualifications, products and services are designed with your career plans in mind. We not only provide essential recognition through professional qualifications but also offer many other useful benefits to our members at every level.

BCS Membership demonstrates your commitment to professional development. It helps to set you apart from other IT practitioners and provides industry recognition of your skills and experience. Employers and customers increasingly require proof of professional qualifications and competence. Professional membership confirms your competence and integrity and sets an independent standard that people can trust. Professional Membership (MBCS) is the pathway to Chartered IT Professional (CITP) Status.

www.bcs.org/membership

### *Further Information*

Further information about BCS can be obtained from: BCS, First Floor, Block D, North Star House, North Star Avenue, Swindon, SN2 1FA, UK.

Telephone: 0845 300 4417 (UK only) or + 44 (0)1793 417 424 (overseas)

www.bcs.org/contact

# Electronic Business

Geoffrey Sampson

The British Computer Society
Publishing and Information Products
First Floor, Block D
North Star House
North Star Avenue
Swindon
SN2 1FA
UK

www.bcs.org

ISBN 978-1-902505-89-3

British Cataloguing in Publication Data.
A CIP catalogue record for this book is available at the British Library.

Typeset by Lapiz Digital Services, Chennai, India.
Printed at CPI Antony Rowe Ltd, Chippenham, UK.

# Contents

Contents

# About the author

**Geoffrey Sampson** is a professor in the Informatics Department of Sussex University, where he teaches e-business. He was educated at Cambridge and Yale Universities. Before moving to Sussex in 1991 Sampson had taught at the London School of Economics and at Lancaster and Leeds Universities; at Leeds he held the chair of linguistics. Sampson has spent secondments at the Royal Signals and Radar Establishment (now Qinetiq), at the British Telecom Research Labs, and at the universities of Geneva and Cape Town.

Sampson's side interests include Chinese philology; his book *Love Songs of Early China* appeared in 2006.

Sampson has been a Member of the British Computer Society since 1988. His website is at www.grsampson.net.

# Acknowledgements

I thank Elsevier Science Limited for allowing me to re-use material from the first edition of this book; and the Sussex University Department of Informatics, for granting me a period of sabbatical leave to write the present edition.

I am very grateful to the many colleagues, friends, correspondents and students who have helped me in compiling one or both editions with information and advice; I would mention by name Billie Andersen, Andy Balaam, Margaret Boden, Bruce Boughton, David Boyce, Lee Braine, John Carroll, Tony Dalton-Richards, Benjamin Dives, Felicity Falconer, Gerald Gazdar, Jo Haslam, Andy Holyer, Denis Johnston, Li Ruizhi, Rudi Lutz, Huw McCarthy, Jan Metzger, Aaron Moss, A.L. Peel, Sophia Peterson, Stephen Sampson, Andrew Spratley and Kevin Tansley. I ask anyone whose name has been overlooked to excuse me.

I thank Mike Cotterell for producing artwork for the figures in Chapter 2, and VNU Business Publications for supplying the newspapers *Computing* and *IT Week*.

# Abbreviations

| | |
|---|---|
| APS | advanced planning and scheduling |
| ASP | application service provider |
| B2B | business to business |
| B2C | business to consumer |
| B2G | business to government |
| BI | business intelligence |
| BPM | business performance management *or* business process management |
| BPR | business process re-engineering |
| C2C | consumer to consumer |
| CITP | Chartered Information Technology Professional |
| CPA | cost per action |
| CPM | cost per mille |
| CPU | central processing unit |
| CRM | customer relationship management |
| EDI | electronic data interchange |
| ERP | enterprise resource planning |
| GBF | Get Big Fast |
| GPL | General Public Licence |
| HTML | hypertext markup language |
| HTTP | hypertext transmission protocol |
| IISP | Institute for Information Security Professionals |
| ISO | International Organization for Standardization |
| ISP | internet service provider |
| IT | information technology |
| JIT | just in time |

| | |
|---|---|
| M&A | mergers and acquisitions |
| MBC | meaning-based computing |
| MiFID | Markets in Financial Instruments Directive |
| MMO | massively multi-player online role-playing game |
| ODF | OpenDocument Format |
| OSDL | Open Source Development Labs |
| PC | Personal Computer |
| PDA | personal digital assistant |
| PDF | Portable Document Format |
| PIP | partner interface process |
| PKI | public key infrastructure |
| PR | public relations |
| RFID | radio frequency identification |
| ROI | return on investment |
| SaaS | software as a service |
| SCM | supply chain management |
| SEO | search engine optimisation |
| SOA | service-oriented architecture |
| Sox | Sarbanes–Oxley Act |
| TCO | total cost of ownership |
| UDDI | Universal Description, Discovery and Integration |
| URL | universal resource locator |
| VC | venture capitalist |
| VoIP | voice over internet protocol |
| W3C | World Wide Web Consortium |
| WAN | wide area network |
| WSDL | Web Service Description Language |
| XML | eXtensible Markup Language |
| Y2K | year 2000 |

# Preface

This book is an enlarged and updated edition of one published in 2004 under the title *e.biz: The Anatomy of Electronic Business.*

The e-business field is so fast-moving that many topics covered at some length here were not mentioned in the original edition. The new edition is longer than its predecessor; nevertheless, to make room for important new topics it was necessary to omit two chapters on less central subjects. These are website design, and the impact of IT on smaller firms (Chapters 11 and 13 of the first edition). Computing degree courses typically include plenty of material on website design, so that it is not necessary to squeeze a brief treatment into a book about e-business. (The references I would recommend are Morville and Rosenfeld (2006) and Niederst Robbins (2006).) Although there are still special problems for small firms in coming to terms with the new technology (and the subject is discussed in this edition), technical developments such as the emergence of software as a service mean that these problems are no longer acute enough to merit a full chapter devoted to them.

Two points of terminology should be mentioned.

People who hear the term *e-business* sometimes ask 'Is that the same as e-commerce?' It is broader. *Commerce* refers to the trading activities that take place at the interfaces between company and company or company and individuals. *Business* includes commerce, and it also includes all the internal activities that enable a company to transform its inputs into its outputs. Information technology – 'IT' for short – is bringing about large changes in both these areas, and both are covered in this book. When I use the term 'e-commerce', this will refer strictly to trading across organisation boundaries.

It is often useful to contrast e-business with business as it was conducted before information technology introduced new business techniques. I call the latter *conventional* business, as in 'conventional warfare'. Much successful business today is conventional in this sense.

At the publisher's request, I have avoided using pronouns in ways that suggest that participants in e-business are always male, though the resulting turns of phrase are sometimes clumsy.

References to sources occur in two forms. When a quotation is taken from an ephemeral news report, for the sake of accountability the source is identified briefly in a footnote. In the case of publications with more lasting significance, citations in Harvard style – e.g. Smith (2005) – link to the detailed reference list beginning on p. 245.

Many items cited are available online. Search engines have become so efficient that it does not seem worthwhile to specify URLs here other than in a few special cases. Where URLs are quoted, the prefix http:// is understood.

*Sussex, August 2007*

# 1 Introduction

## SCOPE AND ASSUMPTIONS

This book is written to help computing students understand how their expertise is changing the nature of business.

This is a new topic. Businesses have used computers for decades. But, for most of that time, they were using the machines mainly to execute, more cheaply and/or quickly, the same processes that were previously carried out manually. Now, computers are often changing the content of what businesses are doing. Although there were isolated earlier cases, it is only for about 10 years that this has been true to any great extent.

Most books about e-business are written for managers who know about business and economics but are mystified by the new technology. This book is written mainly for readers, like my own students, who are at ease with the technical side of computing but may never have had occasion to think about business issues. I hope that businesspeople who come across the book may find it enlightening and helpful, but there is certainly material here that, to them, will seem too obvious to spell out. To computing students, basic economic or business concepts are not always self-evident. There is no reason why they should be.

Technical IT details will be avoided wherever possible in this book. Computing students study them in other contexts. Other readers will often prefer not to learn about them at all.

The book will look at developments worldwide, but its perspective will be centred on Britain and Europe. Unlike most computing topics, in e-business geography matters. And, for e-business, the UK happens to be a supremely significant market. By 2004 Britain had overtaken the USA to become the world leader in terms of the proportion of retail sales taking place online. Tesco.com is the world's largest online supermarket, and is seen overseas as a model of innovation and business success. Britain has a higher proportion of households with broadband (47 per cent in 2006) than the USA (44 per cent) or Germany (33 per cent). The proportion of total advertising spending going to internet advertising in Britain is slightly higher and growing faster than in the USA (and it is far higher than the world average).

In a book about e-business, there is nothing parochial about a British perspective.

## BUBBLE AND REALITY

Now is a good time to write this kind of book. For several years, the topic of e-business was under a cloud, as a reaction to the crazy overexcitement of the dotcom bubble period in the late 1990s – which ended in tears when the bubble burst in 2000 and many startup companies went bust. In the immediately following years, any mention of e-commerce or e-business aroused instant scepticism. But e-business activity continued, and by about 2006 the public was beginning to notice that at last it was really working. The broadcaster Rory Cellan-Jones chronicled the collapse of the dotcom bubble in his 2001 book *Dot.bomb*; by May 2007 he was commenting 'this time the internet companies are making money, not promises... The internet revolution that was promised in 1999 has arrived'.[1]

At the end of the 1990s, the e-business atmosphere was irrational to an extent that is hard to credit, looking back. Investors were baffled by computer technology but were convinced that, somehow, there was a mass of profit to be made from the internet; in consequence, they were throwing a wall of money at anyone who came up with an e-commerce idea.

Daniel Levine asked the venture capitalist (VC) Guy Kawasaki about that mad time:

'There's a sense today that a few years ago all you had to do was sit down for a cup of coffee with a VC, jot down a business plan on the back of an envelope and you could walk out with a check for $30 million. Is that a myth?' [Kawasaki:] 'Well, it wasn't that easy. You also had to boot PowerPoint, but that's it. [laughs] ... Much of that myth is true.'[2]

When the bubble burst and new-technology companies collapsed or saw their share prices fall to fractions of earlier values, some people concluded that e-business was a delusion. But the mere fact of numerous bankruptcies tells us nothing about the future of e-business: such things are usual with disruptive economic innovations. As David Manasian (2003) wrote:

In the 1870s America's railroad industry boomed in much the same way as the world's telecoms industry in the late 1990s, only to collapse in a similar heap of bankruptcies... A few years later ... [railways] revived, changing American business for ever... In the first few years of the 20th century there were thousands of people tinkering with carmaking, most of whom went bust. A decade later only a handful survived, but the car was about to become the icon of progress.

## E-BUSINESS RECOVERS

By now, not only is the technology moving ahead, but share prices of technology companies have in many cases become healthy again.

[1] Rory Cellan-Jones, 'Still waiting for the dotcom revolution', *Daily Telegraph* 9 May 2007.
[2] 'One-on-one with Guy Kawasaki, CEO, Garage Technology Ventures', *San Francisco Business Times* 29 March 2002.

Already in 2004, the sober and penetrating *Economist* magazine was reporting that

> ... the wild predictions made at the height of the [dotcom] boom – namely, that vast chunks of the world economy would move into cyberspace – are, in one way or another, coming true.[3]

Figure 1.1 displays the growth of total UK online spending over the past 10 years. The trend is rising, at an increasingly rapid rate. (Note that there is no sign of the pace having slackened around 2000–1, when post-bubble gloom was deepest.) In January 2008 it was reported that online spending accounted for 15 per cent of total UK retail spending in the year just ended, up by more than 50 per cent over the previous year. For spending by businesses, the 2007 online proportion was 27 per cent. 'For the first time ever, money spent by UK shoppers on the web eclipsed the turnover of Tesco.'[4]

## UK online spending, £bn

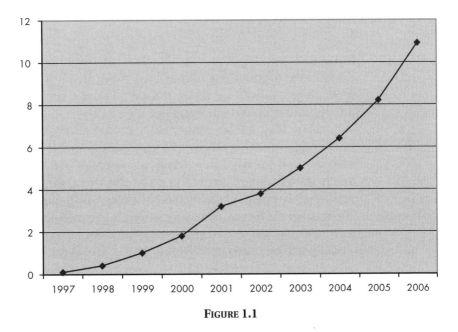

FIGURE 1.1

Conventional retailers are beginning to suffer from online competition. In 2005, British retailers worth £3 billion went bankrupt; the analyst Nick Gladding believed that competition from e-commerce was a significant factor in a third of cases.

---

[3] Paul Markillie, 'A perfect market', *The Economist* 15 May 2004.
[4] James Hall, 'Businesses coin it as net sales rise 50pc', *Daily Telegraph* 18 January 2008.

The Swiss food and drinks firm Nestlé had some 'unique' features that were seen as so crucial to company culture that they were published to staff as things that would not be changed when a new chief executive arrived in 1997. One was that 'IT would not play much of a role in the day-to-day running of the firm – Nestlé's focus on its people, products and brands would continue to be far more influential.'[5] But by 2004 the need to remain competitive forced Nestlé to abandon this sacred cow. It partnered with the German software company SAP in an ambitious attempt to boost operating efficiency by shifting activities on to an electronic 'resource planning' platform.

Ten years ago, companies' annual reports to shareholders contained little or nothing about their use of IT, partly because that was seen as sensitive information that ought not to be revealed to competitors, but partly also because few shareholders would have understood or cared. Now, shareholders in leading companies are demanding to know that their organisations are making the most of enterprise IT. (Confidentiality is becoming less important, because it often appears that competing firms all gain more from common computing infrastructures than any single firm can gain by going it alone electronically.)

## THE IMPORTANCE OF OPINION

Now that the exaggerated enthusiasm of the bubble period, and the exaggerated negative reaction that followed, are both in the past, it might seem futile to dwell on them. But they make a good illustration of the importance of opinion in business.

In technology, all that matters is what objectively is the case. If people think that something works differently from how it actually does work, then too bad for what they think. In business, opinion matters fully as much as objective realities. The *value* of a thing, for instance, is nothing other than what people think it is – the benefits that they currently expect it to yield in the future. The expectations may prove quite wrong, but there is no alternative, 'objective' measure of value. Yet, without value, there would be no business.

## A LEARNING PROCESS

As I write, we are not yet 14 years from commercialisation of the internet. (Some legal constraints on acceptable internet use were relaxed in 1990, but significant commercial exploitation began only in late 1993–early 1994.) For the business world, those years have been an intense learning experience. All business life is a process of discovery, as managers try out ideas about how to become or remain profitable in the face of ever-changing

---

[5] 'Daring, defying, to grow', *The Economist* 7 August 2004.

economic conditions, customer requirements, initiatives by competitors and so forth, and the customers' responses show whether the ideas are good or bad. But the internet – and IT in general – is such a large-scale break from the past that the experimentation process has been unusually challenging. Some assumptions that seemed obviously correct, in the early years of e-commerce, have turned out to be just wrong. Only now are we reaching a phase where some central questions about e-business have been answered fairly solidly, and the continuing learning process may perhaps begin to feel more like 'normal' business life.

As one clear example of this learning process, consider website design. In the early years of e-commerce, it was an accepted truism that the success of a website was tied closely to its aesthetics. A website should make a powerful visual impact. Depending on what type of business it served, it should be exciting, or graceful, or impressive – but certainly not just bland. The man who rapidly became recognised as the leading authority on website design was David Siegel – his book *Creating Killer Web Sites* became the best-selling single title (on any subject) on online bookshops after the first edition came out in 1996, and was translated into 10 languages. Siegel offered all kinds of tips for giving websites a 'wow!' factor. He urged web designers to 'turn a site from a menu into a meal'. He wrote: 'Web pages will sing, they will dance, they will be alive with movement.' At a period when few home users had broadband connections, sites designed according to Siegel's principles were often very slow to load, but that just did not seem important relative to aesthetic considerations. This was not irrational: many business experts believed that the value of websites lay in creating brand images, rather than scoring high on search-engine rankings or actually selling goods.

But it turned out that users did not merely treat findability, efficiency and convenience as higher priorities than aesthetics; they often actively disliked sites that prioritised aesthetic considerations. In an interview with Siegel in 1998, the *Sydney Morning Herald* commented:

> Take Discovery Channel Online, which once boasted one of the Web's most elegant opening pages. The site has returned to a more conventional and less exciting scrollable table of contents. Most lovers of Web design would deplore the change. But as Siegel notes, Discovery carefully tests all elements of its site with its users – and the less beautiful site tested much better.[6]

Siegel told the *Herald*: 'I am not trying to win any design awards for my clients any more.' We have discovered that e-business websites are about fitness for purpose – not art.

---

[6] 'Why Mr Web Design changed direction', Siegel98.notlong.com.

The most respected web design guru of the present day is Jakob Nielsen, who emphasises *usability* rather than aesthetics. In 2003 Nielsen recalled that, up to 1999, usability advocates were 'roundly booed at internet conferences and ignored by the prevalent "killer design" agencies'.[7] As a result, e-commerce sites often failed to achieve business benefits. After the turn of the century the consensus changed, but according to Nielsen:

> ... the damage done during the early years was so bad that four years of progress have been insufficient to bring us to an acceptable level. Basically, the first 10 years of commercial web sites were a lost decade with very few designs that truly worked for customers.

This is just one clear and striking example of how we have gradually been learning how business can exploit the possibilities created by IT, through experimenting and seeing what works and what does not work. We shall never stop learning. But we have come through the early growing pains. Dimly, we may now be able to discern the outline of longer-term trends.

## B2C, B2B, B2G

People who talk about 'dotcoms' usually mean companies that sell to the public – although the URL .com domain is not restricted to retailers. Figure 1.1 showed that e-business activity in this business-to-consumer (B2C) area is on a strongly growing trend. But B2C sales – *e-tailing* – are only one part of the picture.

When the World Wide Web first arrived, B2C was where the excitement lay. Partly, this was because the directness of communication between individual customers and retailers was genuinely the thing about the web that represented its biggest single innovation from a business point of view. Largely, though, it was for the more superficial reason that B2C commerce is the aspect of business that is directly visible to journalists and other opinion-formers.

Any business is an operation that takes in various goods and services as inputs, and turns them into (normally more valuable) goods and/or services as outputs. Things bought by consumers represent the ends of long *value chains* that trace back ultimately to unprocessed raw materials; normally, many companies will have played successive parts in the process by which raw materials are turned into consumer goods. B2C trading is the very last step in the series of transactions that get a good or a service to a consumer, and it is preceded by a long series of business-to-business (B2B) transactions. One American estimate puts total B2B market size at 10 times the size of the B2C market.

---

[7] Nielsen quotations taken from David Neal, 'Good design pays off', *IT Week* 19 May 2003.

B2B trading via the internet never became the stuff of a media feeding frenzy, as e-tailing was; but the evidence seems to be that B2B is actually a more important aspect of e-business, not merely in terms of helping buyers and sellers to find each other but also in terms of allowing established business relationships to function more efficiently. The value of online B2B sales in Britain in 2004 was three times online B2C sales, and growing faster.

Some people distinguish a further category of business-to-government (B2G) trading – trading where government is the customer has features distinguishing it from both retailing and selling to private-sector organisations. Governments, at the national and local level, have recently been among the principal forces driving e-business forward.

## BUSINESS PROCESS RE-ENGINEERING

The impact of IT is not limited to the interactions between companies and other companies or individuals – *e-commerce*. It is also affecting the internal processes by which companies do their work of transforming inputs into outputs. *Business process re-engineering* (BPR) has been a management buzzword for some years, and often it refers to reorganising business operations in ways that are not related to computing in particular. But one important area of BPR involves using IT to run businesses in ways that would not have been possible with manual methods: that is how the term BPR will be used in this book.

(For the difference between 'commerce' and 'business', see the preface.)

Thomas Malone (2004) describes how British Petroleum (BP) addressed a need to reduce its total greenhouse-gas emissions by 10 per cent over the 12 years from 1998. Discovering a pattern of modifications to the company's existing manufacturing operations that would enable that target to be met, while minimising any adverse consequences for the company's costs or productivity, was itself work that BP needed to execute – purely internal, managerial work, but very important work.

Conventionally, senior managers would have set target emission reductions for each of BP's many business units, and then adjusted the targets through a cumbersome, time-consuming (and hence expensive) process of bargaining, as unit managers argued that their particular targets were unrealistic. Instead, the company simply issued managers with permits to emit so many tons of carbon dioxide or equivalent annually (with the total number of permits matching the reduced goal), and let the managers trade the permits with one another via a company-wide electronic trading system. A unit that saw an easy way to reduce its emissions would sell its excess permits to a unit that needed a larger allocation. The result was that BP accomplished the task of adjusting its operations very rapidly (the overall 10 per cent emission reduction was achieved in 2001, nine years early), saving a large amount of managerial work via a technique that would not have been feasible without IT.

This is just one example of how IT is now allowing businesses to run their internal operations in ways that were not possible before. Business process re-engineering is not about permit-trading in particular, but about all kinds of ways in which computers are changing the nature of firms' internal activities.

Business process re-engineering is even less publicly visible than B2B e-trading, let alone B2C e-tailing; and because BPR is not about things being sold, there is no straightforward way to quantify it and measure year-on-year change as one can with B2B and B2C e-commerce. Furthermore, IT-based BPR tended to develop a little later than e-commerce. But many observers suggest that of these three aspects of e-business – B2C, B2B and BPR – the most significant of all may be BPR.

## ABANDONING PRECONCEPTIONS

E-business is a topic that contrasts in flavour with the typical computing student's intellectual background, and it will be as well to spell out some of these differences. This will involve an element of caricature in portraying the 'default' computing student; not all students in this field are alike, any more than students in other fields are alike. Still, there are traits that are relatively common among students of this subject, and they can make it difficult for computer scientists to come to terms with thinking about e-business.

So, to a rough approximation:

*Computer science is 20 year olds in T-shirts.* Even after they move on from graduation into employment, computer people tend to retain the informality of youth. People involved directly with computer technology are usually young, whether because the work requires a mental agility that fades in later life or simply because the systems themselves are new. But an e-commerce startup requires investors – bankers in suits; and a company-internal e-business initiative needs backing by senior managers – suits again. And any business ultimately survives by serving consumers (either directly, in the case of a retailer, or via value chains down which its own output is ultimately transformed into consumer goods or services); consumers come in all ages, so on average they are middle-aged. The tastes and outlooks of people much older than themselves loom larger in connection with e-business than they do elsewhere in a computing undergraduate's studies.

*Computer science is 'You've been doing the same things for ever, but now our computers are going to change everything!'* Computers have caused what is probably the biggest single change in working methods of the past 100 years, but this can lead computing people to imagine that IT is the *only* important thing to have happened. Grant Norris and colleagues (2000: 119) commented:

For many large, global companies, becoming an e-business is the fourth or fifth major organizational change they have undergone since the early 1980s. Many companies have gone through one or more rounds of business process reengineering (BPR); installation and major upgrades of an ERP system; upgrading legacy systems to be Y2K compliant; creating shared service centers; implementing just-in-time (JIT) manufacturing; automating the sales force; contract manufacturing; and the major challenges related to the introduction of the Euro currency.

Some of these developments, such as enterprise resource planning (ERP; see Chapter 8) are themselves IT-based, but others, for instance just-in-time (JIT) manufacturing, have little or nothing to do with computers. (Manufacturing businesses traditionally held large inventories of products so that they could fill orders that arrived unpredictably, but inventory represents capital tied up unproductively. The trend towards JIT has involved developing methods for predicting demand so that goods can be manufactured as needed and not before.) Part of learning about e-business is learning to allot IT its proper place, important but not overwhelmingly dominant, within the wider scheme of things.

*In computer science, technology is king.* Computing students study many topics, but it is tacitly understood that the techie stuff is what really counts. The students most admired by their peers are the technical gurus. E-business uses technology, but the technical details are not what matters. To quote Grant Norris *et al.* (2000: 137) again, they describe the first 'large truth' about e-business thus: 'E-business is about strategy; it is not about technology.'

Charlie Feld and Donna Stoddard (2004), discussing how business can get the best out of IT, put it this way: 'Making IT work has little to do with technology itself.' This point cannot be emphasised enough. The interesting, difficult issues in e-business are how to move businesses forward with the help of the new technology. Somebody needs to know the technical details, but most people involved with e-business, most of the time, can take those details as read – they will rarely be what decides the success or failure of an e-business initiative.

E-business is business that happens to use IT. It is not a branch of IT that happens to be applied to business.

*Computer science is statements such as 'Arrays in C start at zero rather than one'* – truths that must be learned and accepted, with no room for debate or doubt. Business is the opposite; like war, business is guesswork in a fog. Running a business is a matter of trying out best guesses about how to manage available resources so as to squeeze out most value from them in an unpredictable environment. The guesses often prove wrong.

If people could know for sure the consequences of alternative managerial decisions, the activity we call 'business' would scarcely exist. All society would need would be a static administrative activity to oversee the fixed processes by which consumers would be optimally served. In real life, business is what the economist Joseph Schumpeter ([1943] 1976: 83) famously called a 'process of Creative Destruction'. Existing organisations and ways of doing things are for ever being swept aside through the discovery of more efficient methods, or things that are more worth doing. Bankruptcies are an especially dramatic case, but on a less dramatic scale this happens constantly as processes are reorganised within companies that continue to survive.

To quote the most highly respected management guru of the twentieth century, Peter Drucker ([1992] 1998: 114):

> Society, community, and family are all conserving institutions...
> [A business on the other hand] must be organized for the systematic
> abandonment of whatever is established, customary, familiar, and
> comfortable ....

IT has its analogue. Anyone who spends many years in the computing world gets used to painfully learned mastery of particular programming languages, operating systems and so forth being made obsolete by newer replacements. But within any one technical system, all questions typically have cut and dried answers. This can make it frustrating for computing students to read discussions of e-business that say things like 'arguably, $x$' or 'many people think $y$'. It can seem as though the writer has not done their job properly: 'Don't tell us what *might* be so; tell us what *is* so.' When discussing business, that is often impossible. A writer who pretended that things were more certain than they are would be not a good teacher but a poor one.

## AMBIGUITY, SECRECY AND UNPREDICTABILITY

It is not even as though everybody wants to identify the facts clearly. In academic life, to a rough approximation everybody does want that – the motto of many universities is *patet omnibus veritas*, 'truth lies open to all'. In business, people are trying to sell things, and when the things are as complicated as enterprise software systems, plenty of people have a motive for cultivating vagueness. A new buzzword or phrase comes along and is attached to a range of loosely defined ideas, some of which appear to offer the tantalising prospect of revolutionary advances. Provided the definition is loose enough, a vendor can stretch the buzzword to cover a new software product that serves a narrower, non-revolutionary function, and customers may be attracted via the woolly link with the broader prospect.

To a student, this kind of thing is infuriating. But it is how the real world is, and the student of e-business has to accept that.

Another problem about studying any aspect of business is that many facts in business life are secret. For present purposes, though, that problem is less severe than it might seem. The City and Wall Street contain numerous *analysts* – business experts who make their living by compiling data and predictions about company activities and performance; part of an analyst's job is to draw inferences about areas that companies might prefer not to discuss. At the level of an introductory textbook, commercial confidentiality is not really a problem.

Understanding where we are now is one thing; predicting where we shall be going next is another matter. It would be natural for computing students to imagine that although they do not know what is going to happen in e-business in a few years' time, business experts do know. That is not the case.

What the business experts have, and computing students typically do not have, is a framework of concepts that they can use as tools to make sense of what is going on, as the future unrolls into the present. Instead of seeing the business world as just a blooming, buzzing confusion, someone knowledgeable about business can pin categories on phenomena and make generalisations, and this may allow educated guesses about the way things will go next. It is that conceptual framework that this book aims to offer to the reader.

## USER-CENTRED VERSUS SUPPLIER-DRIVEN

If the study of e-business has this alien and, for some computing students, perhaps uncongenial quality, why would they want to study it?

One answer is that this topic may be very different from core computing subjects, but it is actually rather interesting. The most persuasive answer, though, may be that computing students need to study e-business if they want to be employable.

For most of the half-century that IT has played an economic role, that role was supplier-driven. Managers had little detailed understanding of what the technology could do for them but sensed that the potential was large, so the technologists could develop hardware and software with reasonable confidence that, if they marketed it, they would find customers: 'Build it and they will come.' The default job for a computing graduate was one in which he or she deployed mainly technical skills.

Since the turn of the century, jobs like that have been melting away – although this development is new enough that even computing teachers have not always noticed it.

One reason is that, where purely techie jobs do still exist, often they have moved offshore, to Eastern Europe or to India. It is not that IT work as a whole is leaching away overseas – far from it. At present the UK is running a multi-billion surplus in IT services trade with the rest of the world (i.e. they are buying far more from us than we are from them). But the career paths available in Britain increasingly involve much more than mere coding.

A second reason is that the rise of the *software-as-a-service* and *web services* models of enterprise computing (to be examined in Chapters 6 and 12) means that the economy nowadays has less total demand for code development and maintenance than before.

But the most important reason is that 50-odd years of improvements in hardware and algorithms have led to a situation where computer power is now more than sufficient for most practical applications. What business needs now is people who can think about how to bring the technology to bear on real problems – not people who only want to think about the technology itself. Quoting Bruce Harreld, IBM's senior vice-president of strategy:

> As applications have become more sophisticated, there is a greater need now to know how to apply the technology to retain competitive edge. It used to be 80 per cent about technology; now it's 80 per cent about the quality of how it is used.[8]

Senior managers have ceased to be people who are so baffled by the new technology that they can only give techies their head and hope for the best. By now, they have acquired the savvy and confidence to apply normal management disciplines to IT along with other company operations. Discussing a case study of Delta Air Lines, Feld and Stoddard (2004) comment:

> In doing the hot, sweaty work of simplifying its systems and aligning IT with the company's overarching business goals, Delta's senior managers also learned to trust their instincts. They learned that the same business skills that allowed them to see what was wrong with the company's fleet of aircraft could also guide them in managing Delta's armada of technology platforms.

Managers in general have been learning this lesson.

Joseph Langhauser of General Motors spoke for many when he told a conference on the future of computing in 2003 that IT tools had proliferated faster than companies can exploit them: 'We don't need any more IT… We need to figure out the business processes we have.'[9] When Intel released its 64-bit Itanium-2 chip in 2002 and marketed it for business computing, it was nicknamed 'Itanic' because people were sceptical that business

---

[8] Quoted by Brian Glick, 'The next era of IT will be based upon integration', *Computing* 26 June 2003.
[9] Quoted by Tony Kontzer, 'A harsh assessment of IT from Peter Drucker', *InformationWeek* 12 February 2003.

needed the extra power of 64-bit technology. A survey of UK company IT department heads in 2004 found that their top priority was business integration – getting various software systems to work with one another and to support the company's business activities coherently – and that the very last thing they were concerned about was keeping abreast of new technical developments.

Twenty years ago, advances in computer technology were driven by business needs. Today, cutting-edge technology is driven by consumer electronics (e.g. ever better multimedia for gamers), but what business is looking for is better ways to apply existing technology to its practical problems.

## THE NEED FOR SOFT SKILLS

Over the past few years there has been a chorus of calls from industry for computing students to modify their balance of interests, not abandoning 'hard', techie skills but understanding the need to complement them with the 'soft' skills needed in management – people skills, communication skills and business understanding. In 2000, only 15 per cent of IT job advertisements mentioned management skills; five years later that figure had risen to 40 per cent. A weighty 2007 report by Microsoft on prospects for British IT (which it sees as bright) finds that:

> The balance of soft and hard skills is becoming more critical, with soft skills for IT graduates being of more importance than other [technical] disciplines... The 'traditional' Computer Science degree with its emphasis on purely technical skills will not be enough on its own to meet the needs of the IT industry …
>
> (Microsoft 2007: 49)

Many other sources have been filling in the details. In a survey of British IT managers and directors in May 2005, four out of five said that the most important step for company competitiveness is to equip IT staff with comprehensive business skills. The technology journalist Linda More stresses the need for people skills:

> … technology staff are no longer able to hide away in the background – they are expected to be seen and heard. Therefore, the growing requirement is for softer, customer-facing skills along with good communication and presentation abilities.[10]

---

[10] 'Sign of the times', *Computing* 12 April 2007.

Corinne Dauncey, marketing manager of the specialist employment agency Tip Top Job, makes similar points from the job-search perspective:

> Not only do IT professionals need knowledge and experience, but it is important that they are articulate and commercially astute. Technology and business skills are going to become as important as each other.[11]

Part of that astuteness is as straightforward as grasping that professional colleagues expect communications to be expressed in literate English, avoiding jargon. Mark Samuels says:

> Take note, then, IT candidates. Your future is likely to involve a subtle mix of technology and business… Understand what business requires and communicate your resolution in English, rather than machine code.[12]

Many IT employers these days are happy to recruit graduates with non-computing degrees, for the sake of the business and other soft skills where they are often strong – a 2007 survey of British IT managers found that more than half of them do not see computing degrees as essential. So students who have chosen computing as a degree subject surely owe it to themselves to ensure that they can offer at least a modicum of these complementary abilities and knowledge.

## A PROFESSIONAL BASIS

One short textbook cannot achieve all of these things. People skills are outside its purview. What this book does aim to do is to provide a basic business foundation – to give the reader coming from a computing background a sense of what business is and how it works, and an awareness of some of the trends, the technical possibilities and the IT systems that are changing business now and that seem likely to matter in the future. It gives readers the vocabulary and the concepts they need to hit the ground running, when they first become players on the e-business stage.

In case readers are daunted by the above analysis of how the IT job market is changing, it is worth pointing out that there is an upside as well as a downside. While computing was a purely technical domain, business (and government) kept IT experts 'on tap, but not on top' – they stayed behind the scenes, and their status in their organisations was low.

---

[11] Quoted by Linda More (see previous note).
[12] Mark Samuels, 'What on earth does it all meme?', *Computing* 30 June 2005.

Now that they are expected to contribute creatively to business developments, they are beginning to receive the respect due to professionals. Eric Woods of the consultancy Ovum commented about public sector IT in January 2007 that 'It is getting to the point where the IT profession is taken with the same seriousness as any other in government'[13] – which could not have been said 10 years ago; comparable developments are occurring in the private sector.

Many graduates might feel that cultivation of a broader skills base is a price worth paying for the possibility of attaining levels of career status that were not available to IT specialists in the past. And it is scarcely a 'price'. In the long run, wider horizons make for a more fulfilling working life.

## E-BUSINESS IS BUSINESS

I said, above, that e-business is business that happens to use IT. Since e-business is business, longstanding principles that apply to other aspects of business apply equally to it.

That axiom went temporarily out of fashion during the dotcom bubble. For a short while people believed that the internet had changed all the rules. The *Wall Street Journal* celebrated New Year's Day, 2000, with a special edition on the new economy, in which its Washington economics editor Thomas Petzinger announced the abolition of the laws of supply and demand, and the Santa Fe Institute economics professor W. Brian Arthur asserted that earnings were no longer a requirement for a successful company: 'If everyone thinks you're doing fine without earnings, why have them?'

Not many weeks later came the crash, and since then it has been hard to grasp how people could have said such things. The only rational justification for investing is expectation of future profit – earnings in excess of expenditure. As Stan Liebowitz puts it:

> In fact, the internet changes very few of the tried-and-true business strategies. Like other important technological advances, the internet will change many aspects of our lives. But the economic and business rules that worked in previous regimes will largely continue to work in the new regime... It is just our hubris at work when we start to think that our technology can change forces that are not of our conscious creation.
>
> (Liebowitz 2002: 1)

---

[13] Quoted by Sarah Arnott, 'Commitment crucial for public sector IT', *Computing* 18 January 2007.

Nitin Nohria *et al.* (2003) carried out a research project comparing samples of American companies that had been consistently successful over a 10-year period with others (companies that had been unsuccessful throughout the period, and companies that had moved between success and the opposite), in order to identify just which management strategies 'really work'. It seems an obvious question to ask, but it had never been studied in such detail before. Referring to two major enterprise software genres (which we shall be examining in detail in later chapters), they say:

> We learned, for example, that it doesn't really matter if you implement ERP software or a CRM system: it matters very much, though, that whatever technology you choose to implement you execute it flawlessly.

This might suggest that IT is fairly dispensable from a business point of view: use it if you like, but you can get along well enough without it. However, when the UK Department of Trade and Industry (as it then was) published its annual 'Value Added Scoreboard' in July 2006, it found that companies known for IT investment tended to be the ones that produced most output value per pound of input cost. And research published by the Hackett Group (a business advisory firm) in 2006 found a strong tendency for companies that are 'world class' in other respects also to have world-class IT departments.

Taking the various findings together, the most judicious conclusion seems to be that, yes, IT is indeed important to business – but what is *really* important is running the business well. Running one's business technology well is just part of that.

# 2 IT and the Structure of the Economy

## THE MOVE TO OUTSOURCING

IT is not just changing the nature of goods and services, and the methods used to produce and sell them. It is also changing the pattern of organisations doing the producing and selling. Companies seem to be getting smaller – Adam Wishart and Regula Bochsler (2002: 120) wrote about an age 'dominated by herds of tiny fleet-footed firms'. *Outsourcing* – 'buy, don't make' – has become a favoured strategy. What is going on here?

There are actually two separate things going on, only one of which has much to do with IT. One trend is what Americans (whose economy was traditionally far more self-contained than Britain's) call the 'hollowing out' of the US economy. The image is of an apple eaten away by wasps: from the outside, the fruit may look as whole as before, but behind the glossy skin there is now far less substance, as manufacturing operations are shifted overseas. The same is happening in Britain. Shopping for new shoes a few years ago, I picked a pair from Clarks, the famous company based near my childhood home in Somerset, and was startled to see a MADE IN CHINA sticker on the sole. The friend who helped me choose them giggled with the salesperson at my naivety – like many other British firms that used to make the things they sold, Clarks now farms out the manufacturing function to companies elsewhere, and the home company focuses on marketing and distribution.

Developments like this may mean that firms employ fewer people. But this trend has little to do with IT. The impetus towards globalisation comes from the fact that labour costs vary across the world. The progressive reductions in tariff barriers that have occurred by international agreement over the last half-century, rising skill levels in the third world, and perhaps lower transport costs have enabled Western companies to take advantage of low third-world wage rates. Modern communication technology plays a part, but that is a minor consideration.

## DISAGGREGATION

The development we are concerned with is separate. Even when a set of interrelated industrial and commercial operations are still carried out wholly within one country, nowadays they are often executed by a number of smaller companies, each specialising in one narrow niche and interacting contractually, rather than by one large company. Even administrative functions such as payroll and personnel are often outsourced to specialist firms. And there is a trend towards *vertical disaggregation*. Normally there are very many successive steps in the process by which consumer goods are created, ultimately, from raw materials. It was never usual for one company to do everything from one extreme of the chain to the other, but in the new economy firms are taking responsibility for shorter segments of the chain.

Again there is a potential confusion. Any new company naturally starts small and hopes to grow. In an area where new activities are being carried out by new organisations, it is inevitable that the organisations will tend to be small. But many commentators feel that there is something deeper going on. They believe that it is in the nature of e-business to shrink company sizes permanently, not just in the obvious sense that automation means things that previously had to be done by people are being done by machines, but in the sense that the same chains of operations will be divided among larger numbers of players occupying smaller niches.

People were observing that IT seemed to lead to smaller firm sizes even before the web (Brynjolfsson *et al.* 1994). But once the web arrived, some commentators threw moderation to the winds. Downes and Mui (1998) announced a new 'law of diminishing firms', according to which average firm size was destined to decline towards zero – every individual a separate firm.

This, incidentally, is part of the attraction of e-commerce for young people. It is not just that the web is socially 'cool', and they are fascinated by the technology. Those things are important. But there is also the apparent promise that one can get something going on a shoestring that has a fair chance of becoming a worthwhile piece in the economic jigsaw. Many of us would like to run our own show, rather than working at someone else's beck and call.

So why should IT have this impact on economic structure? And will the trend last?

As always where business is concerned, nobody can claim to be sure of the answers. But there is an answer to the first question, which has convinced many observers; and, if this answer is correct, it has an interesting consequence for the second question.

## WHAT TO PRODUCE HOW?

To understand these answers, we need to stand back for a while from the new economy and think about the fundamentals of how any society, traditional or modern, is organised economically.

Suppose one of my students sallies forth from their flat in Brighton this morning to do some shopping: let's say they buy oranges and a TV set. Then they are placing themselves at the apex of an immensely complex tree-shaped structure of specific economic operations. Drawing out the entire tree would be impractical, but Figure 2.1 suggests a small part of what it might look like.

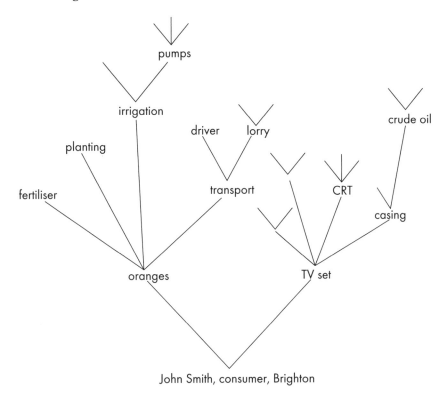

**FIGURE 2.1**

For oranges to be harvested, they must have been planted. Fertiliser will have been applied, and they will have needed irrigation, using machinery manufactured from diverse input elements. To get the oranges to the Brighton supermarket, transport was needed: at the latest stage of the journey, a lorry – itself the result of a complex process of manufacture – driven by a driver who had received training for this work. The television comprises a cathode ray tube, made out of various materials, a plastic casing made ultimately from crude oil (which was sucked out of the ground using very complicated machinery), and so forth.

Because we are all thoroughly used to the fact that the things we want are waiting in shops, it is easy to overlook how astonishing this fact really is. The network of decisions and actions that have placed oranges and a TV set in Brighton shops this morning is unimaginably vast and ramified, and few people involved will have known about more than one small part of the pattern. The man who planted the orange trees had perhaps never heard of Brighton. There was certainly no central authority thinking, 'In 2007 a student in Brighton will be wanting oranges and a television, so we need to see about getting orange trees planted, a lorry built ...'

Notice in particular that the mass of decisions and actions are not determined by the nature of the materials and activities involved. At almost every step, there are many real choices to be made. Almost every *factor of production* (each type of input to one of the production processes) will be capable of many uses: the lorry that transported oranges might have been used for different transport tasks, and the driver could have chosen to train for some other work. Perhaps the final stages of making the TV set involved assembling components that had no use other than as parts of that sort of set, but this is not the typical situation: most input factors will have alternative potential uses, and often many uses. Conversely, the outputs at the various stages could usually have been produced from different patterns of inputs. TV casings are normally plastic, but alternatively they could be made of metal or wood – in the early years of television, wooden casings were usual. The oranges might have reached Brighton by rail rather than road and so on; again, there will be fewer alternative patterns at some stages than others, but mostly there will be alternatives.

So, if almost every input can be used to produce different outputs, almost every output can be produced from different inputs, and nobody is over-seeing the system as a whole, how is it determined what in particular is produced how? Why do my students not find that, often, the things they would like to buy are unavailable, and why does the system not frequently produce far more of some things than anyone needs? The latter does happen sometimes – there are cases where farmers have to plough in a crop because it turns out not to be worth the cost of harvesting; but the wonder is why this is not a much more widespread phenomenon.

## SUPPLY AND DEMAND

The answers to those puzzles are the basic subject matter of economics. They are expressed in terms of the *price mechanism*.

For individual consumers, prices are nasty things that stand in the way of them enjoying all the goods and services they would like to have. For society as a whole, though, prices do important work: they transmit just enough information throughout society to enable people, each of whom knows only one small corner of the economy in detail, to coordinate their actions so that as much value as possible is squeezed out of the resources available, and waste is kept to a minimum. Prices achieve this by reconciling supply and demand.

For any particular product – oranges, say – there exists a *supply schedule*: a graph something like Figure 2.2, in which the *x*-axis represents the quantity of fruit grown annually, and the *y*-axis represents the price at which the fruit are sold. The schedule runs south-west to north-east: the higher the price for oranges, the more will be produced, because owners of land and other production factors will increasingly find that it pays to divert these resources from their current use to the production of oranges. The true line will probably not be nearly as smooth as I have drawn it. There might for instance be a price point where it becomes worth using some particular expensive fertiliser that greatly increases production, and so the graph will kink upwards at that point. But the trend must be broadly south-west to north-east.

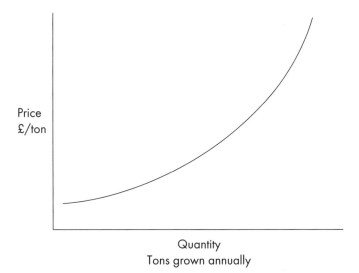

**FIGURE 2.2**

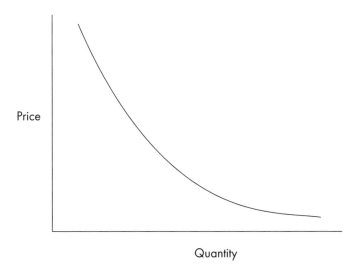

**FIGURE 2.3**

Figure 2.3 shows the *demand schedule* for oranges: the total quantity that would be bought at different prices. This runs north-west to south-east: the cheaper oranges are, the more will be bought. When I was a child, oranges were an expensive luxury: it was a treat to be given one at Christmas. Now they are relatively far cheaper, and people eat them routinely alongside local fruit such as apples.

These graphs are both hypothetical: at a given period, the price for any particular thing is what it is, and we can observe how much is produced and sold at that price, but we have no direct way of checking what the quantities would be at every possible alternative price. So we usually cannot plot supply or demand schedules exactly. But we know at least this much about them: the supply schedule must run south-west to north-east, while the demand schedule must run north-west to south-east.

That being so, if the two lines are plotted on the same graph, they must cross (see Figure 2.4). The crossing point fixes the price that oranges will actually fetch and the quantity that will actually be produced. If people try producing oranges in a way that requires them to charge a price higher than *P*, say by using expensive fertiliser when quantity *Q* of oranges can be produced by cheaper methods, then they will be left with their output on their hands; they will have to cut the price to get rid of them, and shift to growing something else, or to growing oranges more cheaply. If people sell oranges for a lower price than *P*, consumers will want to buy more in total than it pays growers to produce at that lower price; disappointed customers will bid the price back up to *P*. *P* is the *equilibrium price* at which the same quantity is produced that customers are willing to buy, leaving no waste and no shoppers confronted with empty shelves.

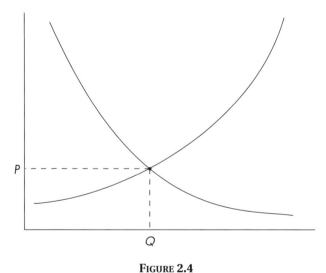

**FIGURE 2.4**

This is an idealised picture – the system does not always work as smoothly as my discussion suggests, but broadly speaking this is how prices are determined.

My example used oranges, a consumer good. But the same principles fix the prices of everything else, including items – say, railway goods wagons – that have no direct value to consumers and are relevant only as inputs to processes high in the network that links raw materials at the top to consumption at the bottom.

## AN INVISIBLE HAND

The result is that prices constitute a *signalling system*, showing the controller of any factor of production how best to apply it. Someone who deals with one little corner of the economic world could never acquire, or cope with, all the detailed knowledge of their potential customers' businesses, the customers' own customers' businesses and so forth that would show why, ultimately, the resource they are responsible for will end up yielding more value to consumers if they sell it to business A, which will make one use of it, than if they sell it to business B, which will use it in a different way. But they do not need to go into all that detail. The price system gives them just enough information to make decisions *as if* they had encyclopaedic knowledge. Business B will not buy at a price that makes it worth supplying it, because for the use business B wants to make of the given resource it can substitute some cheaper alternative. Business A wants to use the same input for a process where there is no cheaper alternative; so business A will pay the required price, and business A gets the resource. Thus the multifarious resources available to society are distributed to the uses where they will produce most value for society.

Adam Smith, the father of economic thought, put it like this, in a passage that must have a high claim to a place among the top 10 texts of all time that explain how the world works:

> As every individual … endeavours … to employ his capital [so] that its produce may be of the greatest value; every individual necessarily labours to render the annual revenue of the society as great as he can … he intends only his own gain, and he is in this, as in many other cases, led by an invisible hand to promote an end which was no part of his intention.
>
> (Smith [1776] 1976: vol. 1, p. 456)

An invisible hand! This is the economists' answer to the question of how society determines what is produced how, with no overseeing authority. In terms familiar to computer scientists, an economy is a self-organising system, and prices are the mechanism by which its organisation is optimised.

In principle, this machinery can determine the price of human labour – what people earn – in the same way as anything else. Obviously, many people feel that 'people are special' and that incomes ought not to be determined entirely by the impersonal mechanisms that fix the prices of inanimate goods. In Britain and many other societies, the state acts in various ways to modify the pattern of incomes, in cash and kind, that would emerge from a pure market economy: medical services are financed by a progressive tax system, income support is provided for the poor, and so on. Economists sometimes warn that policies such as these, though they may be desirable, by interfering with the operation of the price mechanism entail hidden disadvantages that need to be balanced against the clear advantages. But that is the realm of politics rather than economics, and outside the scope of this book.

## POSITIVES AND NEGATIVES OF BUSINESS

For those who are sensitive to it, it is the self-organising complexity of business life that gives it its fascination. Our world contains an astonishing variety of raw materials, human abilities and other resources; no-one knows how best to deploy them all in order optimally to satisfy human needs and tastes, but markets provide a mechanism by which economic agents can feel their way by trial and error towards successful patterns. Each company and each individual knows only one small part of the entire filigree of economic relationships, but through their activities in their particular domains they jointly co-evolve an effective overall system.

There are analogies with biological evolution of species, each of which must adapt to a niche defined largely by the other species it lives alongside, and which accordingly changes as those species too evolve. But the timescale of biological evolution is hard for a human being to grasp; we have to infer it rather than directly seeing it. With business, we watch co-evolution happening before our eyes.

Many readers may feel that this is an unduly romanticised account of business life, which ignores its darker sides. Unquestionably, there are depressing aspects to business in a modern free-market society. Does one's heart really lift, for instance, when the subtle structure of economic relationships called into being by Adam Smith's invisible hand functions so as to output on the one hand an abundance of, say, Turkey Twizzlers and Beavis and Butthead cartoons, and on the other hand decreasing quantities of demanding classical music? (Readers for whom these examples do not work will surely have little difficulty thinking of others.)

This is a real issue. The standard answer is to say that economics cannot take responsibility for consumers' preferences. Many of us might wish we lived in a society of people whose tastes were more refined than the twenty-first-century average, but the task of business is to serve the consumers who actually exist. Readers must decide for themselves how satisfactory that answer is – it would go far beyond the scope of this book to pursue the issue.

Others will see further downsides to business. Many readers will object that the first world's market-based economies may be good at catering to every whim of rich Westerners, but there are also people living in grinding poverty in the third world – because their income is low they have little consumer power, and so business does little or nothing for them. And some will argue that in the process of satisfying current consumers, business recklessly generates pollution that will damage the life-chances of future generations; since they do not yet exist, they have no buying power at all to influence current business activity, and yet surely we ought not to ignore their interests.

These again are real and serious issues. I do not wish to minimise their importance. If there were room to discuss them adequately here, it would be debatable how far business in itself is responsible for the negatives. For instance, one prime contributory factor to African poverty is the way in which the rich world protects its agriculture with tariff barriers, such as the EU Common Agricultural Policy and comparable US regulations, which actively hinder the ability of Africans to develop economically in the ways that are most readily available to many of them. These barriers are political in nature, not created by business, and at present the rich world seems to have no intention of dismantling them. In the case of pollution, too, if business acts in an antisocial way, that may be because politics has not evolved adequately sophisticated ways of arranging to charge companies the true costs of their activities.

But there has to be a limit to what one book can discuss. This is a textbook on e-business, not a tract about the North–South divide or about pollution and climate change. Business is an activity that seeks to find ways of adding value to input resources, within whatever political framework it finds itself. To a large extent it must accept that framework as a given, and this textbook must do the same. The author is quite ready to concede that there are aspects to present-day politics that are far from ideal. But the topic of this book will be e-business as it functions in our society as it is.

## COASE'S THEORY OF THE FIRM

So far in this chapter, we have been considering classical economic theory – the common background for most economic discussion over the past two centuries. It has nothing directly to say about the size of firms, which was the topic from which we set out. For that, we must come forward to a theory stated by Ronald Coase, winner of the 1991 economics Nobel Prize (and British by origin, though he taught at the

University of Chicago). Coase's *theory of the firm* was first stated in a famous article published before the Second World War (Coase 1937).

Figure 2.5 schematically represents one small part of the network of economic transactions in a society: the nodes are individuals, and the links between nodes are transfers of resources between individuals and agreements by one individual to do something for another. In a market economy, many of these links come into being through the system of freely negotiated contracts on which the price mechanism depends. But, Coase points out, within this sea of contractual relationships there are islands (indicated by dotted lines) within which activities and use of resources are decided by managerial instructions rather than by negotiated contracts: the 'islands' are what we call firms or companies. As between individuals and/or firms, economic decisions are made freely in response to price signals. *Within* firms, decisions are imposed by managers implementing plans. Why, Coase asks, should the islands be the size they are, rather than much larger or much smaller?

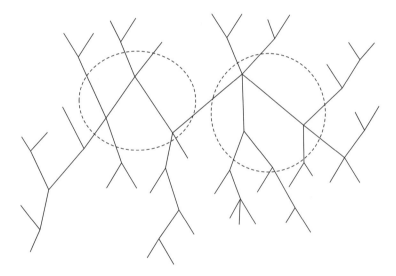

**FIGURE 2.5**

One way to think about this is to consider the logical extremes. What would economic life be like if, at one extreme, the whole of society formed one big island of command relationships?

This case is easy to think about: it is one aspect of the political ideal called socialism or communism. The reason why a market economy does not spontaneously adopt that form is that it requires a level of centralised planning of economic decisions that is thoroughly impractical. If I were writing 20 or 30 years ago, I might have needed to argue this at length; until the 1980s many people believed that a socialist economy was a valid ideal, even if it had never been realised satisfactorily. Since then, it has been generally recognised that socialism simply cannot work: no planners could assemble enough detailed information to devise a reasonable blueprint specifying what to produce how. We have to let such decisions be guided by the price signalling system, which is sensitive to more considerations than any planners could take into account.

But in that case, why have firms at all? Why does the network of Figure 2.5 not consist wholly of freely negotiated contracts between individuals, with no islands of command relationships?

This opposite extreme is harder to think about, because it has not traditionally been discussed, even as a hypothetical ideal. But, with effort, we can envisage a world in which all economic relationships are between individuals. As a university teacher, for instance, I might rent weekly slots in a lecture hall from someone who had borrowed the large sum of capital needed to create a university, and I would charge individual students a subscription fee for the right to attend. If one pursues this scenario very far, a science-fiction quality sets in. But what is it that compels the economic sea to contain islands of command relationships, and why are they as big as they are, and not much larger or much smaller? Before Coase, no-one had asked this question.

## TRANSACTION COSTS

Coase's answer is in terms of *transaction costs*: the costs of creating and maintaining the dense network of links between economic agents. Classical economics focused on the substance of transactions: a supermarket buys a load of oranges from a supplier for $x$ pounds. But the money paid for the oranges is not the only cost paid to bring about this transaction.

Economic agents have search costs: they must put time and effort into locating suitable suppliers and potential customers. There are coordination costs: for instance, time has to be put into ensuring that the hour and location at which a supplier delivers oranges are an hour and location at which the supermarket can receive them. The process of negotiating contracts will often be time-consuming and therefore expensive; and operating the contracts once agreed involves its own costs, for example for sending out bills. (For a telephone company, the greatest cost in supplying a household with phone service is billing.) If things go wrong, larger costs will be incurred – in the worst case, a company has the expense of enforcing its contract in a law court.

These costs are far from negligible. One estimate (Wallis and North 1988) suggests that transaction costs may account for about half of the gross national product. So they must have a large influence on economic organisation.

Now, Coase argues, although transactions between companies inevitably involve costs of these kinds, within a small company achieving the same arrangements is costless or nearly so. If a company employs its own driver, no-one asks 'What would you take to deliver this load to Brighton tomorrow?' and gets involved in dickering over price and comparing alternative quotes. The manager simply says 'Your job tomorrow is to deliver this load to Brighton'. Companies are a device for eliminating transaction costs; Coase sees that as their basic *raison d'être*.

But, as a small company gets larger, organising arrangements internally becomes more complex and expensive. In a large firm that makes many deliveries and employs many drivers, internal searching becomes necessary: 'Who can we give this assignment to?' Internal politics begins to complicate things: 'How can we persuade Deliveries to take on responsibility for recyclables?' The larger the portion of the total economic network comprised within one firm, the higher its internal management costs will be, until eventually, if the firm gets any larger, the extra transactions that are 'internalised' will be as expensive as if they were carried out on the open market. This is Coase's answer to the puzzle about 'island size'. Firms expand until the marginal cost of internal managerial arrangements matches the cost of carrying out the corresponding transactions on the market.

If this is what determines company size, then IT will change things: IT alters transaction costs. Most obviously, the web makes it far cheaper to search for potential transaction partners. Contracting costs and coordination costs may also be reduced; think, for instance, of automatic stock market trading, where buyers and sellers are matched and sales executed without human intervention. IT is giving us what people have taken to calling a *frictionless economy*.

As one concrete example, take the (American) Lamons Gasket Company, which makes more than 100,000 lines of sealing devices – gaskets, packings, nuts, bolts, screws.

> Until recently, simply figuring out what customers wanted to buy and getting the right items to them was a horribly inefficient process at Lamons. Customers would phone or fax in an order, and a customer service representative would have to translate the information into Lamons's part numbers and format. The average order cost less than $500 but took 30 to 60 minutes to get into the system... Then Lamons built an e-commerce Web site, and customers' ability to find, order, and pay for goods improved radically.
>
> (McGrath and MacMillan 2005: 85)

Those 30–60 minutes of expensive staff time were a pure transaction cost, paid by both selling and buying companies (Lamons is a B2B trader) – the time expenditure did not in itself do anything to help the company manufacture more gaskets or more machines incorporating gaskets; it was just a precondition for shifting products one step down the value chain. In this case it is easy to appreciate how IT has shrunk transaction costs.

If transaction costs in the market are lower, the break-even point at which company expansion causes internal management costs to equal them should be reached sooner. So, by the logic of Coase's argument, companies ought now to be smaller.

And this is where we came in. A prediction that follows from a theory put forward in the 1930s is being tested and apparently confirmed, 70 years later.

## COASE AND IT

Ronald Coase's 1937 article said nothing about computers; they had not been invented. The classic statement of the implications of Coase's theory for e-business was a far-sighted paper by Thomas Malone *et al.* (1987); and Brynjolfsson *et al.* (1994) and Hitt (1999) claimed to find concrete evidence that IT was indeed causing firm sizes to shrink. Many well-informed commentators feel that the case is made. The IT revolution means that the trend towards smaller, niche companies is here to stay, and Coase's analysis is the correct explanation linking these two phenomena.

But there is an alternative point of view. The internet has reduced the costs of transactions on the market; but the internet is not the only aspect of IT to affect business, and other aspects might lead to different predictions.

The nearest thing to computers that Coase did mention in 1937 was the telephone – at that point still a relatively novel business tool. Coase's prediction was that the telephone was destined to make firms *larger*: he saw the telephone as reducing the coordination costs of a firm's internal operations. If internal management costs are reduced while external transaction costs are unchanged, a firm can expand further before reaching the break-even point where the two are equal.

Seventy years on, it is not clear why Coase saw the telephone as affecting management costs but not external transaction costs. In those days, trunk calls between different regions were cumbersome affairs involving manual intervention by telephone operators, and so perhaps telephones seemed more significant as company-internal communication devices than as channels of communication between firms. That is a question of mainly historical interest.

But the analogous question about IT and present-day business is very relevant. We saw in Chapter 1 that the initial focus of e-business was on the web as a new medium for B2C and B2B commerce, but that the balance is shifting now towards BPR, using software such as the enterprise resource planning systems to be discussed in Chapter 8, or the 'internal market' software used by BP in the case discussed on p. 7.

Internal BPR reduces a firm's management costs. So, what Coase's theory might lead us to expect is a first wave of business computerisation that impacted mainly on external transaction costs, and hence caused company sizes to shrink, followed now by a second wave impacting mainly on internal management costs, which, by the same logic, should cause company sizes to grow again (cf. Sampson 2003).

There is plenty of evidence bearing that expectation out.

Beginning about 2002–3, on both sides of the Atlantic, there has been a growing wave of *merger and acquisition* (M&A) activity – events where companies of comparable size merge into a single organisation, or a smaller company is bought by a larger company and becomes its subsidiary. This trend has applied to business across the board, not just to high-tech businesses, but it certainly has been very noticeable among the latter. Two of the first big deals, in 2002, were Hewlett-Packard's merger with its competitor Compaq, and IBM's acquisition of the consultancy arm of the accountants PricewaterhouseCoopers. In 2003 the enterprise resource planning company PeopleSoft bought its competitor J.D. Edwards, and then Oracle acquired the enlarged PeopleSoft in January 2005.

Furthermore, although M&As in the IT area used to be mainly 'horizontal' – a company would buy out a competitor, gaining a larger share of the market in its area of activity without necessarily changing the size of the segments into which the value chain was divided – in recent years IT M&As have increasingly been 'vertical'. In July 2005 the security firm Symantec bought data storage and recovery specialist Veritas, and, conversely, the dominant storage company EMC acquired RSA Security in September 2006 (together with 30-odd other companies since 2003). In September 2005, eBay bought VoIP phone company Skype. In October 2005, broadcaster BSkyB bought internet service provider (ISP) Easynet. In December 2005, the broadcasting company ITV bought the social website Friends Reunited. In October 2006, Google bought YouTube. These pairs of companies were not direct competitors; the resulting single companies each account for larger value-chain segments than were handled by the respective companies before the takeovers.

Another new development has been a partial reversal of the outsourcing trend. Five years ago outsourcing was a one-way street, but nowadays many companies are bringing outsourced activities back in-house. The first notable example was Cable & Wireless's 2003 decision to terminate a contract with IBM for IT infrastructure and customer billing systems. There have been many subsequent examples. J.P. Morgan Chase cancelled a contract with IBM in September 2004; Sainsbury's took back control of its IT systems from Accenture in October 2004; Prudential brought data-centre operations back in-house from Capgemini in July 2005 – indeed, by 2005 one consultancy firm claimed that almost two-thirds of organisations had brought some form of outsourced service back in-house.

What we are seeing here is to a large extent the result of progress along a learning curve. When a company first needs to computerise its operations, it has so little expertise that farming the work out to specialists may be the only rational move – even though, inevitably, it means some loss of control. As the company gradually acquires a better understanding of the area, the difficulties of insourcing diminish, and sometimes the point comes where the disadvantages of indirect control outweigh those of equipping the company with the recruits and reorganisation needed to do the work in-house. Often, it will still on balance be preferable to outsource work; but sometimes it will not be, and in those cases it is being reabsorbed. The overall consequence is that, again, companies have been tending to grow larger recently after a period when they were growing smaller – as the theory suggested might happen.

The theory gives us no way to predict the overall net effect of these contrary trends. When commentators first drew links between Coase's ideas from the 1930s and modern e-business, they noticed only the transaction-cost-shrinking aspect of e-business, and so they felt safe in predicting that average firm size would end up smaller. The theory did not provide tools allowing detailed predictions about *how much* smaller, though. If IT reduces both transaction and internal management costs, then it is anyone's guess which of the two impacts on company size will end up outweighing the other – mean firm size might end up rather smaller than before the IT revolution, or it might end up rather larger, or it might stay much the same.

It does seem likely, though, that the extreme forecasts of an overall shift to 'herds of tiny fleet-footed firms' will prove exaggerated. There is no real reason to expect the economic landscape of the future not to be dominated as it has been in the past by big business.

## STARTUPS BECOME BUY-UPS

Many people are attracted by the idea that IT enables little online startups to carve out viable continuing business niches alongside large established players, but some see it as a dream that has already faded. Innovative startups continue to come along – a group of ex-employees of Prudential's online savings bank Egg joined forces in 2005 to found Zopa, a new kind of bank that does not lend its own money but instead puts would-be lenders in touch with creditworthy borrowers. (Because they link individuals to individuals, businesses such as Zopa and eBay are sometimes called *C2C* as opposed to B2B or B2C organisations.) But whereas, at one time, a startup that demonstrated the feasibility of a new e-business concept would typically hope to flourish as an independent company, nowadays the likelier path is acquisition by an established concern. Even Martha Lane Fox and Brent Hoberman's Lastminute.com, which went public in 2000 and was seen as one of the few real successes among the early British dotcoms,[1] sold itself in July 2005 to the Texas-based Sabre Holdings, which counts its revenue in billions. An *IT Week* editorial at the beginning of 2007 commented:

> The romantic notion of David taking on Goliath is outdated and, today, a preferable strategy would be to set aside slingshots, shake hands with the big fellow and do a deal.[2]

## THE VIRTUAL ORGANISATION

Even if firms were to remain somewhat smaller than in the past, there is another way in which IT is allowing effective company size often to be larger than formal company size. Separate companies are collaborating as so-called *virtual organisations*.

Fifty years ago, relationships between companies were distant. They had to be: there was no e-mail or voicemail; documents and artwork were generated and exchanged via chains of clerical assistants and the postal service, rather than being transmitted at electronic speed between the desktops of the staff immediately involved. Firms were like independent city-states, communicating at arm's length through ambassadors. Nowadays, though, it is easier for legally separate organisations to collaborate in an intimate fashion. Virtual organisations are flexible alliances of companies or individuals that come together to respond to business opportunities and then dissolve and rearrange themselves in other alliances as opportunities change again. The rapid, data-rich communications facilitated by IT encourage this kind of flexible independence.

Arguably, this pattern of organisation has advantages in a fast-changing business environment. Small companies can limit themselves to their core competences, where they have a competitive edge, while outsourcing functions where they have no special expertise to other companies that have; yet there is continuity – although the partners are not legally yoked together permanently, they are regular collaborators who know each other's strengths and cooperate on a basis of familiarity.

Furthermore, IT is facilitating new levels of collaboration between large, established companies. Perhaps the most extreme example to date is the French aircraft manufacturer Dassault's new Falcon 7X model, which made its maiden flight in May 2005. The 7X is claimed to be the first fly-by-wire business jet, but it is also the first aircraft designed entirely in a virtual environment:

---

[1] Though it never actually made an annual profit.
[2] 'Join in the startup sell-out bonanza', *IT Week* 8 January 2007.

> A single database was used to define the aircraft's design, including all 40,000 of its parts and 200,000 fasteners. The database was shared between workers at the 30 or so firms which contributed different parts of the plane. Before a single piece of metal was cut, everyone involved ... could walk around the plane in virtual reality and iron out conflicts over what went where... Can a mechanic actually reach a particular component to replace it, and is it physically possible to turn the spanner? Nothing was left to chance.
>
> As a result, the first plane to be constructed was perfect: there was no physical prototype... In aviation, the first few dozen aircraft of a particular design are normally tweaked as unanticipated problems arise[3]

– with the 7X, the tweaking was completed at the virtual-reality stage.

From a computing point of view, the 7X story is a fascinating technical achievement. From the business point of view, what is fascinating is the intimacy of the collaborative relationships between individuals within many independent companies. Desirable or not, this level of collaboration across organisation boundaries simply was not possible before broadband electronic links allowed workers at separate sites to pass engineering drawings, three-dimensional graphics files and other detailed data back and forth freely and rapidly. The set of partner companies in the 7X case were acting in a manner that did make it look rather like a single organisation.

Defining a new aeroplane model would traditionally have been seen as an enterprise-critical function, which a manufacturer would not want to share with outsiders. (Majchrzak *et al.* (2004) mention an occasion in the early 1990s when the idea was initially viewed by executives of a Boeing subsidiary as 'blasphemous'.) The level of collaborative activity that occurred in the 7X case may be an extreme, but it is a natural progression from kinds of IT-mediated collaboration that are by now thoroughly routine.

It has become common for companies to appoint senior executives with the specific role of seeking new alliances with companies whose strengths are complementary. Now that IT has made intimate collaboration across organisation boundaries possible, it is widely seen as highly desirable for business success. Economists have understood for centuries that efficient production depends on splitting up complex tasks between specialists – Adam Smith's classic example (illustrated on the reverse of the current £20 note) was the way in which pin factories divide the work of making pins into many separate activities performed by separate workers. But in Adam Smith's day, practical considerations meant that those different workers had to belong to a single organisation. Now, IT is

---

[3] 'Haute couture', *The Economist* 18 June 2005.

removing that practical constraint in many cases – and organisations, too, perform best when they focus on their core competences, so we are seeing a new wave of division of labour. Michael Capellas, chairman of the then independent computer manufacturer Compaq, said in 2002: 'nobody can do it all. Successful companies will be the ones that are able to build up trusting partner relationships.'[4]

## CONTROL VERSUS TRUST

One consequence of the trend to intimate collaboration between firms is that *trust* has to do a share of the work that used to be done by hierarchy and discipline. An alliance of companies who join forces on a project will make a contract governing the main lines of their collaboration, but a legal contract can never prescribe all the detailed rules and practices that develop within a single organisation; so, 'trust has to substitute for hierarchical and bureaucratic controls' (Lipnack and Stamps 1998). It is widely agreed that the business environment is tending to lay increased importance on trust as opposed to formal control. If so, this is a significant new development.

It is perhaps a surprising one, because in many areas of public life the movement over recent decades has been in the opposite direction. Thirty years ago, professionals such as doctors, schoolteachers and academics were normally trusted to do the best job they could; nowadays, they are monitored and regulated at every turn. The social changes have been so pronounced that they were chosen as the topic of the 2002 BBC Reith Lectures, in which Onora O'Neill argued that the abandonment of the trust principle in public life is creating intractable social difficulties (O'Neill 2002).

It is not easy to see how to reconcile an increasing role for trust in business with the reality of decreasing trust in much of life. We shall find that trust is a recurring theme in the study of e-business.

## FIRMS AS TOOLS

One idea to take away from this chapter is that firms are only tools – they are not ends in themselves, as individual human beings are. Most of us are glad to see effort going into keeping other people healthy, not because of the useful work that those people will do in future (if that were the sole reason, it might be best to kill everyone off at retirement!) but simply because they are fellow human beings with the same rights as ourselves to make as much of their lives as they can. If you work for a company, you are encouraged to see the flourishing of that company

---

[4] Quoted in *SAP INFO Quick Guide* 4/2002, p. 29.

similarly as a good thing in its own right. The economic system works best if employees do to some extent embrace their employers' interests as their own. But, standing back a pace and focusing on the social system as a whole, we see that companies are really no more than instruments that society has evolved to serve the needs and aspirations of the human beings who constitute society.

That means that a book such as this needs to examine not only the e-business strategies by which companies can seek profits, but also the impact of e-business technology on individuals and on society.

Even readers who think they are interested exclusively in how to use IT for profit would be wise to keep half an eye on the wider picture. They may not be interested in the social consequences of e-business; but many voters are, and voters are quite capable of causing government to change the rules of the game that companies have to play.

At present, governments and voters, as well as companies, are feeling their way uncertainly into the new world that IT is creating. A large issue for companies is how governments will remodel the e-business environment, now they are beginning to acquire the confidence to do so.

# 3  E-Commerce Strategies

It is time to make the discussion concrete. This chapter will examine one e-business in depth: Amazon.

Nobody suggests that Amazon is a 'typical' e-business – if such a beast exists. Amazon is predominantly a B2C operation, although nowadays it also has B2B aspects. Historically, a 'typical' dotcom would probably be a company that was launched in the late 1990s and collapsed in about 2001. In that year, *USA Today* described Amazon as 'the company that legit-imized e-commerce', and its founder Jeffrey Bezos boasted 'We are the only e-commerce company of scale'.[1] In terms of consumer recognition, Amazon was from an early date far ahead of the e-commerce pack. Four years after launch, Amazon was the fifty-seventh most valuable brand worldwide, above long-established names such as Guinness and Hilton. Amazon is arguably an outstandingly successful company.

My students sometimes boggle at the word 'arguably'. My reply is: 'If you had started a business a dozen years ago and by now you were counting your cumulative losses in billions, how successful would you say you were?'

Typical or not, Amazon makes a good case study – partly because its high profile means that plenty of data is available. Amazon was first with many e-business technologies. The shopping-trolley metaphor, for instance, which we take for granted nowadays in the e-tailing context, was an Amazon invention. And most business-strategy themes that analysts see as potentially significant for the success or otherwise of e-businesses can be illustrated from Amazon.

Our overall purpose is to examine e-commerce strategies rather than to discuss Amazon for its own sake, and this chapter will look at other companies when that is helpful. But many of the relevant concepts can be exemplified well from the changing fortunes of Amazon.

## AMAZON IS FOUNDED

Jeffrey Bezos was born in 1964; by 1992 he was the youngest senior vice-president of a high-tech-oriented Wall Street firm. Two years later he threw the job up to create an internet bookshop. Bezos founded

---

[1] Quoted by Byron Acohido, 'Amazon: We'll be profitable by year's end', *USA Today* 26 March 2001.

Amazon, aged 30, with a few hundred thousand dollars of his own and relatives' money; the website was launched under the slogan EARTH'S BIGGEST BOOKSTORE on 16 July 1995.

By 1996 venture capital funds were competing to invest, and Bezos shifted his sights up to a higher plane of ambition. In May 1997 Amazon was floated as a public company; that is, in order to get access to far more capital to work with than was available to him as a private company proprietor, Bezos divided company ownership into shares made available for trading by the public on a stock exchange. Amazon's opening share price valued it at $423 million (this was the product of the price for one share multiplied by the number of shares into which ownership was divided – the company's *market capitalisation*, or 'market cap').

The prospectus was explicit about the fact that Amazon was losing money fast and expected to lose it faster for the foreseeable future. A new company normally does run at a loss; one has to spend capital out in order to develop a business to the point where it can return a worthwhile income stream. Bezos planned a large-scale, expensive programme of company development.

## AMAZON'S INITIAL BUSINESS MODEL

In the year that Amazon was founded, 1.5 billion books were bought in the USA. The standard distribution pattern was that publishers sold books to wholesalers, the largest being the Ingram Book Group, with seven warehouses in different parts of America stocking about 400,000 titles; wholesalers supplied books on a sale-or-return basis to retailers, who sold to consumers (large retailers might also supply small retailers).

Amazon's initial business model involved occupying the retailer slot in this value chain: it bought books from Ingram and sold them to the public through its website. Because its 'shop' was a website, it could sell nationally or internationally without the expense of bricks-and-mortar branches with salaried staff. Furthermore it did not need to tie up capital in inventory. In theory, the operation could have been totally inventory-free: when a customer ordered a book, Amazon might have arranged for the wholesaler to ship it to the customer directly. In fact, books moved via Amazon's premises, but paused there only long enough for packing and forwarding.

Thus, the capital and operating-cost requirements both favoured internet selling over bricks-and-mortar book retailing. The *cashflow* pattern was favourable too, since Amazon (like any retailer) would pay its supplier in arrears, but customers paid up-front through their credit cards. By contrast, even when a conventional bookshop does sell a particular book, on average the sale occurs two or three months after the shop has paid its supplier.

A conventional bookshop can stock only so many titles – the largest have room for about 130,000 titles. That is certainly more than enough to include all the best-sellers, but not everyone is looking for those. Each individual lower-ranking title appeals only to a small readership, but collectively the *long tail* of lower-ranked titles have many readers looking for them. Amazon has effectively no constraint on the number of titles 'stocked', and about a third of its sales come from outside the top 130,000 titles. The ability to market long-tail items easily is one of the novel commercial consequences of the internet.

## THE ONLINE BOOK-BUYING EXPERIENCE

Not all differences favoured the online model. Bezos never expected to put conventional bookshops out of business: he knew that people enjoy spending time in them. He said in 1998, 'We will never make Amazon.com fun and engaging in the same way as the great physical bookstores are… You'll never be able to hear the bindings creak and smell the books and have tasty lattes and soft sofas at Amazon.com.'[2]

But there are other things an online bookshop can offer that a conventional bookshop cannot, which might enable the online bookshop to capture a worthwhile share of the market. These things might even expand the total market, so that Amazon's share would not be entirely at the expense of conventional competitors.

One of these is using data on customers' buying histories to predict titles that are likely to interest them. Amazon greets a returning customer by name: 'Hello, Geoffrey, we have recommendations for you.' The recommendations are generated by algorithms that compare a customer's buying history with those of other customers whose purchasing patterns overlap. After one has been an Amazon customer for a while, the recommendations become eerily well-targeted; it takes a strong will to avoid letting book spending get out of control.

We cannot talk about 'business process re-engineering' here – Amazon was new, so there was no previous process to re-engineer. Nevertheless, it is important to understand that what was significant in the Amazon operation was not just about selling through an electronic interface rather than over a counter. It was also about things happening electronically behind the scenes. One of the things that e-commerce is good at is *cross-selling*, often symbolised by the tag 'Do you want fries with that?' Using records of many customers' past buying to predict individuals' future choices among 1.5 million titles is a powerful marketing tool that would be quite unfeasible without IT.

---

[2] Except where otherwise noted, Bezos's quotations are taken from a speech at Lake Forest College, Illinois, 26 February 1998, quoted by Spector (2000).

Another Amazon technique was to draw customers into membership of a *virtual community*. The site ran interviews with authors, book reviews, reader games and contests; readers were invited to contribute their own reviews, which were rated by other site visitors, and at some periods Amazon gave cash prizes to the highest-rated reviewers. (Meanwhile, software was running in the background keeping count of metrics such as *conversion rate* – the proportion of hits on any particular site element that were followed by a purchase – so that site managers could tweak their pages in response to hard evidence rather than gut instinct.) At one point Amazon planned forums that would allow visitors to chat to one another.

Things such as online book reviews serve two purposes. They can help customers decide whether a title is worth buying, in a way that briefly scanning a physical copy cannot. But also, participants are involved in a relationship with the company that might encourage a kind of loyalty that is unlikely with a physical shop. Some commentators have seen virtual communities of this kind as an important marketing tool (cf. Chapter 10). Bezos wanted Amazon 'to seem smart and authoritative – to become not just a store but a *destination*' (Marcus 2004: 4).

In the early years, Amazon's changing home pages were designed by human editors, to draw visitors' attention to discounted best-sellers or to little-known titles that deserved wider exposure; but since 2000 the home pages have been personalised for each visitor individually, composed automatically by reference to the visitor's known buying tastes. (Amazon ran an experiment in which successive site visitors were served randomly with either editor-designed or automatically personalised home pages and a tally was kept of resulting sales: the machine won.)

Amazon adopted many other techniques to encourage customers to accept this novel method of shopping. It was, for instance, the first e-tailer to respond to orders by e-mailing an immediate confirmation. Robert Spector (2000: 152) noted that 'As late as 1999, of the ten most visited shopping sites on the Internet, Amazon.com was the only one that offered on its home page a link to its "shipping policies", where a chart explained shipping and handling fees.' Bezos focused on doing everything possible to please customers, from obvious points such as large discounts and fast (and sometimes free) delivery, to editorial write-ups and site illustrations that aimed to give the visitor 'a sense of the quirky, independent, literate voice, and that behind it all you're interacting with people.'[3]

## GETTING PHYSICAL

The initial business model did not last long. Beginning in 1996, Amazon acquired premises to keep its own stock of the 200,000 best-selling titles.

---

[3] Amazon executive editor Rick Ayre, quoted by Peter de Jonge, 'Riding the wild, perilous waters of Amazon.com', *New York Times* 14 March 1999.

It continued to buy titles ranked from 200,000 down to 400,000 through wholesalers; the long tail of slower-selling books was ordered directly from the publishers. To the original customer service centre in Seattle, Amazon added another on the US east coast; in 1999 five more were added. More premises entailed many more staff salaries.

There were two reasons for this development. One was that Amazon's leading competitor, Barnes & Noble, tried to buy the wholesaler Ingram in 1998. Anti-trust rules (by which the law maintains competition by forbidding an individual company to acquire a monopoly position) prevented the sale from going through, but the attempt drew attention to a vulnerability in Amazon's original business model.

More crucially, though, the inventory-less approach proved inconsistent with Amazon's ambition to dominate the field. When customers knew they could walk into a bricks-and-mortar bookshop and buy a best-seller then and there, they were not likely to wait too much longer for an online purchase to be delivered; only by holding its own stocks of popular titles at strategic locations could Amazon fulfil orders within a day or two. Once Amazon had attracted serious investment, the outside investors (and Bezos, who had originally been thinking in terms of profitability at a lower level of market share) wanted it not just to make a living but also to dominate its market sector. The inventory-less model would not allow that.

## GET BIG FAST

This large ambition was one way in which Amazon became a typical dotcom. The new world of online commerce was seen as vacant terrain ripe for colonisation, like the American West waiting for pioneers to stake their claims; with a one-off opportunity like that, the important thing was to grab as much territory as possible, and worry about profits later. The syndrome was identified by Neil Weintraut (1997):

> [Rather than] build[ing] businesses in a methodical fashion, Internet businesses ... adopted a grow-at-any-cost, without-any-revenue, claim-as-much-market-real-estate-before-anyone-moves-in approach to business. This mentality came to be known as 'Get Big Fast.'

Get Big Fast became such a standard e-commerce principle that it is often reduced to the abbreviation GBF. It might seem to contradict the idea in Chapter 2 that lower transaction costs in internet commerce lead to smaller firms, but there is no real contradiction. Coase's theory is chiefly about the vertical size of companies – how large a segment of the long value chains leading from raw materials at the top down to consumer goods or services at the bottom is typically contained within a single organisation. Get Big Fast relates more to horizontal company size: how large a share of a given market, and how broad a range of 'sister' business activities, are controlled by one firm.

Globalisation of trade, and the global reach of the internet, promote a winner-takes-all business environment. Instead of many similar firms each surviving in its own geographical or specialist niche, it becomes easier for one company to conquer the entire sector and leave few pickings for the rest. E-commerce was seen as creating a large *first mover advantage*: being first away from the starting blocks gave a good chance of sweeping the prizes.

Achieving large scale is particularly attractive for a business whose costs relate mainly to developing a website and software for serving customers online. These costs may be heavy, if the site and software are complex, but they do not rise in proportion to the scale of the selling operation. A physical bookshop that doubled the range of titles it carried would probably need to double the size of its premises, and perhaps almost double its staff of shop assistants. When an e-commerce site is up and running, adding numerous web pages similar to existing ones is only a marginal extra expense.

Considerations such as these are why investors were so happy to put large sums into e-businesses that spent money like water and did not expect to see profits for years.

## TECHNOLOGY LOCK-IN

Investing to Get Big Fast makes sense only if, having won the race and taken a large market share, one can keep it. Any high-street greengrocer could corner custom by giving away a £5 note with every bag of vegetables sold but, once the fivers stopped, customers would drift back to the greengrocers they used before.

It is often claimed that customers for technical products do not – or, rather, cannot – behave like that. They get *locked in* to a technology, so that a company that gets big fast not only corners the market but also keeps it.

The example of technical lock-in that almost everyone has heard of is the QWERTY keyboard. When typewriters were invented (the story runs), engineering limitations meant that rapid typists jammed the keys; this was combated by distributing the alphabet around the keyboard in an arrangement that forced typists to work slower. In the 1930s, when the technology had improved and jamming was no longer an issue, a better arrangement – the Dvorak keyboard – was invented; but it never took off, because the English-speaking world was locked into QWERTY. Manufacturers that might market Dvorak keyboards would find no buyers, because touch-typists were trained on QWERTY; typists that might train on the Dvorak layout could not, because it was not manufactured.

Many people would be better off if we all switched from QWERTY to Dvorak, but there is no way to get there from here.

The suggestion is that this is not just a tale from history but a vivid illustration of a pervasive phenomenon in high-tech markets. Technology by its nature produces lock-ins: so the first mover advantage is huge, and getting big fast at any cost makes business sense.

This idea has been influential among investors in e-commerce. But it ain't necessarily so.

## DO LOCK-INS EXIST?

The flaws in the lock-in idea were exposed by Stan Liebowitz (2002), who pointed out in the first place that the QWERTY story is false. Although the QWERTY layout was chosen to prevent jamming, it is also a good arrangement for fast typing. Impartial experiments comparing QWERTY and Dvorak show little difference.

What is true of keyboard layouts is true more generally, according to Liebowitz. Alleged cases of technical lock-in dissolve when looked at carefully. Either a technology that dominates its market is about as good as (or better than) alternatives that are failing to make inroads; or, if an alternative technology really is superior, then it will displace the market leader.

The most plausible cases of lock-in are cases where the benefit of a technology to one individual depends on how many others use it. If telephone companies were not interconnected, so that subscribing to one enabled you to phone only other customers of that same company, then most people would want to subscribe to whichever company most people subscribed to: that is called a *network effect*. Network effects can be relevant to IT. Even if some better word-processing format were invented, I might be reluctant to switch from Microsoft Word while the people who swap files with me still use Word – it would lead to too much hassle. If those people all made the same calculation, then Word could retain our allegiance; although Liebowitz claims that in practice network effects are not strong enough to prop up inferior technology.

In any case, for e-business, network effects are often irrelevant. If I decide to stop buying from Amazon, then the fact that many people do still use it will not be a consideration for me. Why should I care who *other* consumers buy from?

## FIRST VERSUS BEST

All this suggests that first mover advantage and Get Big Fast may be overrated principles. Being first to market may enable an e-merchant to gain from customer inertia – a later competitor could find it hard to gain market share by being only equally good; but a competitor that offers customers more can win in the end.[4] Liebowitz is in no doubt:

> If you are faced with the choice of either rushing a weak product or Web site to market in order to be first or taking the necessary time to be best, go with best.

Amazon achieved its success through quality of service rather than timing. It soon acquired competitors – Barnes & Noble launched an online operation in February 1997; but market research showed that online book buyers preferred the Amazon experience to that offered by other online bookshops. The consumer rating service BizRate (p. 77) initially gave Amazon one of the highest scores for any e-tailer, and it continues to give it outstandingly high ratings.

On the other hand, experience as e-commerce has recovered from the dotcom crash suggests that there may be something to the first-mover theory. The journalist Ken Young commented in 2005:

> Curiously, many predictions about the internet made before the crash seem to be coming true. Those with 'first-mover' advantage are invariably the sector leaders.[5]

## ELUSIVE PROFITS

The original e-commerce vision was of companies that sink scarcely any capital into inventory or buildings, and simply conjure profits out of the electronic network, by providing virtual links between customers and suppliers.

This vision blurs when web-based companies expand their physical operations, as Amazon did when it began to hold its own stocks of books. The costs of the virtual side of company activities can soon be dwarfed by the costs of the physical side. Gary Rieschel noted:

> … it takes between $15 million and $25 million to build a top-of-the-line Web site. Yet it costs at least $150 million to build a warehouse and distribution system for a consumer Web operation.[6]

---

[4] Fernando Suarez and Gianvito Lanzolla (2005) analyse a range of industries to discover what types of market conditions lead to genuine first mover advantage; their findings imply that the high-tech sector is one where the concept is least likely to apply.

[5] 'E-business bounces back', *IT Week* 12 September 2005.

[6] Reported by Michael J. Mandel and Robert D. Hof, 'Rethinking the Internet', *BusinessWeek* 26 March 2001.

Consequently the economies of scale that are such an attractive feature of e-business become irrelevant, because operating costs are dominated by areas where outgoings rise in closer proportion to growth in activity.

By early 2001, Amazon's annual revenue was running at $2.8 billion, but it had yet to make a profit in any accounting quarter. I do not mean to make light of Amazon's remarkable success at satisfying numerous customers. But, so long as Amazon continued to make losses, on average each instance of customer satisfaction was costing more than Amazon charged in return. The greengrocer was still tucking £5 notes in with the carrots. This was nothing unusual among the market-share-chasing e-tailers of the time; in 1999, net losses for five of the best-known companies ranged between 22 per cent and more than 300 per cent of sales revenues. But people were starting to see that it could not go on indefinitely. Harold Bordwin, a liquidation adviser, commented:

> People have been saying by selling products at a loss, we'll be the category killer, and when there's a shakeout, we'll be able to impose margins. That doesn't make sense to me. It's like the old joke about losing money on every sale and making it up in volume.[7]

Investors agreed, and the bubble burst – many dotcoms collapsed, and others saw their share prices fall to fractions of the previous figure. Amazon survived the bloodletting, but by 2001 its shareholders' patience had worn thin. They wanted to see a move towards profitability.

Bezos responded by cutting back hard to try to get into the black – 15 per cent of employees were let go, and some customer service centres were closed. The idea of striving to give customers the impression that behind all the technology they were interacting with quirky, literate people had gone out of the window a couple of years earlier. James Marcus (one of those literate Amazon editors) quotes the chairman of an editorial meeting in 1999:

> Remember how I used to talk about creating the best possible buying environment for the customer? Giving them the information they needed to make an intelligent decision? Well, that's over ...
>
> (Marcus 2004: 131–2)

From now on they were to think of themselves as 'store managers', not 'editors' (Marcus 2004: 168). Amazon refocused towards income-generating

---

[7] Quoted in W.M. Bulkeley and J. Carlton, 'Reality bites – e-tail gets derailed', *Wall Street Journal* 5 April 2000.

techniques that could be implemented automatically and hence cheaply, no longer worrying too much about whether customers saw the site as a 'destination'.

Amazon did finally achieve profits in the fourth quarters of both 2001 and 2002. (Any bookshop makes far more sales in the period leading up to Christmas than in the rest of the year.) Since 2003 Amazon has been making profits not only in the Christmas quarters but over complete years. But it will take many profitable years before Amazon earns back the $2.3 billion it had lost by 2001, so that the net economic consequences of its existence are the same as if Bezos had stuck to his day job in 1994.

## DIFFERENT PERFORMANCE MEASURES

Simple graphs of Amazon's finances will demonstrate how different an impression one can get of the health of a firm, depending on the statistics that one focuses on. For consumers, the most obvious financial fact about a company is that it takes money in from its customers. The total income received from customers annually is, in Britain, called the company's *turnover*, but since Amazon is an American company I shall use the more transparent American term 'revenue'. Figure 3.1 shows Amazon's revenue over its first decade as a public company.

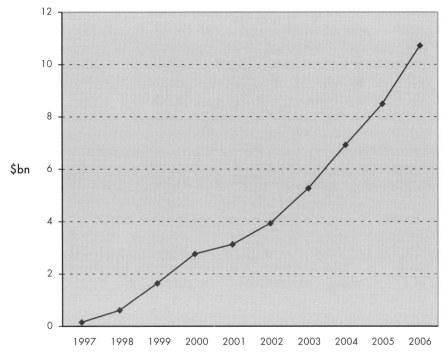

**Amazon revenue (yearly)**

FIGURE 3.1

It is an impressive picture: a rather steady climb, rising to well over $10 billion in 2006. My students who found it odd to query whether Amazon should be seen as a success undoubtedly had in mind something like Figure 3.1: how much more successful could a company be?

However, a firm does not only have income. It also has outgoings, which will commonly use up most of the income. An established company is doing well if it achieves a profit margin of 10–20 per cent – that is, keeps its outgoings down to no more than 80–90 per cent of turnover. Amazon must buy at wholesale prices the books and other goods that it sells on to its customers, and it must find the various other costs of doing business – notably, employees' pay. Figure 3.2 shows Amazon's *net income* over the same period – the income left belonging to the owners of the company (namely, its shareholders), after the company had covered all its outgoings, including tax on profits in profitable years. A very different picture! For several years the company plunged into accelerating losses, until the situation was taken in hand in 2001; and the profits since 2003 have been on a lower scale than the earlier losses.

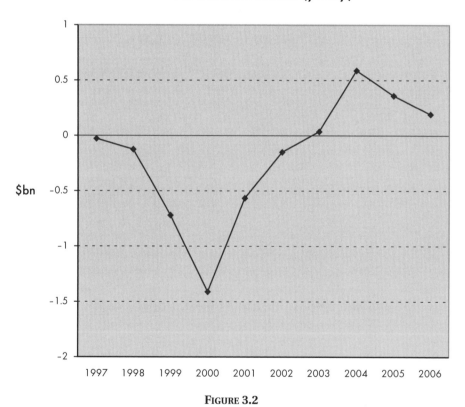

**Amazon net income (yearly)**

FIGURE 3.2

Now look at Figure 3.3, the firm's share price over the same period: what someone had to pay to become a part-owner of Amazon. Whereas Figures 3.1 and 3.2 represent successive chunks of time (years), a share price varies continuously, day by day and indeed minute by minute during stock-market trading hours. I have compromised with the format of the earlier graphs by taking a snapshot of Amazon's share price once every six months, which smoothes out what was in reality an even bumpier ride than that shown in Figure 3.3. (For brief periods in 1999 the price went over $100.)

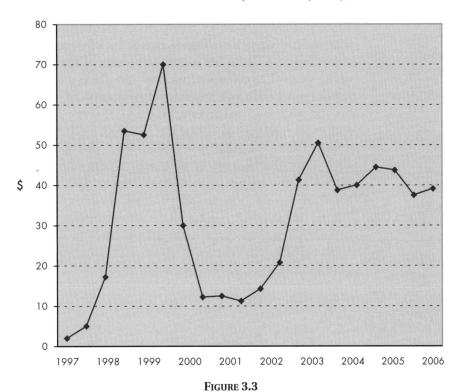

### Amazon share price (half-yearly)

**FIGURE 3.3**

One might imagine that the ups and downs of a firm's share price should mirror its profitability. But in this case the graphs do almost the opposite. The price zooms upwards in the closing years of the old century, while losses were growing deeper, and then collapses in the opening years of this decade, while the company was moving towards profitability; now profitability has been achieved, the share price is drifting around an intermediate value, although seemingly with a gentle downward trend.

Share price and profit do not move in step, because a graph of profit is a record of *past* facts, while share price is determined by buyers' and sellers' forecasts of *future* unknowns. The only reasons to buy a share in a company are to do with its ability to make profits. One hopes to get an income, in the shape of *dividends* (part of the annual profits that are distributed to the owners in proportion to their shareholdings – commonly, another part of the profits will be ploughed back into future company activities); and one hopes for *capital growth* – that is, that one will eventually be able to sell one's shares for more than their purchase price – which in turn depends on other people's expectations about profitability. Everything about a share price is ultimately determined by people's views of the company's future ability to pay dividends, but past profitability (or the reverse) is only one kind of evidence about that. With a new, growing firm it is not very useful evidence.

To a large extent, share price movements reflect a collective process of intellectual discovery, as the community of investors comes to understand better the factors that will govern firms' future profitability. In Figure 3.3, the steep initial climb corresponded to a widespread overestimate in the late 1990s of how easy it would be to exploit the still largely mysterious web for profit. The precipitous fall in 2000 represented the sudden realisation, as people learned more about this new thing, that it was not going to be so easy after all. Then when Amazon did eventually move into profit, the higher share price showed that investors expected this to continue, though they are more sober now than in 1999 about the profit levels likely to be achievable.

Thus, Figure 3.2 has some influence on the shape of Figure 3.3, but only a limited influence. As for Figure 3.1, as an indicator of the overall success of the company it tells us almost nothing taken on its own. Clearly, if we aim to assess the health of a company from financial data, then we must be very careful about which statistics we look at. In a book such as this, we can do no more than scratch the surface of the financial aspects of business. (For a readable introduction to the subject addressed to computing students, see Blackstaff 2001.)

## DIVERSIFICATION

In pursuit of the Get Big Fast principle, Amazon expanded not only internationally (beginning in 1998, when Amazon bought existing British and German online bookshops and turned them into Amazon.co.uk and Amazon.de) but also into many other retail sectors. In 1998 it branched out from books into music, and later that year into DVDs and videos. The following year it began selling toys and electronics; and the trend continued. At different times Amazon has moved into selling pet products, kitchenware, clothes, DIY equipment and other categories – most recently, packs of non-perishable groceries. Some of these ventures failed, but others flourish, to the point where it would be quite misleading, nowadays, to call Amazon an 'online bookshop'. By 2005, Amazon was selling more consumer electronics than books. The slogan has changed from EARTH'S BIGGEST BOOKSTORE to THE WORLD'S LARGEST SELECTION.

Once Amazon had established that it was possible to use the web as a large-scale retailing medium, Get Big Fast was a motive for broadening its range. But broadening was problematic in several ways. Not everything is traded the way books are traded; some things may not lend themselves to internet selling at all; and there was a hidden flaw in the financial logic.

We shall take these points in turn.

## DIFFERENT KINDS OF RETAILING

Amazon's earliest diversification, into selling music CDs, probably required no great adaptation to its business model – music can be sourced and shipped off to customers in much the same way as books. But for some of the other new categories, that was far from true.

Consider toys, for instance. Toy manufacturers do not sell their leading lines in dribs and drabs as publishers sell books, title by title. They try to catch tides of fashion by planning new lines of toys that have a chance of becoming crazes, and they market them in quantity at annual trade fairs. If you were a retailer attending the fair, as James Marcus (2004: 186) recalled, you

> … tried to guess what America's children would be playing with twelve months hence, and placed your bets. If you were wrong, and not a single tot wanted that Jabba the Hutt pedal scooter, you were screwed.

There is no sale-or-return with toys: the retailer would have lost its money.

So however successful a retail operation is at selling one kind of good, there is no guarantee that it will succeed with another kind. Different products pose different commercial problems. Another issue that scarcely arose with bookselling was shipping and delivery. When Amazon moved into home improvements, these were suddenly highly problematic:

> … when the postman dropped by with your table saw, which could weigh up to 1,000 pounds, he was going to have trouble pushing it through the mail slot. To make matters worse, Amazon was charging only $4.95 to deliver that table saw.
>
> (Marcus 2004: 187)

The delivery charge had to be kept down to the minimal level that is cost-effective for shipping books, because if Amazon charged the true cost of delivering the table saw it would be so easy for customers instead to buy it at the American equivalent of Homebase.

Problems such as these abound, and the excellence of Amazon's web interface does nothing in itself to solve them. Getting consumers to order your products is only one of the challenges a retailer has to solve (albeit a large challenge). The problems mentioned here are independent of the electronic sales medium.

## EXPERIENCE GOODS

Another diversification problem does relate to the electronic interface. It is not clear that internet selling is as suited to other products as it is to books (nor that the data Amazon has accumulated on book buyers will be helpful for selling other things).

I was puzzled, after I began buying books from Amazon, to find flyers advertising kitchenware tucked in with the books when they arrived. It was hard to believe that the books I buy make me look a good prospect for pots and pans. In any case, while physical contact is not very relevant for book-buying decisions, in our house if we need new kitchenware we want to see it and touch it before buying. If that means waiting a fortnight to visit a distant shop, that is fine – our saucepan purchases are never urgent. Is the Sampson family unusual there? I doubt it.

Kitchen utensils are what marketing experts call *experience goods*: a customer wants direct experience of them before buying them. With books, on the other hand, normally the buyer simply wants the information or literary content contained in them, and so direct contact is not significant for buying decisions. Stan Liebowitz (2002: 58–86) predicted that, among others, experience goods would not be likely to sell well online.

Admittedly, kitchenware brands tend to be distributed widely; for expensive items, Amazon might hope that customers would assess them in a conventional shop but then save money by buying the identical utensils at a discount online. The point is worth pursuing, though, because for some categories of goods this seems less realistic. How many people are regularly going to try on a suit or a dress in a high-street shop and then say 'I'll think about it' and go home to order the same garment online – could they be sure it would fit identically well? Or what about original art? Surely someone buying an expensive painting wants to be able to look at each brushstroke directly, unmediated by pixel rasters and palette code conventions? Furthermore, at the upper end of the art market, one would imagine that part of what the customer is 'buying' is association with the dignified, opulent tradition embodied in the Bond Street galleries and auction rooms where such pictures are sold.

However, several years after Liebowitz's prediction about experience goods, reality seems to have falsified it. Many clothes retailers are making a success of online selling. By 2006 Dorothy Perkins was selling more via its website than on the high street, and Topshop expected shortly to be in the same position. Even small boutiques are making e-tail work. Twenty-eight-year-old Sara Kumari is a typical clothes e-shopper: 'Occasionally something doesn't fit', she concedes, 'but I just sell it on eBay and get the money back.'[8]

Again, one might feel that direct experience is essential in buying a second-hand car. eBay originally believed that no-one would want to buy a used car online, where they cannot lift the bonnet or kick the tyres. They found different when users began listing real cars in the section eBay provided for toy cars; nowadays eBay Motors is a significant portion

---

[8] Quoted by Clare Coulson, 'Shopping @nd clicking', *Daily Telegraph* 8 November 2006.

of the firm's business. Perhaps even more surprisingly, online art sales are working well too.

The argument that some things are intrinsically un-e-tailable seemed persuasive, but apparently it was fallacious.

## TIGHT MARGINS

A further diversification problem related to *profit margins*. Amazon had built up a huge customer base and knew its customers perhaps more closely as individuals (through their tastes in books) than any other large company. It wanted to exploit that body of data to sell other products for which there is a large difference between price paid to the wholesaler and price charged to the customer. But there is a problem of economic logic lurking there.

Many e-tailers began with the idea that the low overheads of running a website should make it easy to undercut conventional shops. Amazon offers larger-than-normal discounts on book prices, so that its profit margin on books is already smaller than that for conventional bookshops. However, beyond the short term it is not conventional retailers with which an e-tailer needs to compare its profit margins – it is other e-tailers.

With categories of product that consumers are happy to buy online, it may well be that conventional retailers will be driven out of business because they cannot match e-tailers' prices. That has happened much less than some expected; but, even if it does happen, it will not leave e-tailers free to make profits by charging prices that are just a little less than the prices that made conventional retailing viable. Competition between online merchants in the same market sector is likely to be even fiercer than competition between conventional retailers, because it is so easy for buyers to compare prices online. So, even if some goods are currently associated with large profit margins, where online selling of those goods is feasible, the margins will narrow.

Many early enthusiasts for e-commerce were victims of a plausible-looking fallacy. They assumed that if inventing and implementing a novel e-commerce technique allows something to be done more cheaply than it can be done by conventional means, then the saving will accrue as ongoing profit to whoever implements the technique. But in a market economy there is simply no reason why that need be true, and often it is not. Much of the effort that people have put into developing e-commerce has in practice created savings for the benefit not of those people but of their customers. As economists say, consumers are able to 'capture' the gains achieved.

This is one way in which e-commerce functions to shift the balance of economic power from traders towards consumers. In conventional retailing, there is a large knowledge imbalance: merchants selling a particular type of good will normally know far more about the qualities of those goods, how much competitors are selling them for and so forth than individual consumers (who have limited time to research any particular purchase). The web makes that research much easier and quicker, which puts purchasers in a stronger position vis-à-vis sellers.

In China we are seeing the emergence of a further step in this rebalance of bargaining power. Consumers are using the internet to form groups of people who all want to buy the same thing, and who use their resulting bargaining power to negotiate large discounts with the retailers. In Europe, where haggling has not been the way of life that it is in many parts of Asia, this technique has not yet arrived; but it is a logical progression from things that have already happened.

## ALLIANCES

We saw in Chapter 2 that alliances are often seen as key to the success of e-business. Amazon was slower than some to take this road, but in due course it did so. For instance, in 2000 Amazon partnered with Toys R Us to create a website selling toys and video games. Toys R Us bought and managed the inventory and took the risk of goods failing to sell; Amazon was responsible for website development, order fulfilment and customer service.

One special type of alliance-building began much earlier, in 1996, when Amazon started its Associates programme. ('Associate' is Amazon's term; now that the concept has become commonplace in e-tailing, the standard term is 'affiliate'.) Businesses or organisations that run sites devoted to a particular topic link their book recommendations to Amazon; a visitor to the associate site can click to buy a book, and Amazon fulfils the order, paying a commission to the associate. By 2002 Amazon had more than 800,000 associate sites. For Amazon this is a valuable source of new customers.

Furthermore, Spector (2000: 158) points out that Amazon's affiliate programme, being the first in the field, was set up in a particularly advantageous way: once a customer makes a purchase through the programme, Amazon 'owns' that customer and pays no subsequent commissions. Many other e-businesses have imitated the Amazon Associates programme, but in later versions the affiliates have typically required continuing benefits from customer relationships that they initiate.

## INTERMEDIATION AND DISINTERMEDIATION

One way in which commentators often discuss what is innovative about online retailing operations is to describe them as cases of 'digital intermediation' or 'electronic intermediation'. The term *intermediation* and the opposite, *disintermediation,* are used heavily in academic writing about e-business – although, unfortunately, these words are not always used as carefully as technical terms ought to be used.

The idea behind these terms is that computer technology can enable value to be created by inserting a new step at some point into a value chain (intermediation); or conversely that the technology can make some existing step redundant (disintermediation). In Chapter 2 we saw that IT may be causing value chains to split up into different-sized segments from before; that does not imply a change in the total number of steps, but only in how many steps are executed within the bounds of a single organisation. The idea of electronic (dis)intermediation is that the value chains themselves might change length, in terms of the number of steps by which goods or services reach the consumer.

Although these terms are used widely, they involve confusion. Some may feel that, in a book such as this, it would be better to avoid ambiguous terms and to write about e-business only in language that does not lend itself to misunderstanding. Unfortunately, that would leave readers defenceless when they encounter these words elsewhere – and they are used so frequently that many readers will encounter them. It seems better to be explicit about the confusion and help readers to see what is really going on behind the ambiguities.

It is reasonably easy to quote cases that fit the definition of disintermediation, as I explained it above. One example would be airline websites such as Travelocity, which have made it easy for consumers to buy flight tickets directly from airlines, 'disintermediating' the high-street travel agencies that used to represent the only practical way for most individuals to book flights.

In the early years of e-commerce it was less easy to identify clear cases of electronic intermediation. Nowadays, good examples are price-comparison sites such as uSwitch. When I surmised recently that our family was paying over the odds for gas and electricity, I gave uSwitch details on our pattern of usage: uSwitch calculated recommended deals with new suppliers, and opened accounts with them on our behalf. Instead of dealing with the utility companies directly, I used uSwitch as an *electronic intermediary*. The commission that the suppliers must have paid uSwitch (to make its business viable) was evidently worth their paying, as the cost of achieving better take-up of their offerings than if consumers had to research them individually.

Cases such as Travelocity, which cuts out a link in a conventional value chain, and uSwitch, which inserts a link, are reasonably clear. We surely need to distinguish cases such as these from cases where the number of links remains constant but an e-business takes over some link from conventional competitors.

## CONFUSION OF TERMS

This is where confusion has often arisen, particularly in the early years when there was little 'true' e-intermediation. As one example, consider a far-sighted study of the future of e-business by Alina Chircu and Robert Kauffman (2001). The substance of Chircu and Kauffman's predictions has turned out very accurate, but the language in which the predictions were made is misleading.

What Chircu and Kauffman said, in effect, was that when *pure-play* (that is, electronic-only) startups threaten the trade of established conventional competitors, in the long run the established firms will commonly see off the threat by adding an electronic side to their operations and becoming *clicks-and-mortar* hybrids. However, the way Chircu and Kauffman put this was to say that e-only 'intermediaries' may in the short term 'disintermediate' conventional businesses but the latter will succeed in 'reintermediation'. This is deeply confusing – and, although nowadays there are plenty of examples, such as uSwitch, of true electronic intermediation, e-business commentators continue to use this confused terminology.

For Chircu and Kauffman, Amazon was a case of 'intermediation', because it competed successfully with conventional booksellers. But, broadly speaking, Amazon's presence does not increase the number of steps along the value chain linking authors and publishers to readers – it just replaces a conventional link with an electronic link.

Chircu and Kauffman gave two more examples that they regarded as 'intermediation'. One was the American website Priceline, which enables tourists to buy hotel rooms, flights, package holidays etc. by naming their own price, which suppliers fitting the tourists' requirements decide whether to accept. If one assumes that the conventional way for a tourist to book a room is to contact a hotel directly, then Priceline does add an intermediate step, which benefits tourists by making it easy for them to arrange discounts, and benefits hotels by helping them fill their rooms. But with most other things sold through Priceline, such as package holidays, tourists typically would have used an intermediary before the internet: the innovation relates to the novel bargaining power that Priceline bestows on the consumer.

Chircu and Kauffman's third example of intermediation was eBay, which provides a C2C virtual marketplace where individuals can sell one another more or less anything – including, in particular, flea-market-type junk whose owners would often have been unable to find buyers at any price without the internet. eBay is an interesting e-commerce example – apart from anything else, it is one of the few e-businesses that has been profitable from the start. However, eBay does not insert an extra link into an existing value chain. The exchanges that eBay facilitates are often ones that would not have taken place at all without IT.

## INCREASING LIQUIDITY

In the case of both Priceline and eBay, the economically significant consequence of the internet is not changes in the length of value chains but making the market more *liquid*. Mutually beneficial exchanges happen that would not have happened before. Without Priceline, hotel rooms would remain empty because would-be travellers would not discover that the hotel was willing to accept a low price to fill them. Without eBay, items that some collector is glad to pay for would end up on the dump.

The internet can have dramatic consequences for market liquidity. Many of us are willing to pay estate agents thousands to sell our house, because we buy and sell houses so infrequently that we lack the knowledge to strike a good bargain. Walking down a pleasant street, who knows which householders are starting to think about moving and might be willing to accept an offer? And is the street as pleasant as it seems, or are there hidden drawbacks? Since 2006 the USA has had Zillow, a website where you can click on any house in an aerial photo and get a well-informed estimate of its current value; for your own house, you can post a figure that would persuade you to move. Suddenly, everyone has at their fingertips information that they could only previously accumulate through lengthy chats with neighbours and the like.

Increasing market liquidity is an important effect of e-commerce. It is a separate issue from changing the number of links in value chains. The two issues do not always go hand in hand, although sometimes a single e-commerce development may have both consequences.

## CLICKS AND MORTAR VERSUS PURE PLAY

The term 'reintermediation' ought to refer to cases such as high-street travel agents who are threatened with redundancy finding ways to re-establish their role in the face of competition from operations such as Travelocity. But what Chircu and Kauffman mean by reintermediation is strategies by which conventional businesses resist competition by e-only counterparts. When Chircu and Kauffman predict that disintermediation will commonly be followed by reintermediation, they do not mean that middlemen will succeed in reasserting their roles in cases where the internet is enabling their customers to deal with their suppliers directly. That seems implausible. My guess is that high-street travel agencies must wither away as the internet penetration of households increases. What Chircu and Kauffman mean, rather, is that conventional businesses will commonly find ways of fending off competition by dotcom startups. A successful business needs more than innovative technology. It is normally easier for the conventional company to acquire the technology, than for the e-business to acquire the other necessary assets, such as customer base, a well-regarded brand, expertise in the goods or services traded and access to a suitable distribution network.

The substance of Chircu and Kauffman's prediction is turning out by and large to be quite correct. A symbolic record was set on the American Thanksgiving Day in 2005 when, for the first time, the conventional US retailer Wal-Mart got more website visitors than Amazon. According to *The Economist* in late 2005: 'Increasingly, the websites run by conventional retailers – once considered dinosaurs of the bricks-and-mortar age – are growing the fastest.'[9]

For an interesting example of the contrast between online-only and clicks-and-mortar approaches to e-tailing, consider the grocery business.

Various e-only food retail companies began operations in the late 1990s, delivering customer orders from warehouses that looked very different from conventional supermarkets: they were organised to make the picking-and-packing process efficient, and there were no displays arranged to tempt shoppers, because there were no shoppers. The most highly regarded of these startups internationally was Webvan, launched in 1999 to serve the west coast and Chicago areas of the USA. Webvan succeeded in attracting more investment than any other e-tailer apart from Amazon.

By contrast, when Tesco began its online service Tesco Direct in 2000, it did not sink money into dedicated warehouses; orders were made up from the same supermarket shelves from which conventional shoppers were filling their trolleys. American media were amused at the naivety of these Limeys. The e-commerce magazine *Industry Standard* wrote, in Tesco Direct's first year:

> The Tesco Direct service is so low-tech it's bizarre. Orders are sent to the Tesco store nearest the customer's home, then 'pickers' pull the desired items off the shelves. You read that right – no warehouse... Tesco [had] better invest in infrastructure, including 'dedicated picking centres' free of day-to-day shopper traffic ... [because] the Web is an unforgiving place.
>
> (Quoted by Murphy 2003)

The Limeys had the last laugh. In 2001, Webvan went bankrupt – while Tesco Direct had already become a profitable arm of its parent company; it is now making important contributions to Tesco's growth and profitability.

Tesco Direct had no ideological objection to dedicated warehouses, and in 2006 it opened one in Croydon. Chief executive Sir Terry Leahy explained:

---

[9] 'Clicks, bricks and bargains', *The Economist* 3 December 2005.

> We found that in the south of London we were short of stores from which to operate our dot-com business and it was holding back our growth.[10]

For that matter, it is not a given that the online-only approach must fail in this market. In Britain, Ocado (launched in 2002) has been running as an online-only grocery, in partnership with Waitrose; at the time of writing it has not yet turned a profit, but investors remain optimistic. In 2006 the electrical goods retailer Dixons decided to *become* a pure-play e-tailer, using the expertise and other resources it has built up over the years as a high-street chain to sell in future exclusively online.

What has evaporated, though, is the idea that 'the internet changes everything', and that conventional business techniques are all ancient history. Nowadays, e-business is seen as another family of tools to add to the existing business arsenal. They are new and shiny tools, but someone who acquires a power drill does not throw away their saws and hammers.

## THE TECHNOLOGY PROVIDER ROLE

A further prediction of Chircu and Kauffman's 2001 paper was that, because established firms were likely to out-compete pure-play e-companies, the best longer-term strategy for the latter would often be to stop trying to win that competition, and instead to adopt the role of technology provider, developing and licensing the systems that conventional companies need in order to become clicks-and-mortar businesses.

Amazon began going down that route early. Already in 2000 Amazon licensed its 1-Click software and trademark for use in Apple's Online Store, and in 2001 Amazon contracted to provide e-commerce arms for Borders (the second US bookshop chain), which had tried to set up its own online operation without great success, and for Waterstone's in Britain. The arrangement with Waterstone's ended in 2006, when that company decided that it needed more direct control over its e-shop, but meanwhile Amazon had been doing similar deals with a wider variety of retailers. Since 2002 Amazon has been providing e-commerce infrastructure for the US department-store chain Target. In 2005 Marks & Spencer decided that its in-house e-commerce operation was failing to achieve its potential and outsourced it to Amazon.

Recently, Amazon has been developing the technology-provider side of its business in other ways. In 2002 it initiated a 'web services' business (see Chapter 12), allowing website developers to incorporate features from Amazon's site into their sites – for instance, an outside website could

---

[10] Quoted in Madeline Bennett, 'Tesco reviews web range as online sales near £1bn', *IT Week* 1 May 2006.

give its own visitors the ability to search Amazon's database. Later, Amazon began its Simple Storage Service (S3), which provides online digital storage at 15 cents a gigabyte, and Elastic Compute Cloud (EC2), which rents out processing capacity on Amazon's machines to smaller companies. In September 2006 Amazon announced Fulfilment by Amazon, under which other companies can use Amazon's personnel and facilities for shipping goods and dealing with returns, and WebStore, an off-the-peg e-shop solution for small traders. Amazon's new Unbox operation is a video-download service – an area where it faces little competition as yet and profit margins are high. When Amazon managed in 2006 to promote an unknown novel to best-seller status, it took an option on the film rights and looked for a studio to partner with in order to produce the film.

Selling e-commerce technology to other companies may be a good strategy in its own right. However, Amazon has made no moves to withdraw from e-tailing. By moving into diverse kinds of technology-provision business, while maintaining its original e-tailing operations, Amazon has now become a rather amorphous company. Nicholas Carr commented in 2005: 'For investors, it's becoming difficult to figure out exactly what kind of company Amazon is.'[11]

It might seem a good idea for a company to pursue every opportunity it spots to develop new income streams, even if the opportunities lead in different directions. Business experts standardly regard that as a bad idea, though. Running any one business is such a complex, challenging task that the only chance of doing it well (so the consensus runs) is to focus on developing the specific type of business one knows. The usual phrase is that a firm should 'stick to its knitting'.

Challenged on this, Jeffrey Bezos claims that the technology selling that Amazon has moved into 'is the knitting':

> This is what we've been doing for 11 years. The only thing that's changed is that we're exposing it for others.[12]

Well, perhaps. Bezos is saying that the core focus of Amazon is the technology it has created, initially for its own use and now additionally to be sold to others. But, as we have seen, even a technology-based company is not just about technology. The technology that Amazon is now marketing may be the same as it has been using for its internal purposes, but the business of marketing that technology will undoubtedly differ in various deep respects from the business of book retailing, and indeed from retailing in general.

---

[11] Nicholas G. Carr, 'Amazon.com's split personality', *BusinessWeek* 9 June 2005.
[12] Quoted in 'The e-commerce giant wants to be more than just a retailer', *The Economist* 5 October 2006.

## CONCLUSION

At the time of writing, Amazon's turnover is continuing to climb, but profits have fallen because of continued heavy investment in technology, together with the free delivery it offers on many purchases (attractive to consumers, but expensive for Amazon). In February 2007 the analyst Safa Rashtchy commented on Amazon's latest quarterly figures, 'The revenue growth was impressive. But over all, the picture hasn't changed. They're still asking us to have faith.'[13] Over the three years to early 2007, Amazon's profit margin (the proportion by which revenue exceeds outgoings) has varied between 3.5 per cent and 5.1 per cent – unimpressive, set against Wal-Mart's 5.5 per cent. Whether the company will turn the corner and become a good investment remains a very open question.

There is no risk of the name Amazon vanishing. When a brand has achieved the level of impact that Amazon has achieved, it is too valuable to be allowed to die. Even if the company that uses the brand changes the nature of its business radically, or is taken into new ownership, the brand will be maintained.

What the future holds for Amazon the company, on the other hand, is less clear. Perhaps Jeffrey Bezos's current multi-pronged strategy will succeed; or perhaps in five years' time Amazon will label a very different business from the one we know.

This uncertainty itself makes Amazon an appropriate e-business case study.

---

[13] Quoted by Laurie J. Flynn, 'Amazon's revenue rises but profit drops', *International Herald Tribune* 2 February 2007. There was a sharp uptick in share price when Amazon's second-quarter results were released in 2007.

# 4 E-Business and the Institutions of Society

## INSTITUTIONAL BARRIERS

Back in 1998, much of the technology that makes e-commerce possible was already in place. A study by the University of Freiburg looked into why businesses were proving slow to exploit it; the findings remain enlightening today. The study (Schoder *et al.* 1998) examined almost 1000 large and small companies in German-speaking Europe; as in the economy generally, most were dedicated to B2B trading, and a minority to B2C. Even those companies that already used the web were often using it merely as a publicity medium.

The survey responses made the reasons clear. Most companies believed that their business could in principle be ported to the internet; few of them saw the complexity of the technology, or the speed at which it was changing, as barriers. Instead, overwhelmingly they cited problems about lack of business conventions in this new domain, and inadequate legal regulation together with unclarity about how existing laws applied.

E-commerce presented companies with opportunities, but also with risks – the researchers classified these as:

- *Client risk* – difficulty in assessing the reliability of customers who make contact via the web.
- *Financial risk* – the value of goods or money that might be lost through internet trading.
- *Legal risk* – problems about assigning responsibility for various elements of electronic transactions and enforcing contracts.

For these managers, legal risk far outweighed client risk and financial risk combined.

The Freiburg findings made clear how crucial for the evolution of e-business are matters that relate to *social institutions* rather than to the technology itself – matters such as law, accepted ways of doing things and attitudes. The social institutions of the conventional business world developed over centuries. It will be a long time before society has adapted its institutions to the new medium sufficiently to create a stable framework for e-business.

## WEALTH, POVERTY AND SOCIAL INSTITUTIONS

The fundamental importance of these issues becomes unmistakable when we consider why some societies are rich and others poor.

Differences in prosperity between countries are huge. Burundi has an annual income per head of US$200 and falling – despite a lush agricultural environment. Canada's income per head is more than 100 times higher, though in the colonial period it seemed such a useless territory that in 1763 the British debated whether it would be better to take Canada or the small West Indian island of Guadeloupe from the French as reparation for the Seven Years' War.

William Easterly and Ross Levine (2003) analysed economic and social indices to discover how responsibility for prosperity differences between countries should be divided between three factors: geography (e.g. access to the sea); government policies, which may favour or hinder economic advance; and social institutions, such as political stability, established systems of property rights and so forth. One might guess that all three factors contribute to prosperity or its opposite, but Easterly and Levine found that good institutions are the *only* factor that matters directly. With good institutions, Burundi might be as prosperous as Canada; with bad institutions, Canada – or Britain – could be as wretched as Burundi.[1]

This suggests how much there is to play for in the evolution of e-business. Relative to what may emerge from the new technology, we are in a situation like that of eighteenth-century Canadian colonists: the future is ours to build. Getting the institutional framework for e-business right may not just affect progress marginally; it may make the difference as to whether e-business ends up as a minor innovation or explodes into a revolution of wealth-generation whose characteristics cannot be guessed at. Let us examine some sample areas where institutions are already proving problematic.

## DIGITAL SIGNATURES

A good example of a social institution on which conventional business depends is the *signature*. This is purely a convention, but an important one; yet it is tied to pre-electronic technology. The speed and convenience of online business interactions are lost if nothing can be settled without signatures in ink on paper. One case study found that

> ... it takes ten days for a bank to process a simple student loan that should take one day, because the bank has to print out the on-line forms and courier them to the applicant for signatures, then wait for them to be returned by post only to scan them back into digital form.[2]

But the convention of writing one's name by hand is only a means to an end. The business world could happily live without signatures, if it could agree on some electronic convention that serves the same purpose.

---

[1] It is fair to point out that Easterly and Levine's conclusions have been called into question by Glaeser *et al.* (2004).

[2] 'Just sign here', *The Economist* 10 June 2006.

For 30 years the IT industry has been attempting to develop a system of 'digital signatures', but no system has yet achieved general acceptance.

What is the business function of signatures? There are at least two:

- *Authentication* – the signature helps the recipient of a document to be sure that it comes from whom it purports to come from.
- *Non-repudiation* – if someone places an order or agrees a bargain, after they sign a written statement of the transaction they cannot later claim that it never happened or that the details were other than they were.

Handwritten signatures obviously do not achieve these goals perfectly – a signature can be forged. But the signature convention is a good start, universally understood and readily usable; and further devices strengthen the convention, in cases that are crucial enough to need extra support – in some situations a signature is formally witnessed.

There is an electronic technique that, on the face of it, seems to match and indeed improve on the business benefits offered by signatures, as well as having large additional benefits relating to confidentiality. This is *public key cryptography* (e.g. see Levy 2000), invented in 1978 by Ron Rivest, Adi Shamir and Leonard Adleman.[3]

Without going into the details, public key cryptography depends on the mathematical fact that working out the product of numbers is easy, even if the numbers are large, but going the other way – factorising a large number – is difficult. Any individual, say Alice, who uses the system is assigned a pair of large integers, one of which is published as her 'public key' while she keeps the other secret as her 'private key'. By using the various key numbers to transform messages, anyone can send Alice a message using her public key, which Alice can decipher using her private key; and Alice can use her private key to send anyone a message, which they can decipher with Alice's public key – the fact that Alice's public key makes sense of the message guarantees that only Alice could have written it. Alice can send Bob a message that only Alice could have written and only Bob can read by enciphering it twice, with her private key and with Bob's public key – Bob deciphers it using Alice's public key and his own private key.

Any change to a ciphertext means that it deciphers not into a different message but into gibberish. Decipherment of a message without the relevant key is believed to be mathematically impossible.

In principle, public key cryptography offers a near-perfect method of authentication. Physical signatures may be forged, but if someone keeps their private key secret there is no way for anyone else to produce a ciphertext that can be deciphered with the first person's public key. Someone who receives a message legitimately can read it but could not have

---

[3] Although the technique is credited to Rivest, Shamir and Adleman and called the 'RSA algorithm' after their initials, Levy points out that it was invented earlier by scientists at GCHQ Cheltenham, who were forbidden to publicise it for national security reasons.

written it. And business communications often need to be confidential. Provided the intended recipient of a public-key-encrypted communication keeps *their* private key secret, no-one else can read it.

Traditionally, 'cryptography' depends on a single secret key that is agreed between the parties to communication. That allows communication only between agents who are already in a mutual relationship. But public key cryptography allows reliable, secure communication between anyone and anyone, whether or not they have had prior contact.

## PUBLIC KEY INFRASTRUCTURE

From a technical point of view, public key cryptography seems to offer an ideal digital replacement for signatures; but the necessary infrastructure has never developed. For public key cryptography to work, society needs not just the mathematical concept but also a system of trusted authorities distributing keys to organisations and individuals.

In Britain, the Post Office opened a digital certification business, ViaCode, but closed it in 2002 because slow uptake made it financially unviable. Other organisations such as the banking clearinghouse BACS (now VOCA) have experimented, but no trials have taken off sufficiently to achieve general acceptance. There is a catch-22 problem. Digital certification is expensive until it is adopted by enough users to bring down the cost, but while costs remain high and the user community is small, companies prefer to make do with less satisfactory solutions. Individuals are unlikely to get involved at all, until some system has been adopted near-universally by organisations. In the student loan case, even if the loan company had a set of public and private keys, at present there is no chance that the student will have them.

The problem is not just about expense, but also about public understanding and trust. Boaz Gelbord (2000) pointed out:

> Though much easier to forge, the old written signature is a system that everyone understands; we are all more-or-less equally qualified to check if a signature matches the one on the back of a credit card ... people are reluctant to place their trust in a system that requires a high level of mathematical knowledge to understand.

As a result, despite the theoretical attractions of the technique, and despite the fact that some have felt that e-business can never take off properly without it, recently the concept of a public key infrastructure has come to be seen as 'last season's colour', to quote one industry observer.[4]

---

[4] Richard Sharpe, 'PKI products fill a gap in the validation market', *Computing* 29 April 2004.

Other approaches are being tried. In June 2006 a Seattle firm, DocuSign, announced a novel process available to anyone with access to a web browser. But digital signatures are clearly one example of an institution needed for e-business progress that is easier to describe than to create – although the barriers are social, not technical.

## FULFILMENT

Another area involving practical hurdles, particularly for e-tailing, is *fulfilment*.

Fulfilment is the business term for the process of responding to orders by ensuring that customers get the goods. At Christmas 2000, when internet shopping was hot news, journalists wrote stories about how they had decided to join the IT revolution by doing their gift shopping online, only to garner a sheaf of 'sorry you were out' notes from courier companies. People can make special arrangements to receive the odd one-off delivery, but shifting to online purchasing as a routine is less easy. Tesco's online business allows consumers to specify two-hour delivery slots, which can be in the evenings or at weekends; their online-only competitor Ocado offers one-hour slots. This may be practical for grocers, where every town or village generates numerous orders every day, but it would be uneconomical for other sectors with lower density of ordering. The Royal Mail has experimented with various schemes: it tried installing 'drop boxes' so that consumers ordering goods online could have them delivered to lockers at their workplace or in public places, and it ran a 'Decide & Deliver' scheme, which made it easy for shoppers to direct deliveries electronically to convenient locations such as a neighbour's house or a workplace. But by late 2003 these experiments had been abandoned. (If one will have to lug goods home from a drop box, where is the advantage of electronic shopping over the high street?)

Fulfilment is not problematic exclusively for retailing. In the B2B domain there is no difficulty about receiving deliveries; but online trading can generate novel patterns of order flow, which may be hard for the supplier company to satisfy promptly – yet the online medium creates heightened expectations of prompt fulfilment.

That, though, is not a 'social institutions' issue. B2C fulfilment is: it depends not only on what is economically viable for retailers but on what patterns of delivery can be made to fit into consumers' lives. James Roper, chief executive of the e-tailing industry body IMRG, went as far in December 2005 as to say 'Delivery is the last frontier in e-commerce.'[5] It has not really been solved adequately yet.

---

[5] Quoted by Phil Muncaster, 'Delivery scheme aids e-shoppers', *IT Week* 12 December 2005.

## GAPS IN THE LAW

A chief institution distinguishing prosperous from impoverished societies is the rule of law. Businesspeople often say that a business can succeed in any environment, provided it is settled and predictable. Law is a central part of the framework that offers that predictability.

One large issue is how the laws of many separate countries apply to a global medium; and another is the kind of law that regulates business on behalf of society as a whole. Those aspects of law will be discussed in Chapter 5. But for business, the most crucial kind of law is law that defines the rights and duties of one economic agent with respect to other economic agents: a company's entitlements and obligations vis-à-vis competitor companies, supplier or client companies, and consumers. Even within a single national jurisdiction, e-business raises novel problems for these long-established areas of law.

No statute can hope to anticipate every circumstance. English and American law acquires precision from the accumulation of precedents – decisions in earlier cases that settle how some broad principle is to be interpreted in particular contexts. A technology as new and wide-ranging as IT suddenly creates wide areas where no precedents exist, and so no-one can say for sure how the law applies. Any aspect of business may reveal an uncertainty in existing law, but IT is quite special in the size of the gaps it is uncovering.

A few concrete examples from different areas of law will give the reader a sense of how broad the uncertainties about e-business law currently are.

## THE LAW OF CONTRACT

A good example of e-commerce revealing a legal gap was the 2002 Kodak case, relating to the law of contract (for business, perhaps the most crucial area of law). The online Kodak store offered a 'special deal' on a digital camera, mistakenly quoting the price as £100. The normal price would have been over £300, and so this figure was remarkably low – but, arguably, not so low that customers were bound to realise it was an error. Thousands of orders were placed in the few days before the offer was taken down.

In face-to-face shopping, the law is clear. If the wrong price tag is put on goods by mistake, customers cannot hold the shop to that; but once they take the goods to the till and their money is accepted and rung up, it is too late for the shop to say that a mistake has been made. In this case, the Kodak site automatically registered customers' credit-card details and e-mailed order confirmations, but the error was caught before the cards were debited or the cameras shipped out. Had binding contracts been created? Kodak said not: what happened was like bringing goods to the till but not yet paying. Legal experts said various things. In due course, Kodak blinked and honoured the orders at the low price.

From the company's point of view, that was doubtless the right decision: their reputation is worth more than the monetary loss. For e-business generally, it is unfortunate, because an important area of commercial law remains unclarified. Consequently it is that much more difficult than it might be to set up an online trading operation with confidence that the commercial risks have been assessed accurately. (In 2003 Kodak closed its online store.)

In December 2006 another company took the opposite line in a similar situation. Amazon advertised a 'buy one, get one free' promotion on DVD boxed sets, but a software bug meant that a shopper who put two sets in their trolley received the discount twice – that is, the total bill was nil or only a tiny amount. Many such orders were actually sent out. When Amazon noticed, its response was to charge the intended price to customers' credit cards retrospectively, after inviting them to return the goods if they preferred. Many commentators felt that Amazon was on shaky legal ground. Between them the two cases demonstrate the unclarity of this area of law.

## TRADEMARKS AND SEARCH ENGINE RANKINGS

Trademarks are another legal area where e-commerce is creating new uncertainties. One example relates to listings on search engine sites such as Google.

The American company Mark Nutritionals produced a slimming programme under the registered trade name Body Solutions. In 2002 it sued several search engine companies for trademark infringement, because searches on the words 'body solutions' did not yield result lists in which URLs for Body Solutions appeared in the first screen. It happened that Mark Nutritionals went bankrupt before this case was resolved. But then in April 2004 essentially the same issue was revived when the American Blind company took Google to court because its AdWords system (see p. 166) allowed competitors to buy the words 'American' and 'blind', with the result that searches for 'American blind' would not produce the American Blind site in Google's paid-for listings (Battelle 2005: 180–6). Google's position (initially, at least) was that it would respect companies' ownership of phrases registered as trademarks, but not of generic words that happened to occur within those phrases. At the time of writing this case continues.

One understands the trademark owners' displeasure. At the same time, it is hard to imagine how search engine companies could operate in the future, if the decision goes to the plaintiffs. For one thing, as Danny Sullivan put it in connection with the Mark Nutritionals case:

'Orange' is the name of a mobile phone company in the UK, while 'Apple' is the name of a ... computer company... Can searches for these words not carry ads without the permission of Orange or Apple?[6]

## INTELLECTUAL PROPERTY

Clear structures of property rights are crucial for business. The IT revolution has scarcely affected property in the core sense – land and physical goods; but it has large implications for intangible property, such as copyrights and patents. In an information-based society these categories are increasingly important.

Currently, the impact of IT on intellectual property law is throwing up more issues in the area of patents than copyright. In particular, there is a controversy about extending the patent system to business processes.

Traditionally, patents covered things such as novel machines and physical processes. A program could not be patented, because it was not a machine. The routines that a business uses to get its work done were certainly not thought of as patentable things – they were just part of company culture.

In America this position was reversed by two court decisions; one in 1981 allowing patents on software had little effect in practice, but the floodgates were opened by a decision in 1998 (the State Street Bank appeal, cf. Lessig 2002: 208–9) allowing patents on business processes. By 2002 the patent-monitoring company Derwent Information claimed to have catalogued 200,000 business-method patents internationally. Copyright law forbids one company from copying another company's proprietary software code, but American patent law now forbids a company from writing its own code to implement the same process.

In Europe the situation is different. Some individual European Union member countries do allow software patents, but a proposal to introduce them EU-wide was debated fiercely by advocates of both sides of the question and eventually (to many onlookers' surprise) overwhelmingly rejected by the European Parliament in July 2005. (There are already signs, though, that this may not have been the last word from the EU.) In Britain, the non-patentability of software was reaffirmed by the High Court in rejecting an appeal by the news agency Bloomberg in March 2007.

In principle, one can argue either way. Patent law was created for a purpose – to stimulate the invention of valuable new technology by giving inventors a financial incentive. In a modern society, where individual software researchers are typically salaried employees and the companies

---

[6] Danny Sullivan, 'Lawsuit over paid placements to define search engines', *SearchEngineWatch.com* 19 February 2002.

that employ them are straining every corporate muscle to find and maintain competitive edges vis-à-vis their competitors, arguably the incentive is redundant. The economists Michele Boldrin and David Levine (2006) argue that both copyright and patent law are pointless institutions in modern circumstances. But even people who do not hold that extreme view are often sceptical about software patents. Tim Berners-Lee urges that software patents cannot fail to hamper software progress that is in everyone's interests, because innovators would not be free to build on their predecessors' ideas in the normal way: 'Programming is always about reassembling existing stuff – novel ideas are rare.'[7]

A contrary point of view is that software patents are needed to compensate companies for the fact that automation makes their processes transparent. When a firm's business processes are executed manually, they are largely inexplicit; new recruits pick them up as much through tacit imitation as systematic training, and patents would be redundant even if available because it would be so hard to identify what a competitor might want to copy. Computerisation entails spelling everything out explicitly. David Kaefer of Microsoft urges that 'Software patents take the place of trade secrets that we relied on before.'[8] IT creates a need for different firms' systems to link up with one another and be interoperable, so one company must reveal its processes to others, and hence software and business-process patents have become a necessary device for ensuring that separate interlinked organisations can each claim their proper share of income: 'Patents are more a form of currency than they are a brick wall.'

## THE PATENT SYSTEM BREAKING DOWN

The argument is complicated by the fact that, in the USA where software patents are now routine, the system of issuing patents is close to breakdown. For a technology to be patentable, the law requires that it must be genuinely new and not obvious. When a patent is requested, these tests have to be applied by officials called patent examiners; and applying them adequately is difficult (how can one reliably check that no-one, anywhere, is already using a given technique?). Refusing a patent takes work to assemble evidence justifying refusal, while granting one is easy, so when patent offices are hard-pressed they grant patents that should not be granted. This is happening a lot in the USA at present, and there are many stories about the resulting absurdities. US patent no. 5,965,809, granted in 1999, defines a technique for determining a woman's bra size by running a tape measure round her bust.

In principle, this problem is independent of the question of whether software should be patentable. But allowing software patents opens up

---

[7] Quoted by Brian Runciman, 'Berners-Lee visits key web issues', *Computing* 6 April 2006.
[8] This and the following Kaefer quotations taken from 'A market for ideas: a survey of patents and technology', *The Economist* 22 October 2005.

such a large new domain of potential patent applications, and the obviousness and 'prior art' tests are so difficult to apply in the abstract world of software, that patent offices are virtually guaranteed to be overwhelmed and issue too many patents. Currently there are many complaints about companies getting patents in the USA for computational techniques that are both obvious and already widely used.

There was considerable disquiet in 1999 when Amazon patented its 'one-click' online purchase method and successfully sued its competitor Barnes & Noble for infringement – the idea of storing a customer's address and credit-card number so that subsequent purchases can be executed without retyping the information seems obvious. One of Amazon's founding programmers, Paul Barton-Davis, has himself argued that company's action was excessively cynical, because the setting up of Amazon

> ... relied on the use of tools that could not have been developed if other companies and individuals had taken the same approach to technological innovation that [Amazon] is now following.
>
> (Quoted by D. Carr *et al.* 2000)

However, Barnes & Noble's appeal failed; and many other American patents have been issued for e-business concepts that seem as trivial as one-click.

## RESPONSIBILITY FOR PUBLIC COMMENT

Talking is a casual, spontaneous activity; people inevitably sometimes talk rather wildly – that is expected, and allowances are made. Traditionally, people were expected to be more responsible about publishing the written word, but publishing was an activity requiring such time and care that this expectation was reasonable. Now, the internet enables people to produce written wording as casually as chatting, while giving it the permanence and visibility of publication. An increasingly significant area of legal unclarity concerns responsibility for spontaneous wording posted on the web.

'Web 2.0' is one of the most fashionable current buzzwords; exactly what it means is often rather vague, but one of the ideas it covers is that user-generated content is destined to be a crucial feature of websites, including commercial sites – companies will be positively encouraging their customer communities to contribute to their sites via blogs, chatrooms and the like. There are powerful business arguments for moving in this direction (some of which will be examined in Chapter 10), but a large problem is that individual consumers will not always be as circumspect about what they write as company staff, who have professional lawyers helping them to avoid statements that might attract costly libel suits.

If a hot-headed member of the public makes a defamatory remark about one company on another company's website, is the latter company responsible? Is the situation legally analogous to a slanderous telephone conversation, for which the phone company is certainly not liable – or is a website host, or an ISP, analogous to a library, a bookshop or a magazine wholesaler, which can be held responsible to some extent for libels contained in the publications they distribute?

At present, English law seems to take the latter view. In consequence, ISPs and websites are tending to play for safety by taking down postings at the first hint of legal challenge, even though it is not clear that a court would in fact hold them liable (and the relevant wording might in any case count as legitimate fair comment).

One clear example was the tussle in Britain in 2007 between the controversial childcare expert Gina Ford and the parenting website Mumsnet.com. Gina Ford's writings advocate a hard-nosed approach to disciplining newborn babies – an issue that quite inevitably arouses strong feelings. A number of parents expressed hostility to Miss Ford on Mumsnet message boards, often in exaggerated, hurtfully sarcastic terms; she responded by attempting via a libel suit to get the Mumsnet site closed down.

To defend itself against closure, Mumsnet felt it necessary to ban any mention of Gina Ford and her methods – which from a business point of view may have been wise (Mumsnet had to protect not only itself but also its members, who in theory might have been sued individually for what they had written); but the decision made it difficult for the community of new parents to sort out how best to answer a range of questions that are vital to the welfare of a generation of children. This is a case where safety-first for the company involved leads to real loss for society as a whole.

After the lawsuit was settled out of court in May 2007, Mumsnet allowed discussion of Gina Ford's ideas to resume, provided that it avoided personal abuse. But it is not clear how successfully Mumsnet will be able to enforce this condition in practice on its tens of thousands of members (it would surely be prohibitively expensive to employ legally trained editors to pre-censor members' postings) – and it leaves other companies that run websites uncertain whether a court would really hold them responsible for customers' opinions in a similar situation in future. To quote Pia Sarma, one of Mumsnet's lawyers:

> While Mumsnet and Gina Ford chose to keep their debate out of the Courts, perhaps it would have been helpful for the law in this area if they had battled it out.[9]

---

[9] Pia Sarma, 'The law flounders in the digital age', *Daily Telegraph* 10 May 2007.

## THE PROBLEM OF TRUST

We saw in connection with digital signatures that the problem of achieving e-business-friendly institutions is not only a problem about creating the technical infrastructure and persuading companies to adopt it. It is also a problem about public knowledge and trust. This problem applies more generally. Business needs a legal framework in the background, but most day-to-day business interactions are not enforced by law; they depend on players weighing one another up and trusting their judgements.

By now, trust is recognised as a crucial barrier to the development of e-commerce. Stephen Timms, then UK e-commerce minister, commented in 2002 that, in discussions about e-business progress, 'The issue that comes up time and time again is trust.'[10] Five years later this continues to hold true. A February 2007 survey found that the UK's online economy is 'in danger of stagnating if businesses do not build more confidence in their customers.'[11]

Traditional business functions as well as it does because the average citizen inherits knowledge about how the world works and how to assess risks, who or what to trust and who or what not to trust, through hearing what his elders say and seeing how they behave. If nobody took anything at all on trust, economic life would surely grind to a halt. The social theorist Francis Fukuyama (1995) has argued that the level of trust endemic in a society is an important determinant of its prosperity. But e-business is a domain where this cultural inheritance does not help. Often, older people understand the domain less well than younger people.

After I opened an account with a highly regarded online British savings bank, whenever I logged on to operate the account I would see a message saying that the bank's 'Verisign security certificate' had expired. The first time, I queried this via e-mail and got a gobbledygook reply; after that I ignored the messages. Was this reasonable? Was it foolish? I haven't a clue, and I have no idea who could tell me. That is a very common situation currently.

In the online world, there is a near-total absence of the subtle cues – the way people dress and speak, the quality of stationery, the appearance of company premises or vehicles – which in offline interactions help us to form or revise our judgements about how much confidence to place in people or organisations. The cues that do exist are often ambiguous or misleading.

The problem is made worse by the fact that patterns of trust are different in different human societies, which are linked by the internet more directly than ever before. Fukuyama pointed out that the default level of trust among unrelated individuals is higher in America,

---

[10] Quoted by Emma Nash, 'Now is the time to start building trust', *Computing* 31 October 2002.
[11] Tom Young, 'Online businesses need to build customer confidence', *Computing* 21 Februray 2007.

Germany and Japan than it is in France, Italy or China, for instance. Statistical analysis of data on 28 countries by Huang *et al.* (2003) showed that even the level of internet penetration correlated closely with societies' trust levels.

## FRAUD

Lack of trust in online business relationships is not just about avoiding fraud. The fact that we have a well-developed environment of trust in the conventional business world means for instance that people have a good feeling for who can be relied on to do high-quality work (or to put things right promptly if something goes amiss), who is likely to remain in business long enough to be able to provide after-sales service in time to come, and all kinds of important issues that are unrelated to downright criminality. But clearly, one of the most crucial aspects of all is confidence that one is not going to be a fraud victim. Even if dishonesty were no commoner online than in conventional business, e-business would be severely hobbled by lower levels of trust. And, proportionately, dishonesty is far commoner online than offline. In conventional business life, people assume that most interactions are legitimate and they need to keep their eyes peeled only for the occasional fraudster. In the online world, chillingly, some sites report that up to 70 per cent of transaction requests are fraudulent.

One need not be a naive newbie to be fooled by the phishing sites that became frequent from about 2003 onwards. In experiments conducted by Dhamija *et al.* (2006), 'Good phishing web sites fooled 90% of participants', and 'neither education, age, sex, previous experience, nor hours of computer use' correlated with vulnerability to phishing. One 2004 survey found that as many as two-thirds of UK internet users would not buy products online for fear of fraud, and this was far from irrational – as many as a million Britons had already been fraud victims while shopping online. (In the USA, almost 2 million online adults had cash stolen from bank accounts just in the 12 months to mid-2004.)

By 2007, a technique even more insidious than phishing, *drive-by pharming*, was emerging. Victims' web browsers are remotely reprogrammed to consult domain name servers controlled by the fraudsters; when the victims try to visit a perfectly honest website, using its correct URL, they are taken instead to a fraudulent copy of the site. If this becomes common, the average web user might feel so defenceless that trust in e-commerce could scarcely survive at all.

## LAW, IT, AND PHILOSOPHY OF MIND

Fraud is also an area where IT has been creating legal issues different from those discussed on pp. 65–70: here, IT has not so much exposed a gap in the law as forced the law to confront a philosophical problem that never arose while business transactions were always between human beings.

In ordinary speech, part of what we mean by fraud is that someone gets deceived. The English law of fraud has defined the crime in that way. In the e-business world, fraudsters are often deceiving machines rather than people – yet *can* one 'deceive' a machine? If I keep a toe on the floor when I step on the bathroom scales, they will register the wrong weight; I might be deceiving myself, but would anyone say that the scales are deceived?

This might sound like academic logic-chopping, but it was creating real doubts about the possibility of prosecuting serious crimes. The new UK Fraud Act, which came into force in January 2007, laid down explicitly that deceiving a computer is indeed a criminal offence. For professional lawyers, to whom a computer is perhaps a mysterious magical agent, this may seem straightforward. To a computer scientist, who knows perfectly well that the box of tricks is no more than a capacious and speedy but mindless bit-shuffler, a law like this sounds uncomfortably reminiscent of earlier laws that solemnly defined and punished witchcraft. As society acquires more familiarity with the nature of computers, it will be interesting to see how well this clause survives the test of courtroom combat.

## EROSION OF PRIVACY

The less trusting we feel, the keener we are to safeguard our privacy. Whereas unfamiliarity leads to lack of trust in online interactions, with privacy the current situation seems to be opposite: often, people are happy to engage in online commercial interactions only because they have little grasp of how much privacy they are forfeiting.

To get a feeling for how closely our web-browsing habits are monitored, for instance, David Manasian (2003) suggests the experiment of setting one's browser to warn about 'cookies' rather than silently accept them,

> ... then browse the web for a few minutes. You will soon be bombarded with messages telling you that almost every website you visit is trying to plant cookies – small text files that collect information about your browsing habits – on your computer... Your every move on the internet is being recorded by someone, somewhere.

Many of us who were vaguely aware of receiving cookies imagined, naively, that the information they gathered remained between us and the individual cookie-planting website, making them fairly harmless – but that is far from true. Cookies collect valuable marketing information, which is sold by the sites that harvest it to companies that share it with other sites.

> The largest of these, DoubleClick [acquired by Google in April 2007], has agreements with over 11,000 websites and maintains cookies on 100m users. These can be linked to hundreds of pieces of information about each user's browsing behaviour.

Google wants to use the detailed information about individuals that it gleans from their search histories and from DoubleClick cookies

> ... to provide services that customers do not know they need, even offering advice on what kind of job to take or what to do tomorrow.[12]

Amazon, too, is planning a system that will assemble a database of intimate economic, sexual and religious information about its customers – we know this is what Amazon wants to do, because in August 2006 it applied for a patent on the method it will use to do it.

Web surfing is only one area of life where Big Brother is watching us, or soon will be watching us, in a way that was hardly conceivable only a few years ago. Barcodes on goods are beginning to be replaced by radio frequency identification (RFID) tags, which in terms of business efficiency have three advantages: they are tiny ('half the size of a grain of sand'); they can be read automatically at a distance rather than needing to be scanned manually; and their huge codespace allows individual items, not just product types, to be given unique identifiers. (The Auto-ID standard for RFID codes provides 96 bits; every sheet of paper could easily be given its own unique RFID code, if there were a reason to do so.)

When Benetton announced plans to embed RFID tags into its garments for stock-monitoring purposes in 2003, commentators woke up to the fact that consumers could be

> ... bombarded with intrusive advertising[,] since a history of customer's purchases and their identities would be linked with the tag even after they leave the store.[13]

Burglars would be able to check out the contents of houses without needing to get out of their car.

---

[12] Tom Young, 'What price individual privacy if personal data means better service?', *Computing* 14 June 2007.
[13] Elisa Batista, 'What your clothes say about you', *Wired News* 12 March 2003.

> Future divorce cases could involve one party seeking a subpoena for RFID logs – to prove that a spouse was in a certain location at a certain time.[14]

Benetton faced a customer boycott. And there were similar protests when Tesco not only began experimenting with RFID tags in place of barcodes on small, high-value items (the initial experiments used packs of razor blades), but also used the tags to trigger photographs of anyone taking the items off the shelf, to provide evidence in case of shoplifting. In face of consumer resistance, the companies retreated. But despite tactical retreats in some sensitive cases, it is hard to believe that the technology will not spread. Benetton may have given up tagging its stock, for the time being at least, but Prada had already begun putting RFID tags into its luxury garments, apparently without attracting adverse comment. And Tesco, though it abandoned the idea of automatically photographing razor-blade buyers, has been forging ahead with the use of RFID data (cf. Chapter 11).

Some public fears seem overblown. Many of the worries about RFID tags in clothes could be cured by making the tags obvious and inviting people to discard them after purchase, and now that Marks & Spencer has begun making heavy use of RFID tagging it is doing just that. But RFID tags are not the only way in which IT is undermining privacy. Particularly in the UK, CCTV cameras have become so widespread in public places that (according to an estimate in 2003) the average Briton is recorded 300 times a day. Automatic face-recognition technology is advancing rapidly. Credit cards leave data trails, and as mechanisms for issuing bus and train tickets, admission tickets and the like are computerised these things will add to the detail available on everyone's movements.

The mountain of data produced by supermarket loyalty cards has led to a situation where 'supermarkets know more about your shopping habits than you do';[15] although marketers argue that such data is collected in order to help companies serve their customers better, private-sector exploitation of personal information is not always quite that benign. For instance, call centres use postcode profiling derived from census data so that:

> Calls to banks and retailers from people living in areas perceived as wealthy are put through immediately to the best-spoken, best-trained and most courteous sales staff. Callers from less affluent postcodes can find themselves pushed to the bottom of the queue, where they wait in automated-voice hell.[16]

---

[14] Declan McCullagh, quoted in *vigilant.tv* 14 January 2003.
[15] David Derbyshire, 'They know where you live (and everything else about you)', *Daily Telegraph* 13 June 2005.
[16] David Derbyshire, as previous note.

Businesses have always given more valuable customers preferential treatment in face-to-face transactions, of course, but the differences are less extreme; the favoured customers themselves might not stand for such blatant discrimination happening before their eyes, and it is not clear that we want our society to move towards such crude stratification.

## THE PUBLIC AWAKES

All these things have come about so quickly that the public is only now beginning to react; but the signs are that many people dislike them. David Manasian (2003) believes that 'privacy is likely to become one of the most contentious and troublesome issues in western politics'. Particularly since the atrocities of '9/11' in the USA and '7/7' in London, some people are willing to concede the need for a degree of surveillance by the state – without feeling any happier when private-sector organisations do similar things or when the state goes further than the terrorism risk requires. By 2007, even some police chiefs in Britain – not normally a profession that leads agitation for the cause of civil liberty – were arguing that we risk becoming an Orwellian society.

One loud wake-up call was a mistake made by AOL in August 2006, when it accidentally placed online a large database of customers' search queries. Since many people use search engines to try to resolve delicate issues in their personal lives, the loss of privacy for some was devastating. One Texas woman's numerous queries amounted to a history of how she nerved herself up to be unfaithful to her husband, and then wished she hadn't. As Andrew Keen (2007: 167) says, what AOL did was 'the equivalent of the Catholic Church mailing out 658,000 confessions to its worldwide parishioners'. But Roman Catholic confessors are bound by a centuries-old code designed to prevent abuses. AOL did not intend to make its query database public, but there are no particular rules limiting how it uses it internally. And anyway, once sensitive information is recorded in writing, leaks are almost inevitable.

Privacy may now be a lost cause. Scott McNealy, chief executive of Sun Microsystems, says simply 'You have zero privacy anyway. Get over it' (quoted in Sterne 2001: 210). In many cases it seems likely that economic pressures will cause people to collaborate in relinquishing privacy. Irving Wladawsky-Berger, a senior vice-president at IBM, comments that the insurer Norwich Union is able to use RFID to

> ... track how cars are driven and charge variable insurance rates based on that information... If the customer says, 'I don't want you to track my driving', then in that case the insurance rate is higher. That's life.[17]

---

[17] Quoted by James Watson, 'Real-time automation will keep everyone in the know', *Computing* 18 March 2004.

For a significant premium reduction, probably almost everyone will allow their driving to be monitored – and once the public accepts this in some cases, our assumption that we have a right to privacy will dissolve, for better or worse.

It is even possible to see an upside to the death of privacy. By 2007 several startups, including AttentionTrust and GestureBank (both of San Francisco), were experimenting with models under which individuals charge commercial organisations for access to personal information that, at present, organisations harvest without payment.

A related technical development is that surveillance has been 'democratised' – the security expert Bruce Schneier commented in 2004 that 'surveillance abilities that used to be limited to governments are now, or soon will be, in the hands of everyone.'[18] Some feel, in effect, that if everyone can play Big Brother, no-one will dare to: David Brin (1998) argued that 'mutually assured surveillance' will ensure that personal information is not abused (as the prospect of 'mutually assured destruction' kept nuclear arms unused during the Cold War years).

But many citizens will find it difficult to be as optimistic as Brin. And they may well feel that the prospect of making a little extra money on the side would be a poor exchange for surrendering the privacy that, until recently, they took for granted. At the B2C level, resistance to the transparent society could be a very significant factor limiting future participation in e-commerce.

## CONSUMER RATINGS

Many approaches are being tried in order to create the level of confidence in e-commerce that has long existed in conventional commerce.

One straightforward technique is to publish customer ratings of online merchants. The best-known service of this kind is the American site BizRate, launched in 1996. Participating e-merchants arrange for BizRate to poll consumers electronically when they make a purchase (and again some days later, to allow for assessment of delivery performance, etc.). Purchasers give the merchant marks out of 10 for criteria such as 'ease of finding what you were looking for', 'clarity of product information', 'on-time delivery' and 10 or 12 others. Rolling 90-day averages are published as a display of smiley and sad faces. Participating companies display the BizRate 'Customer Certified' logo.

BizRate is a commercial operation: to keep things fair it does not charge e-tailers for listings, but it sells them the detailed customer comments from which its published ratings are distilled. Nevertheless Americans take BizRate seriously as a source of unbiased information about e-tailer quality.

---

[18] Quoted in 'Move over, Big Brother', *The Economist Technology Quarterly* 4 December 2004.

BizRate puts effort into ensuring that its ratings cannot be manipulated by the merchants themselves posing as customers.

The value of an operation like this depends on its coverage. In 2003 BizRate claimed 'over 2000' participating merchants, which must mean that many had not chosen to participate (it also claimed 1,300,000 active reviewers). A few years later, BizRate's website is less specific about numbers of merchants and reviewers.

Customer feedback seems to be a rather successful mechanism for creating trust in online commerce. Paul Resnick *et al.* (2000) argued that this mechanism actually functions much *better* in practice than one would predict. On eBay,

> ... the overall rate of successful transactions remains astonishingly high for a market [so] 'ripe with the possibility of large-scale fraud and deceit' ...

Resnick *et al.* attributed this to buyers' and sellers' surprising willingness to rate each other fully and honestly on eBay's Feedback Forum.

## SITE CERTIFICATION SERVICES

Apart from services such as BizRate that assess e-tailers on features that are apparent to consumers, there are also non-profit certification schemes that focus more specifically on privacy and trustworthiness, which are harder for shoppers to judge for themselves. These certification services are better developed in the USA than in Europe; the earliest, largest and best known is TRUSTe. (Another is BBBOnLine, run by the US Council of Better Business Bureaus.)

TRUSTe is a non-profit organisation sponsored jointly by companies such as PricewaterhouseCoopers and Microsoft, which has been working since 1997 under the slogan 'Make privacy your choice' to encourage the growth of e-business by fostering user trust and confidence. It has several methods, for instance its Watchdog system provides a resolution mechanism for disputes about customer privacy, but its chief activity is certifying the practices of online companies with respect to customer privacy, via a badge (the 'trustmark') that a site displays to demonstrate that it has been audited and found to meet the TRUSTe norms. In 2007 about 2500 sites were participating.

There has been serious criticism of TRUSTe, however, with sceptics suggesting that the requirements for its trustmark are so minimal as to make it worthless. In 1999, when it emerged that the RealJukebox site was distributing software that surreptitiously gathered personal data from users' hard discs, TRUSTe decided that since the privacy violation was linked only indirectly to site visits it lay outside the scope of a TRUSTe audit. Batya Friedman *et al.* (2000) compared this to

> ... a hotel garnering a five-star rating simply by promising not to guarantee its customers good service and then faithfully keeping its promise.

A survey by Benjamin Edelman (2006: sec. 1.2) suggests that TRUSTe has not raised its game since.

In Britain the Consumers' Association ran a certification scheme, '*Which?* Web Trader', with aims comparable to TRUSTe's, but the scheme closed in 2003 because it failed to cover running costs. Other schemes have been created to fill the gap: within months of the demise of the *Which?* scheme, the government-backed TrustUK organisation introduced one replacement system, SafeBuy, and the internet security and payments company VeriSign introduced another, Trust Mark. But there is a chicken-and-egg problem: traders are willing to pay certification fees only if they think the hallmark awarded will be recognised by their potential customers, and the public does not learn to respect marks displayed only by a few traders. TrustUK was surprised to encounter considerable resistance, by companies that had been covered by the *Which?* scheme, to paying a modest annual fee of £250 for its replacement.

Some commentators feel that there is little indication so far that any website certification mark is achieving worthwhile recognition. There are scraps of evidence suggesting that this may be too pessimistic. Michael Baye and John Morgan (2003) found that on comparison shopping engine sites, merchants displaying hallmarks enjoyed a price premium over uncertified merchants. The European online travel company Opodo experimented in 2006 by putting up pairs of order pages, differing only in presence or absence of the VeriSign certificate – they found that the hallmark yielded a 10 per cent increase in sales.

However, other research implies that even if people are coming to respect some of these hallmarks, they perhaps should not. Benjamin Edelman (2006) carried out an objective statistical analysis of American website certification. This showed that sites certified by TRUSTe are on average slightly *less* trustworthy than other sites. Merchants whose behaviour leaves something to be desired are evidently keener than most to win and display an external seal of approval. (For the Better Business Bureau's BBBOnLine certificate, the statistics were the other way round; but that seems to be because the BBBOnLine certification process is so demanding that to date it had covered only a few hundred sites, and probably could never be scaled up enough to become a widespread standard.)

In the world of conventional commerce, the British Standards Kitemark is very widely known and respected – but it has achieved its current role over a period of more than 100 years, during much of which the commercial world was a far more staid place than it is today. In the visually frenetic, ever-changing world of the web, it may be difficult for any electronic 'kitemark' to achieve comparable status.

## WINNING HEARTS AND MINDS

Many other initiatives have been taken to address the challenge of developing trust in the online world. It would be tedious to try to list all the approaches that have been tried. At the time of writing, financial institutions are pinning many hopes on so-called *two-factor authentication*: bank clients are issued with a small physical device that generates ever-changing codes, and to access their account on the bank website they are required to input the current code. Because the code expires as soon as it is used, key-logging malware cannot subvert the system. The upmarket bank Coutts (nowadays a subsidiary of the Royal Bank of Scotland) has used this system since 1999; in 2007 some of the high-street banks are beginning to follow suit. But there are questions about how readily the average high-street bank customer will accept the need to keep track of a physical gadget – the wealthy clients of Coutts may not be representative; and indeed about how much defence against fraud the system will really provide.

The crucial point is that technology can do only so much to create the preconditions for e-business to flourish. Social, psychological and institutional considerations are at least equally important. There is no shortage of technological initiatives to address the problems about trust and privacy; but technical fixes will achieve little, unless they succeed in winning general acceptance.

From what we have seen, it seems that acceptance is occurring less rapidly than some had hoped. It may be unrealistic to expect attitudes and assumptions that have evolved naturally over centuries to be matched by online analogues within a few short years.

# 5 Jurisdiction, Regulation, Taxation

## E-COMMERCE ACROSS FRONTIERS

In the heady early days of the web, idealists envisaged it creating a new world in which national borders and governments would lose their significance. Some may remember the 'Declaration of the Independence of Cyberspace', published in 1996 by John Perry Barlow (lyricist for the Grateful Dead), beginning:

> Governments of the Industrial World, you weary giants of flesh and steel, I come from Cyberspace, the new home of Mind. On behalf of the future, I ask you of the past to leave us alone. You are not welcome among us. You have no sovereignty where we gather.

People really thought it might be so – but of course it never could be. Sovereignty must always be exercised somehow, by good governments or by bad governments. And for the foreseeable future, the domains within which sovereignty applies will be divided up geographically.

For e-business that creates two problems. One is that a company trading over the internet will be exposed to unfamiliar foreign laws. Even for a large, successful company this issue is far from trivial. For instance, the PayPal internet payment system, owned by eBay since 2002, is a kind of banking operation; and banking is an industry that has been strictly regulated everywhere for a long time. eBay's 2006 annual report, in its required analysis of risk factors that could affect future operations, admits that eBay is not sure what banking laws apply to PayPal outside the high-business-priority territories of the USA, the EU, Australia and China:

> In many [other] markets, it is not clear whether PayPal's … service is subject to local law or, if it is subject to local law, whether such local law requires a payment processor like PayPal to be licensed as a bank or financial institution …

A second problem is that, even where relevant laws of each country are clear, *jurisdiction* may still be uncertain: whose laws apply when parties to a transaction are based in different countries? (The excerpt from the

81

eBay annual report related to both problems: 'whether such local law requires ...' is an issue about individual countries' laws, while 'whether PayPal ... is subject to local law' is an issue about jurisdiction.)

Jurisdiction is not a new problem. Any international trading requires agreement about what law applies to disputes. But before the internet, when effort was involved in communicating across national boundaries, it was not a pressing problem. To B2B traders the issue was obvious and was provided for in contracts: either the jurisdiction applicable to disputes was specified explicitly, or by default the laws of the seller's location applied. Consumer goods were rarely bought by mail order from abroad.

Now that the web makes it easy for consumers sitting in their own homes to buy things from across the world, many governments feel that it is unacceptable for their legal protection to depend on the seller's home law. It is not practical for private individuals to invoke the protection of a foreign legal system. Repeatedly, governments have responded to e-commerce by trying to impose their own legal requirements on sellers anywhere selling to their citizens.

In 1997, for instance, California introduced a law that imposed, on anyone selling to buyers in California, detailed requirements about matters such as disclosure of seller's street address and refund policy – the rules specified not just what should be stated but in what size of lettering and where on the website. The rules may have been reasonable; but if each of the almost 200 nations of the world (and indeed the 50 separate state jurisdictions of the USA) were to impose independent requirements at this level of detail, it is not clear how merchants could comply – or how compliance could be enforced.

## THE E-COMMERCE DIRECTIVE

Some observers saw this Californian legal initiative as a naively overambitious early response to a novel technology. But more recently the EU has been moving in a similar direction. The European E-Commerce Directive was implemented in the UK in 2002. Under this law, in theory a retailer in one European country, say Britain, selling to consumers in another, say France (or even, possibly, in a non-European country), can be required to defend disputes under the legal principles of his home country but in a court in the consumer's country. Many doubt that this will work. One lawyer asked 'Is a French court going to ignore French law? It is just not going to happen.'[1]

Furthermore, the Directive imposes detailed requirements that might be technically unachievable. If mobile computing takes off so that people use PDAs or mobile phones for shopping, there is no way that small screens could display the masses of detailed information required by the Directive.

---

[1] Quoted by Jean Eaglesham, 'A troubled deal on the internet', *Financial Times* 10 February 2002.

Another 2002 EU law, the Brussels Regulation, gives consumers the right to sue in their home courts a trader who 'by any means, directs [commercial or professional] activities' to their country, so that legal remedies depend crucially on whether a website has features relating to audiences in a particular country. If prices are shown in pounds, it might be easy to decide that British buyers are targeted; does the same follow if, say, the site uses British rather than American spelling?

In July 2005 the EU began negotiating with the United Nations to draw up a UN Convention to harmonise e-commerce legislation internationally, evidently hoping that by taking this initiative it might achieve a global convention in which European principles are influential.

Clearly laws such as these can provide a clear structure of rules only once their various ambiguities and impracticalities have been clarified through test cases. One legal expert summarised the current situation by saying:

> There appears to be an inescapable conflict between choice of law provisions designed to favour the development of ecommerce ... and giving priority to the interests of consumers ... different [European] Commission Directorates appear to be promoting different policies.
>
> (Lloyd 2004: 646–7)

Furthermore, in an international context, the legal structure that emerges will be shaped as much by what can be enforced in practice, as by legislators' original intentions.

## A FRAMEWORK FOR GLOBAL ELECTRONIC COMMERCE

One way to create a successful legal basis for global e-commerce would be through agreement by the main commercial nations on common abstract principles, which individual countries would implement within their national law systems. President Bill Clinton's administration in the USA attempted to give a lead: in 1997 it published *A Framework for Global Electronic Commerce*, which urged the governments of the world to join America in embracing policies that would minimise the risk of interfering with the benefits expected to flow from e-commerce. Thus, principle 1 of the *Framework* was 'The private sector should lead'; principle 2 was 'Governments should avoid undue restrictions on electronic commerce' – so, among other things, 'governments should refrain from imposing new ... taxes and tariffs on commercial activities that take place via the Internet'. One might see the *Framework* as proposing a regime that comes as close as real life could get to the idealistic vision of independent cyberspace.

At the time, the *Framework* principles were influential – Mougayar (1998: 68) commented that 'the world seems to be listening'.

One reason why the world was willing to fall in with the *Framework* principles in the late 1990s was the widespread conviction that the internet would soon generate immense wealth, though no-one was quite sure how. The priority was to avoid injuring the goose that was going to lay golden eggs, and there was no telling what seemingly harmless regulation might prove injurious.

Another reason was that the hands-off attitude promoted by the *Framework* chimed with ideas about government that had become popular independently of IT. In about 1980 there had been a reaction against 'big government'; people came to feel that welfare states were incapable of fulfilling their promises, and so it was better to limit the state to the minimal roles of maintaining security and the rule of law, and to leave it to individuals to pursue their own welfare. In Britain this was symbolised by the premiership of Margaret Thatcher – but Lady Thatcher was only the most prominent representative of an international climate of opinion.

The fact that the internet crosses national boundaries freely, and gives individuals and small enterprises access to domains that previously were limited to a few big players, means that government regulation is often difficult to impose. For believers in small government that is an excellent thing, and the internet is a useful ally in the task of reducing government interference.

## INCREASED E-BUSINESS REGULATION

It is easy to see how the *Framework* attracted support when it was published. But there are converse points of view. A decade later, after the goose has laid fewer and less-golden eggs than expected, some of these counterarguments may seem weightier.

Although the international trend has been to remove purely commercial constraints on competition, there has been another tendency since the 1990s to increase regulation in the name of goals such as 'health and safety' and 'equal opportunities'. This tendency affects e-business along with other domains.

## SECURITY STANDARDS

The idea of regulating e-business on safety grounds has emerged in response to government perceptions that the sector is irresponsible about security (even though surveys regularly show that security is IT managers' top priority). In 2003 the Slammer worm caused damage estimated at $1 billion worldwide, although a patch had been available for eight months previously. Doubtless some of the damage affected customers or trading partners who were not responsible for failure to deploy the patch. Various standards, such as British Standard 7799 (now developed into an international standard, ISO 17799), specify requirements for secure information management; but companies are slow to adopt them – in the wake of the Slammer episode David Hendon of the Department for Trade and Industry announced that only 80 BS 7799 certificates had been issued to UK firms to date.

Hendon commented 'There comes a point at which society can't allow the corporate equivalent of train crashes to keep happening.'[2] He suggested that standards such as BS 7799 may be made mandatory. And 2006 saw the first move by the British government to introduce regulation in this area, when it sponsored the creation of the Institute for Information Security Professionals (IISP), which in April 2007 began certifying individuals as qualified to practise.

Many professions take statutory entry restrictions for granted; someone who offers to work as an engineer or an architect without a certificate from the appropriate professional body will be in trouble with the law. To date, IT has not been like that – anyone has been free to sell their services to whoever is willing to buy them. The British Computer Society, which governs the profession in Britain under royal charter, accredits university degrees and issues qualifications such as CITP (Chartered IT Professional) to individuals identified as competent, but at present few employers pay attention to that line in a recruit's CV.

Now, the IISP is set to change that for people working in IT security. And, if security specialists have to be licensed, many will ask why the same should not apply to IT professionals in the health sector or the transport sector. The day may come when no IT employment is open to those lacking a statutory qualification.

But, if compulsion does arrive, it will surely have significant impacts on e-business beyond the purposes that motivate its introduction. Laws introduced for good reasons often turn out to entail unanticipated consequences. The reason why companies have been bypassing BS 7799 is not that they do not care about security – they certainly do – but that they are sceptical whether this is an effective way of achieving it. A few months after David Hendon's remark about train crashes, the House of Commons announced that its own administration was not planning to implement BS 7799.

## DISABILITY DISCRIMINATION

Disability discrimination is a good example of regulation in the name of equal opportunities. The UK Disability Discrimination Act came into force in 2004; among many other things, it requires websites to be accessible to disabled (e.g. blind) users. Until test cases have been fought out, it is not

---

[2] Quoted by Gareth Morgan, 'Whitehall security standard warning', *Computing* 20 February 2003.

clear exactly how this will translate into specific requirements. The World Wide Web Consortium (W3C) has been attempting to flesh out the general principles through its Web Accessibility Initiative, and courts might treat conformance with W3C guidelines as meeting the legal requirements – though this is not guaranteed, since the W3C has no statutory authority. (In Britain the Disability Rights Commission regards the W3C guidelines as seriously inadequate.)

Adequate or not, the W3C guidelines are not simple. The current draft comprises about 30 web documents, each containing many screenfuls of complex text, together with numerous supporting documents. Conforming will presumably be a serious challenge to small businesses running websites on a shoestring; a 2005 EU survey found that even in the government sector, only 3 per cent of sites fully conformed and 70 per cent failed at the most basic level. Furthermore, there is no guarantee that well-intentioned rules designed to make life easier for disabled people might not make it impossible to develop new e-commerce services that would benefit society as a whole.

Bodies such as the Royal National Institute for the Blind have an interest in bringing test cases to show reluctant businesses that they must take legislation like this seriously – though, by the time of writing, no cases have yet been brought in Britain. (In Australia there has been one: a blind man, Bruce Maguire, complained that the Sydney Olympics website was inaccessible to him because graphic material was not equipped with text alternatives. The commission that judged the case found for Maguire in 2000; when the Olympics committee failed to respond, it was fined A\$20,000.)

On the other hand, even in conventional commerce, there is anecdotal evidence that smaller companies nowadays are finding regulatory legislation too complex and onerous to attempt to comply with; and people who make laws tend not to be people who have a good feeling for what is practical in IT. So it is a very open question how far this type of regulation will take hold in the e-commerce sphere, where there is the extra complication of global reach.

## CONFLICTING IDEALS

Making life easier for disabled people is at least an ideal on which there is broad international public agreement. Some societies see it as a higher priority than others, but so far as I know no society actively rejects the principle. The situation for e-business is even more difficult when different societies have conflicting principles.

## THE NAZI MEMORABILIA CASE

One example was brought into focus by the Yahoo! Nazi memorabilia case. France, like some other Continental countries, has fierce laws against activities that condone Nazism. US law upholds freedom of expression for all political points of view. These approaches came into conflict when in 2000 French anti-Nazi groups sued Yahoo! for allowing items such as SS daggers to be advertised on its auction site. The French court ordered Yahoo! to prevent surfers in France from viewing these adverts, with a penalty of about $13,000 a day for non-compliance. Then in 2001 an American court cleared Yahoo! by ruling that the First Amendment to the US constitution (on freedom of speech) trumps more restrictive overseas laws, with respect to content generated by Americans within the USA. The direct contradiction between these decisions went away because Yahoo! meanwhile voluntarily removed the offending adverts. That enabled all concerned on this occasion to ignore the fact that (as it was put by Vint Cerf, an internet pioneer who acted as an expert witness for the French court):

> ... if every jurisdiction in the world insisted on some form of filtering for its particular geographical territory, the world wide web would stop functioning.[3]

The *Framework* approach to conflicts such as this is that the principle of freedom should win. To the American compilers of the *Framework* document, that was equivalent to saying 'the principle that makes it easiest for e-commerce to flourish should win'. Seen from elsewhere, though, the same approach might be perceived as 'the principle that suits the USA best should win'. In 2007 the USA seems to be successfully resisting a World Trade Organization ruling that it must not prevent its residents using overseas gambling websites. Logically this is very akin to the Nazi memorabilia case, but with the USA on the other side.

## PRESERVING NATIONAL CULTURES

That same contrast of perceptions arises in an area that is less acutely inflammatory than Nazi souvenirs, but more significant: the extent to which national cultures should be protected against the levelling effect of globalisation.

Many countries have in the past taken steps to preserve their distinctive cultures through, for instance, legally restricting the proportion of foreign television and films that can be shown. France, with its remarkable history and civilisation, has been a leading example. The *Framework* urged that, on the internet, that approach should be outlawed. Countries that want to promote home-grown content should subsidise it from general taxation, rather than limiting the flow of content from elsewhere.

---

[3] Quoted by Mark Ward, 'Experts question Yahoo auction ruling', *BBC News Online* 29 November 2000.

To the French that might sound like 'French taxpayers must pay to keep France French'. They might wonder why they should have to. The *Framework* principle maximises freedom; but the media happens to be a more important revenue-earning sector of the economy in the USA than in most countries, and so the principle is again one that favours American national interests. (Ironically, apart from France, the nation whose media laws do most to preserve local content against foreign imports is the USA.)

This may be a less important issue than it looks to politicians, though. As entertainment media mature, there is plenty of evidence that consumer preferences lead to more localisation of content than governments would dare to impose. 'The days when "Dallas" or "Kojak" filled British prime-time are long gone';[4] broadcasters across the EU are now far over the legal minimum quota for EU-made programmes.

## THE HAGUE CONVENTION

The present trend seems to be to move away from the free-for-all approach towards the opposite extreme – that anything on the internet that would be objectionable in one jurisdiction should be eliminated everywhere. This poses obvious difficulties for e-business, because of the need to get to grips with numerous exotic regulations. To many, the trend will also be objectionable morally or politically. Plenty of people might be happy with global bans on, say, Nazi souvenirs or paedophile sites – but those are the easy cases. The same people might find it unacceptable if, for instance, alcohol adverts or discussion of interest rates were outlawed because some Islamic nations object to these things.

Contradictions between national legal principles, as in the Nazi memorabilia case, might be eliminated through acceptance of a convention under development since 1992 by the Hague Conference on Private International Law, which would require courts of each signatory country (the UK and the USA are two) to enforce one another's decisions in the areas of commercial and civil law. This is perhaps more practical than the approach taken by the European E-Commerce Directive, which requires courts to make decisions using other countries' laws. But, as one commentator put it in 2001:

> ... imagine this: you live in England and create a website based in England that breaks no English law. Then, because of a court ruling in Turkey, the English courts close you down simply because the website can be viewed abroad and the Turks don't like it.[5]

---

[4] 'The one where Pooh goes to Sweden', *The Economist* 3 April 2003; cf. 'Cultural imperialism doesn't sell', *The Economist* 11 April 2002.
[5] 'Webster', 'Superbyw@ys', *The Oldie* August 2001.

Richard Stallman, founder of the GNU project, has produced a trenchant analysis (Stallman 2001) of the various uncongenial implications of the Hague Convention.

For the moment, those implications are in abeyance; after a decade of discussion, in 2002 efforts to agree such a far-reaching convention were dropped, essentially because of the distance between the legal assumptions of the USA and Continental Europe. But some lawyers believe that similar developments are almost inevitable, sooner or later. (Certainly, plenty of cases are coming along to which the Hague Convention would apply if it were in force. In April 2007 the Thai government was outraged by a clip posted on YouTube mocking their king; YouTube refused to take it down because it did not break American law.)

If this is indeed the route that the world eventually chooses, e-commerce might be limited to what is totally bland and inoffensive – very different from the anything-goes, let 'er rip attitude of the 1997 *Framework*.

When such contrasting principles can be influential at times only a few years apart, it is too early to predict what kind of stable legal regime for e-business will eventually emerge. But by now it seems clear that John Perry Barlow's 1996 Declaration of Independence was wide of the mark. In November 2004 *The Economist* reached the opposite conclusion: 'In the continuing battle between cyberspace and national sovereignty, the offline world has won.'[6]

## COMPLIANCE BECOMES AN IT ISSUE

A very recent trend in the legal environment of e-business is that new laws – in the USA, in Britain and in Europe – are telling firms what kinds of computer systems they must install and even requiring them to push the envelope of what is technically feasible.

This is a large innovation. For most of the time that business has used computers, decisions to adopt particular equipment and software have been made purely in terms of business advantage. The law did not care whether a company carried out its processes manually or electronically. Suddenly laws have begun to impose requirements on businesses that can be met only via IT, and that often need systems different from what the firms would adopt of their own accord. Already in early 2005 a survey by Dell found that more than a tenth of IT spending by British business was attributable to 'compliance' – meeting regulations, rather than making profits – and the proportion was rising fast. Only some of the new laws had come into effect by then; the impact of compliance issues on enterprise computing has continued to grow. By 2006 Gary Flood was writing with pardonable exaggeration: 'some business leaders find it hard to recall a time when they bought computers for any other reason'.[7]

---

[6] 'House of cards', *The Economist* 20 November 2004.
[7] 'Hot on the audit trail', *Computing* 24 August 2006.

Probably the best-known, and one of the earliest, laws in question is the US Sarbanes–Oxley Act ('Sox') of 2002, introduced to combat corporate fraud in the wake of the Enron and WorldCom scandals. Sarbanes–Oxley is a wide-ranging law, but for our purposes its most important feature relates to stringent requirements about auditable controls over detailed financial reporting processes. Companies must be able to demonstrate the reliability of figures in their accounts to a degree of refinement that, in the past, many were not capable of, and that is possible only with the right kind of IT systems. 'Sox' is American, but from 2006 on plenty of British firms have had to comply with it, because they are listed on an American exchange or are outsourcing partners of an American company. (In due course the EU will probably introduce Sox-like regulations on this side of the Atlantic.)

But Sarbanes–Oxley is just one of the first of a flood of new laws impacting on IT departments. It would be impractical to give a full list here. The UK Regulation of Investigatory Powers Act, updated in 2003, requires telephone companies and internet service providers to retain records of phone calls, e-mails and so on for a year and to produce specific items from the resulting data mountain promptly as required – the EU Data Retention Directive, which came into force in October 2007, extends requirements in the same area and is likely eventually to apply not just to telcos and ISPs but even to organisations such as hotels and public libraries. The Basel II accord requires financial institutions to provide detailed auditable management of credit risk. MiFID (the EU Markets in Financial Instruments Directive) has applied since November 2007 and imposes transparency and 'best-execution' obligations on transactions for clients, with retention of data for up to five years. And the list goes on.

The novel regulations require auditability of data, often to an extent that companies did not previously feel necessary for their own purposes. For instance, various legal proceedings now require *e-discovery* – a company may have to produce copies of every e-mail, voicemail and so on received or sent by staff relating to the subject of the proceedings (together with evidence that the list is complete), but e-mail has typically grown up in the past in ways that were too diffuse to allow this. In May 2006 the Morgan Stanley bank was fined $15 million for inability to achieve satisfactory e-mail discovery in current proceedings. Malcolm Wheeler, a corporate lawyer in Colorado, counts e-discovery as 'the single most significant change to the legal system' in his 40-year career;[8] one of his clients had to pay 31 lawyers to spend six months ploughing through electronic documents to check that they had found everything that needed to be shown to the plaintiff.

Perhaps even more importantly, the new regulations often impose requirements on process. Not just the data manipulated or produced by business processes, but the nature of the processing itself, is becoming

---

[8] Quoted in 'Of bytes and briefs', *The Economist* 19 May 2007.

subject to regulation. Before IT, business processes tended to be too inexplicit to come within the purview of law, but once they are executed by software they are easier to pin down explicitly and to regulate.

## COSTS OF COMPLIANCE

One issue for business – and for the societies in which business is embedded – is the sheer expense involved. The cost imposed by Sarbanes–Oxley (in terms of reduction in companies' market value) has been estimated as $1.4 trillion (Zhang 2005). Even by American big-business standards, that is a huge amount. Of course, if Sox eliminates a great deal of fraud, that benefits honest members of society, but one can be sceptical about whether *enough* fraud will be eliminated to justify the cost.

Another issue is that this kind of business-process regulation risks interfering with individual firms' sources of competitive advantage. Even if legislators strive to avoid such interference (which, in an enlightened modern democracy, they normally will), they cannot eliminate the risk. A company is an immensely subtle, complex organism, and nobody, including its own managers, knows for sure exactly which aspects of the way a successful company works are crucial to its success. So one cannot be sure that requiring everyone to carry out some function in a particular way may not damage that success and reduce the efficiency with which the company uses its input resources to serve society in its particular business niche.

A third issue is that legislators are proving remarkably optimistic about the technical possibilities. After decades when people outside the IT profession found computers thoroughly mysterious, now they all have computers in their own homes the public's attitude has swung to the other extreme: they imagine that it is straightforward to produce software to achieve any desired goal, however complex and vaguely specified. The EU Data Retention Directive was agreed in 2006 to come into force in August 2007; 10 months short of that deadline a consortium led by the data-storage specialist company EMC announced that it had developed a 'proof of concept' system supporting the Directive guidelines. That is, their system demonstrates that it is theoretically possible to meet the guidelines, as an academic research project might prove that it is scientifically possible to eliminate malaria from Africa: that is a long way from actually doing it. Furthermore the new rules can impose unrealistic requirements on hardware as well as software. According to Bob Fuller of Dresdner Kleinwort Wasserstein:

> MiFID assumes that IT works 24/7, and doesn't say what happens if it fails. You have to deliver 100 per cent availability on your systems.[9]

---

[9] Quoted by James Watson, 'Banks urged to stay ahead of the MiFID game', *Computing* 2 February 2006.

*The Economist* quoted EMC as reckoning in 2004 that this category of legislation 'calls for one of the [IT] industry's periodic technological revolutions'.[10]

Companies have been subject to numerous legal constraints for as long as business has existed. But the idea of law routinely requiring business to achieve things that are at the edge of technical feasibility is a twenty-first-century novelty.

## AUTHORITY HAGGLES WITH BUSINESS

Because of this technical overoptimism, and because of business complaints about excessive compliance costs and interference with legitimate management choices, the new regulations are commonly not permanently set in stone from day one. Instead we see a kind of haggling process between authority and business, in which compromises are gradually worked out between what authority would like and what business can live with. New rules announced in April 2005 would have required British company reports to disclose numerous non-financial factors that could affect future performance, meaning that companies would need to be able reliably to distil relevant information from oceans of unstructured text data; but shortly before the requirements were due to take effect they were withdrawn as excessively burdensome. The USA relaxed some of the most stringent Sarbanes–Oxley requirements in November 2006. And the new regulations are often taken less than entirely seriously because there has been such a profusion that they sometimes contradict one another. Michael Fabricant, shadow e-commerce minister, commented in 2003 that:

> We are approaching the Byzantine situation in Russia, where one decree conflicts with another and industry does not know what it is supposed to do.[11]

For instance, the Data Protection Act forbids companies from retaining various categories of information that the Regulation of Investigatory Powers Act requires them to keep. The lawyer George Gardiner summarises the position bluntly:

> Nobody can comply with every law; it's a question of prioritising business interests and watching out for which regulator has the big stick.[12]

---

[10] 'File that', *The Economist* 6 March 2004.
[11] Interviews by Sarah Arnott and James Watson, *Computing* 18 September 2003.
[12] 'Weighing up security and compliance', supplement to *IT Week*, 24 April 2006.

Presumably the situation will eventually settle down, so that business is faced with stable regulations whose inconsistencies have been pruned away. We have a while to go before reaching that position.

Law serves society best when it acts as a longstop mechanism that impinges minimally on upright individuals and organisations getting on with their proper business. But by now, as the American legal expert Larry Downes (2004) puts it:

> ... in a global marketplace fueled by information, law and regulation increasingly determine winners and losers. That means company leaders ... must hire lawyers who know how to use law as a strategic weapon... Law is the last great untapped source of competitive advantage.

If your company's e-mail archive allows thorough e-discovery and you know that a competitor's does not, perhaps you can use that fact to win a legal tussle even if the substance of the competitor's case is better than yours. This might seem excessively cynical – but business is business. Society, though, needs winners and losers to be determined by issues of substance, not by skill in exploiting a complex and inconsistent regulatory regime.

## TAXATION

An obvious way in which government intervenes in business is by taxing it. The activities of government have to be paid for, and two significant sources of revenue are tariffs on goods entering a country, and taxes such as corporation tax and value-added tax on internal business activities. (Tariffs often serve a second purpose, in protecting domestic industries against foreign competition.)

The *Framework* document advocated international agreement to levy no tariffs at all on goods that are delivered over the internet, such as films and music (so-called *online delivered content*; see Chapter 7); and not to impose any novel taxes on e-commerce. Domain names or ISP subscriptions, for instance, are the kinds of thing that a government looking to maintain its revenues might be tempted to tax – they are easily identifiable, and (unlike cases of pensioners living in large houses faced with massive council-tax demands) obligation to pay is likely to be matched broadly by ability to pay. The *Framework* urges that this temptation should be resisted.

As online delivered content becomes a larger proportion of the total flow of trade, and as e-commerce develops new forms to which, probably, existing taxes will sometimes fail to apply, the overall effect must be to put downward pressure on total government revenues.

Many economists would see this as thoroughly healthy. Few dispute that spending by governments is inherently inefficient. Other things being equal, a lower-tax economy will be a more vibrant economy. But, of course, countries with high-tax regimes have them not because they think taxation helps the economy to flourish but because they want their state to do various expensive things for the populace, such as providing health services. That is a political choice. Someone sceptical about the *Framework* principles might ask whether we want to allow the new technology to pre-empt political decisions.

There has been a trend, in line with the *Framework* recommendations, to reduce or abolish tariffs on IT-related goods. But then, recent decades have in any case been a period of repeated international rounds of tariff reductions. Economists argue that tariffs are a bad thing: people every-where prosper more if each country concentrates on producing whatever it is naturally fitted to produce, rather than diverting effort towards inefficient production of goods that can be made cheaper elsewhere. Again, although this argument has been influential, some prefer on political rather than economic grounds to defend industries that could not survive if they were fully exposed to overseas competition – as small farmers in France and Germany are defended by the EU Common Agricultural Policy. Conceivably, in future the world in general might choose to turn back towards 1930s-style protectionism. If so, it is not obvious that the world would see good reason to exempt goods traded via the internet.

The *Framework* principles on taxation may well be the best way to help e-commerce to flourish. They are not politically neutral principles.

## TAX NEUTRALITY

Many states of the USA derive their income largely from what Americans call 'sales tax'. When Britain had an equivalent tax, it was called 'purchase tax', and this is a more accurate name: in mail-order sales across American state boundaries, the tax is determined by the location of buyer rather than seller. It has to be that way: if the seller's state determined tax levels, businesses would migrate to low-tax states and a decision to increase sales tax would guarantee economic decline. (Consumers are unlikely to move just because of minor differences in sales tax levels, on the other hand.)

This illustrates the point that tax systems should be neutral. So far as possible, they ought not to alter the patterns of economic activity that evolve naturally. The *Framework* document advocated tax neutrality with respect to the internet, but the very fact that taxing e-commerce is discouraged means that the overall tax system is not neutral as between electronic and conventional trading – it favours the former.

The US states have since 1998 accepted a moratorium on sales taxes on internet transactions. This seems unfair to conventional merchants: e-commerce may often be a good thing, but people should shift to using it because they find that it does in fact serve them better, not because governments have made it artificially cheaper. (There is no doubt that the 'artificial' motive has had an effect; Goolsbee (2000) showed that Americans living in high-sales-tax places bought more over the internet than those living in places where sales tax was low.) The moratorium is problematic also because it erodes the total tax base. Either other taxes have to be made heavier to compensate, or total government revenue declines.

For the American states, the latter effect is creating large problems (not just because of the e-commerce tax moratorium but because, in general, consumption is increasingly switching to services, while state sales taxes apply mainly to goods). In consequence, for American state governors it has become a high priority to overturn the internet moratorium. Although the moratorium has been extended more than once, at the time of writing it looks likely that many US states will soon be imposing sales taxes on online sales.

## A TAX-FREE ZONE?

If tax regimes were easily adapted to changing economic patterns, an optimist might argue that governments will not lose by reducing taxes on e-commerce, because that will help the companies that engage in it to flourish and become more profitable, and hence they will pay more in corporation tax (the equivalent for companies of income tax on individuals). In reality, though, tax regimes have a momentum of their own and cannot be radically recast from year to year – in practice a government that depends mainly on sales tax probably could not suddenly switch to dependence on corporation tax instead. And anyway, it is a large assumption that eliminating one kind of tax will stimulate enough extra economic activity to produce fully compensating increases in other tax yields.

So the idea of allowing e-commerce to become a tax-free zone involves major difficulties. Yet so too does the idea of treating e-commerce for taxation purposes as just another form of trade.

From 2003, the EU required non-EU internet traders to charge VAT on sales to EU consumers on behalf of the tax authorities of the consumers' respective countries. This eliminated a large unfairness, when non-European traders could undercut Europeans' prices by selling VAT-free. But the downside is that a serious compliance burden has been created for the traders. Consider, for instance, eBay, which charges consumers essentially for putting them in touch with one another – if their e-mail addresses ended in, say, .com or .net, eBay might not have known where they lived, and perhaps had little reason to want to know. Now, it has to know. VAT rates are different in different EU countries, so eBay must collect tax at the correct rate in each case, and deal with the many different requirements of various European national tax regulations – and it must do all that to serve distant societies to which an American company owes no natural allegiance. eBay doubtless has the resources to manage this, but for a small company it might be truly daunting.

American mail-order retailers are used to dealing with the different sales tax regulations of the various states; it must be a demanding aspect of their work, but at least there are likely to be family resemblances between state tax regimes within one country, and all the tax laws are written in English. How would American, or British, e-tailers cope if they had to take account of tax laws in, say, Moldova or Laos, which might not be written in English or even in our alphabet? As Emilie Fridensköld (2004: 192) sees it, if most other countries followed the lead of the EU and imposed VAT on digital products consumed within their territories, then the sheer complexity of the resulting requirements would bring global B2C commerce to a halt: 'Systems would then become unworkable as online vendors would have to deal with hundreds of different VAT regimes.'

If e-commerce becomes a major fraction of world trade, it will pose large questions about the financing of governments. It is not clear that anyone has come up with thoroughly persuasive answers yet.

# 6 **Does IT Matter?**

## AN AXIOM QUESTIONED

So far we have been assuming that, for better or worse, computing technology must have a major impact on the fortunes of almost any company. The impact is not always positive. A company that invests in IT in a misguided fashion may find itself in difficulties – plenty have collapsed. In other cases, companies are finding very profitable ways of exploiting IT. One way or the other, it is surely clear that computer technology *matters*.

This apparent truism has now been called into question. Some influential observers are arguing that 'IT doesn't matter'. We do not have to agree with this surprising point of view. (The ideas lurking behind the sound-bite are really too complex to be treated as straightforwardly correct or incorrect.) But we certainly need to understand why the sound-bite is being voiced, and what the arguments are, pro and con.

## ELUSIVE PRODUCTIVITY GAINS

For many years, people were sceptical about whether computers were achieving much for business at all. Businesses invested heavily in computers from at least the 1970s, initially not in order to 're-engineer' their activities but to automate and speed up activities that previously were carried out manually. So, by the 1980s, it seemed that IT ought to be achieving some measurable impact on productivity (the average value of output produced by a given quantity of labour). Yet Robert Solow famously remarked in 1987 (the year when he won the economics Nobel Prize) that 'You can see the computer age everywhere but in the productivity statistics.'[1] In the 1990s, Tom Landauer set out to quantify how much impact computerisation had had on industrial productivity – what the *return on investment* (ROI) had been. His depressing conclusion was that, for the economy as a whole, ROI from computerisation since the mid-1970s had been low or zero (Landauer 1995; see also Goldfinger 1997: 195). Computerising business implies not only spending on equipment and software but also paying for people to maintain it, dealing with the business consequences of the glitches that arise and so forth. Often, it seemed, these cost factors out-balance the benefits from automating manual functions.

---

[1] 'We'd better watch out', *New York Times Book Review*, 12 July 1987.

The period from the 1970s to the early 1990s in the USA was in fact one of unusually low productivity growth.

Shortly after Landauer's research, Robert Gordon (2000) asked whether the 'IT revolution' was all that revolutionary. He concluded that, relative to earlier, genuinely disruptive technological innovations, such as electricity and the internal combustion engine, the economic and social consequences of the computer were actually rather modest.

## INSTALLATION PERIOD AND DEPLOYMENT PERIOD

With hindsight, Landauer's and Gordon's sceptical assessments were formulated just as the tide was turning. Since the late 1990s productivity has been growing unusually fast, certainly in the USA and probably also (though here the figures are debated) in Europe and Japan.[2] And it is clear that the bulk of this upturn is linked directly to IT.

This seems paradoxical, because the years around the turn of the millennium when this productivity acceleration occurred were also years during which investment in IT *fell* sharply, as businesspeople started to wonder whether computing had been over-hyped, and then saw the dotcom bubble burst and stock markets enter a slump for several years. How could IT-based productivity growth coincide with decreased spending on IT?

The answer relates to a point made in Chapter 1: e-business is not about technology for its own sake, but is about finding worthwhile ways to deploy technology. When a new technology is invented, it takes people a long time to discover how best to use it. What seem like obvious applications will often involve niggling but important problems about fitting in with how human beings work.

Carlota Perez examined the course of five successive technological revolutions known to history, beginning with the British Industrial Revolution around 1800. She found that these revolutions fall into two phases: an *installation period* while the new technology spreads but the revolution remains 'a small fact and a big promise', followed by a *deployment period* when 'the whole economy is rewoven and reshaped by the modernizing power of the triumphant paradigm ... enabling the full unfolding of its wealth generating potential' (Perez 2002: 36). At the turning point between installation and deployment periods, we regularly see 'a phase of frantic investment ... stimulated by a stock market boom that usually becomes a bubble that inevitably collapses'.

From Carlota Perez's point of view, what Landauer and Gordon observed was the period when IT was still a small fact and a big promise: business was spending on computers, because it appeared certain that, somehow or other, they had the potential to make a vast positive difference, but the

---

[2] The US productivity trend has slowed again since 2004.

process of learning how to exploit this potential, and how to adapt or change existing practices so that they become compatible with the new technology, was long drawn out. At the turn of the millennium we had the frantic boom and bust; and only now are we at the start of the deployment period, when the benefits begin to be realised – through using IT to re-engineer business processes, not just to automate existing manual processes. Often, this will not involve spending out on yet more equipment, but rather using existing equipment in better ways. Robert Gordon published a new paper in 2004 that in effect acknowledged that his sceptical assessment of the IT revolution had been premature.

One can argue that the installation period for business IT has actually lasted much longer than we have been suggesting. The world's first business use of computing was the work done for the then leading British restaurant chain J. Lyons by their purpose-built computer LEO (Lyons Electronic Office), beginning in 1953. (Lyons Corner Houses, with their distinctive gold-lettered fascia, used to be ubiquitous in British cities, although they eventually failed to compete with the fast-food operations that arrived in the 1970s.) As Kelvyn Taylor sees it:

> LEO was an integrated business platform, not only running the actual manufacturing logistics, but offering what we'd now call BI, CRM and ERP capabilities.[3]

(ERP, CRM and BI are major categories of enterprise software, discussed in later chapters.)

So people had been experimenting to find good ways to make the technology work for business for a full half-century before the dotcom bubble collapsed. If Perez's installation period lasted as long as that, then there is little reason to expect the deployment period to be completed overnight.

## PRODUCTIVITY IS NOT THE SAME AS PROFITABILITY

By now, it is generally accepted that IT is increasing productivity. But that does not mean that the question I used for the chapter title has gone away. The title is borrowed from that of a 2004 book by Nicholas Carr, which extends a debate he initiated with an article, 'IT doesn't matter', in the May 2003 issue of the *Harvard Business Review*. Carr's piece must have been one of the most controversial articles on any aspect of business to have appeared in that distinguished journal for many years. It provoked immediate

---

[3] Kelvyn Taylor, 'LEO roars back into IT fashion', *IT Week* 28 May 2007. On the history of LEO, see Ferry (2003).

responses, often hostile, by dozens of others. In the field of e-business probably no other publication has sparked off half as much debate.

Nicholas Carr was not seeking to revive Robert Solow's suggestion that IT has failed to increase productivity. Carr broadly accepts the newer research that has found productivity gains, though he begins his book by commenting that there is much that remains mysterious – we cannot say

> ... why the recent productivity gains have been so unevenly distributed, appearing in certain industries and regions that have invested heavily in information technology but not in others that have also spent great sums on computer hardware and software.

(And Carr echoes Robert Gordon's earlier paper in suggesting that the impact of computers on society has been modest, relative to nineteenth-century technological innovations. 'Ask yourself which you'd rather do without: Your computer or your toilet? Your Internet connection or your light bulbs?')

But even if computers do make companies more productive, that will not necessarily make them more profitable. If competing companies each become more productive – that is, they produce more output from less input of labour and other factors – then the benefit from the productivity increase cannot be captured by those companies as higher profits. Instead, the benefit will go to the firms' customers. The individual firms will compete away the extra profits by lowering their prices to retain their market share.

When one firm has an advantage that makes it relatively productive, and that rival firms for some reason cannot copy, it can undercut the competitors' prices slightly to secure a large market share, and capture most of the productivity benefit as profit. But if all the firms share the same advantage, then it will be profitable to none of them. For instance, one business sector where IT achieved large productivity gains at an early date was retail banking. According to Diana Farrell (2003):

> On-line banking spread so rapidly ... that no individual bank was able to reap any competitive advantage – the benefits all went to customers.

## THE HUNT FOR COMPETITIVE ADVANTAGE

It is this issue of *competitive advantage* that centrally concerns Carr. To someone running an individual firm, competitive advantage is a much more immediate issue than productivity. Productivity is an abstract arithmetical concept of interest chiefly to professional economists. Competitive advantage, on the other hand, refers to all the features of a particular company that help that company to win customers who could alternatively take their custom elsewhere. It is competitive advantage that enables one company to increase its market share, expand its operations, provide jobs for more employees and return larger dividends to its shareholders, while another company that lacks competitive advantages will shrink and perhaps go out of business.

When Carr says 'IT doesn't matter', what he means is that IT is ceasing to be a source of competitive advantage.

This is very different from saying, as Robert Solow did, that IT was failing to make firms more productive. But it is equally shocking. Carr points out that the 1990s were the decade when senior executives suddenly became excited about the strategic business significance of IT, after 20 years when they had thought of it as a mundane activity, the province of secretaries and technicians. He illustrates the point by quoting from the autobiography of Jack Welch, the chief executive of General Electric until he retired in 2001, and by a clear margin the most admired American businessman of recent times. Welch ignored the internet until, on a family holiday in 1999, his wife

> … sat him down at her laptop and showed him how to send e-mail and use a Web browser. Welch was immediately 'hooked'... Within a year, he had spearheaded a 'destroyyourbusiness.com' initiative aimed at overhauling GE's traditional business models, had demanded that the company's top 500 executives find young 'Internet mentors' to coach them about new technologies, and had asked Sun Microsystems CEO Scott McNealy to join GE's board as a kind of technology guru... 'Everyone began to think digitally,' Welch recalls. 'It was a great mind-set shift for the entire organization.'
>
> (Carr 2004: 5–6)

By 2001 Welch was claiming annual cost savings of over $1 billion through electronic BPR.

This mind-set shift became a business cliché. Typical was a comment quoted from the Blackstone Technology Group website: 'the implementation of future-focused information technology solutions has become a true source of competitive advantage'. By the time Carr was writing, remarks like that ranked as uncontroversial truisms.

## COMPUTING POWER DOES NOT EQUAL STRATEGIC SIGNIFICANCE

The trouble (Carr argues) is that this idea makes an assumption that sounds reasonable but is wrong. The assumption is that as the power and pervasiveness of IT increase, so its strategic significance increases. Not true. A competitive advantage for a company is something that the company has or does that gives it an edge over its rivals.

Competitive advantages arise from things that are special or rare, not from things that are ubiquitous. So, the more pervasive IT becomes in the economy as a whole, the less it can be a source of competitive advantage. Ironically, the period when business leaders grew excited about the strategic possibilities of IT was just about the time when the strategic relevance of IT was melting away.

A hundred years ago (Carr tells us), just as companies had board members (vice-presidents, in American terminology) responsible for fundamental issues such as finance and logistics, so they often had vice-presidents for electricity. Electricity was a new technology that was reshaping industry, and successful exploitation of it required high-level attention. Nowadays it would be absurd for a company to have a vice-president for electricity, but not because electricity has become less important. Electricity is vital for the operations of any company, but it no longer needs high-level attention, because it has become a *commodity*.

'Commodity' has a special meaning in business and economics: it refers to a resource that is available in any desired quantity and whose properties are standardised and well-known, so that distinguishing features of particular examples are of little interest. Houses, say, are not commodities: someone buying a house cares a lot about its individual appearance, size and internal layout, its surroundings, the views from its windows, and so forth. Butter is a commodity; after one has chosen salted or unsalted, and perhaps Danish or New Zealand, a pound of butter is essentially a pound of butter and the only remaining issue is price. Electricity is clearly a commodity: plug in and you can draw as much current as you need, at a standard voltage, and there is no chance that one supplier might provide 'better' electricity than another. According to Nicholas Carr, IT has been moving rapidly in the direction of becoming an anonymous commodity like butter or electricity. Like electricity, every firm will have to use IT, but there will be no way for one firm to use it to gain an edge over rivals.

Carr makes another comparison, with the early years of railways. When railway technology was first exploited by business, he says, there were opportunities for individual firms to use the technology to gain competitive advantages. For instance, a firm might build its own railway to link its site more conveniently to those of its suppliers or its distributors. But as the technology became cheaper and spread, a move like that became pointless; a company would have reasonably convenient access to rail transport almost irrespective of where it was located, and so no special edge was gained by building a private line.

That did not mean that railways offered no benefit to industry. They provided a large benefit, but it was a benefit to industry as a whole. The spread of railways made entire industries more productive, but at the same time railways became 'invisible' with respect to individual firms' competitive strategies.

## IT NEEDS TO BECOME ORDINARY

Looked at in this way, the statement that 'IT doesn't matter' is not a criticism of IT. On the contrary, the fact that (as Carr sees it) IT is now moving in the same direction that railways went, to become a standard, universally available commodity, is an excellent thing. If railways had remained a jumble of separate proprietary lines, perhaps with different gauges or in other respects incompatible with one another, some of those lines might have done a good job for their individual owners, but the economy as a whole could never have reaped the benefit it gained from a nationwide network of lines built to a common gauge and operated under common standards. According to Carr (2004: 11):

> IT needs to become ordinary – needs to lose its strategic importance as a differentiator of companies – if it is to fulfill its potential.

And computing is 'becoming ordinary'. Carr discusses the ways in which both hardware and software have been evolving from individual systems with their own specific strengths and quirks into commodities.

We saw above that, when the J. Lyons restaurant chain decided in the 1950s that it needed a computer, it designed and built its own. Later, it became absurd for a user firm to build a computer independently, but even in 1980 companies were choosing among a range of alternative hardware architectures and operating systems offered by different manufacturers. By the start of the twenty-first century, IBM PC architecture and Windows had become pervasive standards. This standardisation is not necessarily wholly beneficial – some argue that a computing monoculture makes us unnecessarily vulnerable to viruses and other malware, rather as the nineteenth-century Irish over-reliance on a single food crop made them vulnerable to the famine caused by potato blight. But clearly this development implies a change from individualistic computing towards computing as a commodity.

Other aspects of computing have been shifting in the same direction. Various peripherals, such as storage devices and networking equipment, were made to proprietary specs by different suppliers in recent years but are nowadays moving towards standardisation – in 2003 two leading storage companies, EMC and IBM, agreed to make their equipment interoperable. In the 1960s, a firm wanting to computerise some of its operations would write the application software it needed itself; nowadays, a high proportion of all business software comprises off-the-shelf packages used by many companies. IT seems to be well along the path of commoditisation, which, according to Carr, any novel technology needs to take before it can deliver full value to society.

People who see computing as leading to a large-scale IT revolution often assert that take-up, particularly measured by numbers of internet users, has been far faster than in the case of earlier communication technologies such as radio and television. In fact this seems to be untrue – telephone uptake in the late nineteenth century was slow, but more recent technologies including radio and television spread at about the same rate as the internet (Hannemyr 2003). But even if it were true, Robert Gordon argued in his 2000 paper that this would not be a reason to expect that especially revolutionary consequences still lie in store in the future. Any new technology will be subject to diminishing returns – the most valuable uses will be implemented early and, as time goes on, further applications will deliver smaller benefits. So a technology that spreads especially fast would be expected to see returns diminish especially quickly. In 2000, Gordon (2000: 50) found it 'quite plausible that the greatest benefits of computers lie a decade or more in the past, not in the future'.

## CONTRARY OPINIONS

Clearly, one would not expect a statement as challenging as 'IT doesn't matter' to go unanswered. Many people disagreed with Carr, sometimes heatedly. Steve Ballmer, chief executive of Microsoft, retorted 'Our fundamental response to that is: hogwash.'[4] That comment did not move the debate much further on, but others offered more reasoned counterarguments. An obvious objection is that software is inherently unlike electricity. Electricity is simple and homogeneous – once one specifies a few variables such as voltage and AC versus DC, there is nothing more to say. Software could not be more different – it is endlessly diverse and complex, and thus very far indeed from a 'commodity' in the economist's sense. But Carr's response is that, yes, in principle each firm could develop its own purpose-built software, different from all other firms' software – but in practice they will not do that, any more than nowadays they design and build their own computers. Once standard software packages are available, the fact that they are cheap and well-understood means that they are what business will use.

Even if software as well as hardware is commoditised, though, for Tony Scott (chief technology officer of General Motors) that does not imply that it cannot be used to achieve competitive advantage: 'even technology that's a commodity still provides business flexibility'.[5] The analysts Gartner felt that Carr was going wrong.

---

[4] Quoted by Tom Sullivan, 'Ballmer bullish on IT future', *InfoWorld* 24 July 2003.
[5] Quoted by Rick Whiting, 'CIOs sure think it matters', *InformationWeek* 23 May 2003.

> ... by equating IT with hardware and networks; rather, the essence of IT is information. Successful firms will use information and IT intelligently and in new ways to solve business problems and create customer value.
>
> (Quoted in Smith and Fingar 2003: 118)

A vivid analogy was expressed by Chad Dickerson, chief technology officer of *Infoworld*:

> ... the successful assembly of IT 'commodity inputs' is not a commodity itself. Think of IT like the food that comes into a restaurant – yes, the meat and vegetables most restaurants use are commodities that anyone can buy themselves, but what the restaurant does with the food is what really matters.
>
> (Quoted in Smith and Fingar 2003: 120)

John Seely Brown and John Hagel III write:

> IT may become ubiquitous, but the insight required to harness its potential will not be so evenly distributed. Therein lies the opportunity for significant strategic advantage.
>
> (Stewart 2003: 2)

To an extent the two sides are perhaps talking past each other. Deployment of IT, whether particular hardware or particular software, may be commoditised to the point where it cannot in itself give individual firms a competitive edge. At the same time, firms can still discover new ways of out-competing one another and, now that IT underpins so much business activity, many of the successful competitive tactics will be things that could not have been done without computers. Only, the things that matter for business success will be high-level things, far removed from the ground-level nuts and bolts of hardware or program code.

Certainly, if Nicholas Carr or Robert Gordon believe that the strategic business value of IT has already evaporated, they are wrong. Perhaps returns will diminish in due course, but we have not reached that point yet. Research by the Economist Intelligence Unit published in 2005 found that standardisation is causing technology to become more, not less, important at the strategic level. Business used to adopt technology mainly in order to cut costs, but most of the several thousand international business executives surveyed said that, now, technology has shifted from a cost-cutting tool into a tool of competitive advantage.

## SOFTWARE AS A SERVICE

If Carr's ideas are even partly right, presumably they should lead to specific, observable changes in the enterprise computing landscape. (*Enterprise computing* and *enterprise applications* are the slightly pompous terms standardly used for computing and software applications used for business purposes.)

The rise of the *software-as-a-service* (SaaS) model may represent the beginning of such a change.

Software as a service means that a firm that wants to use a particular application package does not have to buy a copy of the package with a licence for however many workstations will need to work with it and implement the software in a client/server environment at its own site. Instead, staff of the firm interact remotely with the package running at the site of a company set up to provide this service – an *application service provider* (ASP). Rather than a large up-front licensing fee, a firm using the application pays for the amount of usage it actually clocks up month by month.

Terminology varies. IBM talks about 'on-demand' computing. Some writers refer to the 'utility service' model, likening software consumption to the use of electricity or gas (the analogy that Carr stresses). All of these terms – SaaS, the ASP model, on-demand computing, the utility service model and 'hosted software' – cover essentially the same thing.[6] If SaaS is destined to become the usual way for firms to satisfy their IT needs, then Carr's controversial claims might be largely vindicated, because software supplied by outside ASPs to a range of different companies is standard software – there is no possibility of customisation, as there is when a company buys and implements software in-house. SaaS has by no means become the default model yet, but many believe that this may be where enterprise computing is heading.

The best-known company in the SaaS field is Marc Benioff's Salesforce.com. Salesforce specialises in one particular (but an important) enterprise application area, namely *customer relationship management* (CRM). CRM will be discussed in detail in Chapter 9 but, briefly, it supports a firm's sales and after-sales service staff by organising data on sales leads, past purchases, and so forth, so that when a member of the firm's staff is in contact with a customer or potential customer, the former has the relevant

---

[6] On the other hand, the similar-sounding term 'grid computing' (which has also been a lively topic in recent years) refers to something rather different. With grid computing, the physical CPU cycles involved in executing an organisation's IT work do not all occur on a predictable machine but are shared across the various machines in a network, depending on where capacity is available. Software as a service is about separating the processing from the user, not about shifting processing between machines unpredictably. Grid computing is interesting chiefly from a technical rather than a business point of view, and it is not discussed further in this book.

facts at his or her fingertips. By October 2006 Salesforce had half a million subscribers, with turnover growing at over 60 per cent year on year, and was looking like an unstoppable bandwagon.

## SAAS AND SMALLER COMPANIES

The SaaS model is particularly attractive to smaller companies. The initial wave of enthusiasm for e-business tended to focus on use of the technology by large, internationally famous companies, and on companies that were small because they were IT-based startups, helping to create the new business techniques. Often overlooked was the host of pre-existing small companies active in areas that had no special relationship with the new technology. But one of the worrying things about e-business, for those who looked deeper, was its potentially damaging impact on small existing companies.

Any innovation involving a large, fixed overhead cost impacts more heavily on smaller than on larger firms, because there is less revenue-earning business to spread the overhead across. It is often said, for instance, that extra state regulation tends to be especially problematic for small businesses: the rules often cost almost as much to implement in a 50-person company as in a 5000-person company. And when e-business began to take off, it was noticeable that smaller firms tended to be much slower than larger firms to adopt the technology. In principle, enterprise software might deliver the same advantages to a small firm as to a large one; but the software packages were often very expensive, and – more importantly – assessing them, deciding which might be worth using, implementing them and educating staff to use them takes a huge amount of time and effort that a small company typically has not got going spare.

For a major international company, asking an individual employee (or even a two- or three-person team) to spend six months or a year investigating a computerisation possibility is not a big deal. If the eventual recommendation is negative, little is lost. In a small company, every single member of staff is commonly at full stretch getting the day-to-day work done. So, if business needs to adopt enterprise software in order to remain competitive, there was a fear that many small firms might go to the wall.

## THE IMPORTANCE OF SMALL FIRMS

Perhaps some readers will think that that would not be too serious – it would be bad luck for the firms affected, but no great tragedy for society at large. That would be naive. Small firms are individually small, but there are a lot of them: collectively they are a major chunk of a national economy. Whether or not the *average* size of firms is changing (as discussed in Chapter 2), the average at any time comprises a small number of very large firms and a far larger number of smaller firms. Almost half of all private-sector British jobs currently are in firms employing fewer than 50 people.

What is more, simple numbers understate the significance of small firms for a national economy. It is widely accepted that small firms are qualitatively important also, as the principal sources of innovation – and a nation that fails to foster innovation in the twenty-first century is unlikely to enjoy a bright future. If a new business idea is implemented by creating a new company, then it will obviously begin small. But apart from that, the culture of small organisations tends to be more open to change than that of large organisations. When a company grows really large, it is hard for it not to succumb to a culture in which rules and precedents become more influential than intuition and original thought in responding to the changing business environment.

That is one reason why 'the top is a slippery place' and the industrial giants of one generation often disappear or lose their lustre a generation later. In Britain in the decades following the Second World War, there was an idea in the air that large companies were unassailable – but that was never really true, and to the extent that it was more true then than at other periods was because government intervention artificially protected the big boys against small innovative competitors (Jewkes 1977). That was also an era when Britain found it difficult to earn its living in the world. Since the political transformation of the 1980s, which turned the UK into one of the world's most vibrant economies, it has become evident that big companies can and often do lose their way and collapse, unless governments prop them up or they manage against the odds to keep reinventing themselves.

One concrete index of the relatively innovative nature of the small-business sector is that it plays a disproportionate role both in creating new jobs and in giving new workers their first foothold on the ladder of employment. In the USA, a 2002 Small Business Administration factsheet reported that small businesses were providing about three-quarters of net new jobs added to the economy, and about two-thirds of individuals' first jobs. Both of these fractions are considerably higher than the overall share of employment attributable to small businesses.

Consequently, if computerisation is damaging to the small-business sector, this is not something that any of us can afford to take lightly. We have seen why one might expect such damage. Small-company ethos may be receptive to the idea that the way things were done in the past need not be the way they are done in future; but ethos in itself does not create time for planning radical business process revamps or capital to spend on equipment.

When IT began to transform business processes, around the start of the twenty-first century, there was some evidence that small firms were failing to cope. The proportion of British private-sector jobs in small firms had been on a rising trend since about 1970, but it suddenly went into reverse; rather than almost half, the figure was down to 30 per cent in 2001, and many small firms ceased trading online. One plausible explanation is that small firms were trying to adopt techniques that proved to be beyond their grasp.

In the past few years this concern has been fading. If e-business was responsible for the turn-of-the-century fall in small-firm employment, then the small firms are fighting back; by 2004 the jobs figure was almost back to the 1995 level. One reason for thinking that small firms will manage in the long term is that the growth of the SaaS model is beginning to make adoption of enterprise software applications less daunting for small firms. In that model, using enterprise software is more like turning on a tap and drawing as much as one needs of a standard resource. The large overhead of implementing the software is borne by the ASP, and if a small firm's monthly usage is only a tiny fraction of a large firm's usage, then it will pay a correspondingly tiny fee.

In pure money-saving terms the choice between SaaS and on-premises software is not clear-cut. The analyst firms Quocirca and Forrester published research in August–September 2006 that found that, when all costs are taken into account, the SaaS model may offer savings in the short term and for small firms, but over a five-year period, or for a deployment of 500 or more seats, the traditional on-premises model works out cheaper. In Salesforce's early years, many people saw its service as attractive only to smaller companies and assumed that large firms would always want to own and run their own software. That is turning out to be a false prediction, though. CRM software is by now often deployed under the SaaS model at companies with thousands of seats, and in household-name companies, such as British Airways and Carphone Warehouse. In these cases, simple cost-saving is probably not the reason for the choice of SaaS.

## HOW FAR WILL SAAS SPREAD?

Salesforce itself specialises only in the CRM genre of enterprise application. As we shall see in later chapters, there are many other kinds of e-business software; one current question mark is whether genres other than CRM (such as the enterprise resource planning – ERP – software to be discussed in Chapter 8) will prove equally adaptable to the SaaS model. One recent development worth watching was the launch in November 2006 of Workday, founded by Dave Duffield, who ran the ERP supplier PeopleSoft before it was taken over by Oracle in 2005. Workday plans to offer a full range of enterprise applications under the SaaS model; it is beginning with 'human resources' software.

Meanwhile, suppliers of enterprise software under the traditional model, such as Oracle and Microsoft, are at least tentatively dabbling in the SaaS approach. They cannot afford to ignore it; if it succeeds, their existing business models will be undermined.

Even if SaaS proves technically feasible for all aspects of enterprise computing, it does not follow that companies will want to use it for everything. One reason why they might not is that it means handing over crucial business data to outsiders – under contractual guarantees of confidentiality, of course, but with crucial material a manager might not find that adequately reassuring. And where a company gains a competitive edge from the way it uses IT, exchanging that for the use of standard packages running on an ASP's servers might be a poor bargain even if it saved money. *The Economist* predicts that 'Big companies will probably keep "mission-critical" systems in-house.'[7]

If the only applications to be farmed out to ASPs are those that have no special significance for the competitive position of the ASPs' clients, then the SaaS model will tell us little one way or the other about the soundness of Nicholas Carr's claim that 'IT doesn't matter'. But some people believe that on-premises software is eventually going to become a quite unusual phenomenon. If that is true, it might suggest that Carr has the right idea.

---

[7] 'Work–life balance', *The Economist* 23 December 2006.

# 7 Shifting to an Intangible Economy

## INTANGIBLE GOODS AND ASSETS

E-business is about the *processes* of business becoming intangible. Streams of bits are replacing paper invoices transported in post-office vans and trains, wooden advertising hoardings, and other heavy, slow-moving paraphernalia of business life. But hand in hand with this there is another economic evolution under way, by which much of the *substance* created and distributed by economic activity is becoming intangible.

The idea that the balance of the economy is shifting towards intangible goods is a modern cliché, seen as important not only by IT professionals but by hard-nosed public figures with no special motive for exaggerating the importance of new technology. Here is Gordon Brown, then Chancellor of the Exchequer, giving his pre-budget report in December 2006:

> Twenty-five years ago the market value of our top companies was no more than the value of just their physical assets. Today the market value of Britain's top companies is five times their physical assets, demonstrating the economic power of knowledge, ideas and innovation.[1]

That is, in the 1980s the value of a large company derived purely from that of its premises, the machinery it owned, and so forth; nowadays the value of these things is dwarfed by that of the knowledge, information and other intangible assets comprised within the company and used in its activities.

Those intangible assets are not just information held and processed electronically. The expert skills, business awareness and factual knowledge possessed by a company's staff, for instance, are probably more important. But IT lies at the heart of the change. The market value of a public company is at bottom what people think it is: the price that people are willing to pay for its shares. Before the IT revolution, companies already depended heavily on intangible knowledge assets – they were certainly far more than mere collections of inanimate buildings and equipment; but things such as knowledge were largely invisible to people buying and selling shares in the market. Intangibles were simply there, like the air we breathe. It is IT that has turned these things, in many cases, into identifiable assets, stored in particular places, created and exchanged

---

[1] Reported in the *Daily Telegraph*, 7 December 2006.

via well-defined transactions, and quantifiable. Once people came to see that companies own intangible as well as tangible assets, they began to value the intangible assets accordingly.

Furthermore, IT turns out to have an especially important role with respect to other intangible aspects of a company's life. Brynjolfsson *et al.* (2002) examined how firms' overall market values were affected by computerisation, at a time when business IT was already beginning to move beyond merely automating existing clerical activities. The figures suggested that computerisation in a business acted as a catalyst for organisational developments that in themselves are considerably more valuable than the cost of the IT investment. As they put it, spending a dollar on premises or machinery makes a company on average about one dollar more valuable; but spending a dollar on computers makes the company some 5–20 dollars more valuable.

## CAPITAL ASSETS VERSUS PRODUCTS

What the chancellor was discussing in the speech quoted above, and what Brynjolfsson *et al.* were studying, was firms' *capital assets*: the resources they own on a long-term basis in order to carry out their activities. But the goods traded down value chains, transformed by one firm after another until they reach their final destination as consumer goods, are increasingly becoming intangible also.

In the case of consumer goods, this is apparent to everybody. Think, for instance, of things such as radio and television programmes, computer games and education; they are not all IT products (in that list, only computer games are), but they are all intangible rather than tangible goods, and between them things like that are certainly accounting for an increasing proportion of consumption. One statistic, for instance, is that in 2004 the average American spent about nine and a half hours a day watching television, listening to radio or consuming other media. (It seems staggering that people have so much free time, but the figures come on good authority). Surely, a generation or two earlier, this category of consumption would have been sharply lower.

E-commerce is often about making arrangements online to trade goods or services, which are then delivered by more traditional means, but in some cases what is traded is itself something in electronic form that is delivered online. This is not yet a large fraction of e-commerce (in 2005 it was estimated at 2 per cent by value of UK online sales outside the financial sector, versus 71 per cent for physical goods and 26 per cent for services), but the proportion is growing.

Intangibles are growing in importance also as input factors of production. Some further statistics are that the relative share of raw materials and energy input in manufacturing output was falling by about 1 per cent per year over the second half of the twentieth century, while the relative share of information/knowledge inputs has been rising at a similar rate since the 1880s. By the 1990s, to take two sample physical manufactures, intangible inputs accounted for 70 per cent of the cost of producing butter, and over 70 per cent of value added in car manufacture.

The statistics just quoted are taken from Charles Goldfinger (1997), a particularly insightful analysis of the shift to an intangible economy: much of the following discussion will be based on Goldfinger's work. That shift does not relate exclusively to IT, and it began long before the computer was invented; but IT is giving the shift a large fillip, by creating new categories of economic good and by making it easier to decouple intangible goods from the physical objects in which they used to be embodied. Although intangibles always were somewhat exceptional with respect to the standard assumptions of economics, before the computer revolution this was a marginal problem. Most economists ignored it most of the time. Now, it is no longer marginal and cannot be ignored.

## INJURING THE INVISIBLE HAND

For the IT specialist, the shift towards an intangible economy is important because it relates to new applications of his expertise. For owners of intangible property, IT is opening up new ways of making that property yield revenues, as well as undermining established business models.

But, for people interested in economic aspects of the functioning of society, the shift towards an intangible economy matters because it is changing many of the assumptions on which economic calculation is based. Adam Smith's 'invisible hand', which uses the price mechanism to bring about the optimal deployment of society's productive resources, may be becoming rather arthritic under the impact of IT.

## INTANGIBLES ARE ECONOMICALLY ODD

Goldfinger identifies a number of different respects in which intangible goods are economically 'special'. Intangible goods can be:

- *Non-destructive:* the same product, for instance a film or a piece of music, can be consumed repeatedly.
- *Joint:* an intangible good is frequently inseparable from a tangible good – reading a novel involves handling a physical book, and watching a film involves getting hold of a DVD.
- They are often *volatile*, in the sense that their value can be highly time-dependent. To someone working in the City, a particular piece of financial information may be worth millions in the morning but valueless that same afternoon. On a pay-per-view television system

113

the average viewer would be far more willing to pay to see today's news programme than yesterday's.

- There is a problem about *infinite regress*: if the good to be consumed is information, then often the only way to discover whether it is worth consuming is to consume it.

These special properties of intangible goods create many problems for price-setting. Traditionally, prices of goods were determined by reference to the cost of production and/or to what buyers were willing to pay. Both factors are problematic in the case of intangible goods.

Production costs do not yield a straightforward method of setting prices, because with intangibles there is typically no proportionality between inputs and outputs. For oranges, producing two tons requires about twice as much input of various categories as producing one ton. But a popular piece of music may be consumed – listened to – by tens of millions of fans, and yet it may have required no more input to produce than is required by a flop that few people hear.

Willingness to pay for intangibles is problematic for two reasons. One is the infinite regress problem. How are consumers to decide what they are prepared to pay for something, if they have no way of assessing its worth without paying for it? The second reason is that intangible goods are typically so easy to copy or share; consumers will not be willing to pay the true value to them of an intangible good if they can get it without paying. This does not relate just to 'piracy'. Many cases of sharing intangible goods are perfectly legal and usual. A student union lounge may subscribe to one copy of a newspaper that is read by dozens of students. But we all know, too, that the ease of copying electronic files often makes it near-impossible to enforce laws that attempt to control copying.

Traditionally, the difficulty of price-setting for intangibles was often masked by the fact that intangible goods were inseparable from their physical embodiment, which could be priced in a normal way. So, for instance, books would commonly have prices set in terms of physical size and quality of paper and printing – rather than in terms of the value of the information they contain, or the literary quality of the writing. As a way of pricing the content, this is not economically rational (price signals set this way will have no particular tendency to match production of different kinds of content with the varying levels of demand for them), but at least it works after a fashion. Once intangible goods are digitised, on the other hand, it is very easy to decouple ('unbundle') them from their physical embodiment. It is then impossible to overlook the pricing problem.

We saw in Chapter 2 that a successful economy depends on a complex web of price signals, by which for instance orange-growers, and the people involved in the various stages by which television sets are manufactured, are led to serve (among many others) a Brighton student unknown to them. If the signals are blurred, because of the peculiarities of intangible goods, then this matters to individual companies because it will be hard for them to know how to act in order to be profitable; and it matters to all of us as consumers, because less value for us will be produced from the resources available than could be produced if the signalling system were functioning well.

## NEW IDEAS ABOUT ECONOMIC GROWTH

The special economic properties of intangibles are more than just a nuisance for pricing. They have led to a fundamental rethinking of the conceptual basis of economics.

Traditionally, economists agreed that all factors relevant to economic life could be classified under the three headings of 'labour', 'land' (meaning natural resources) and 'capital'. Writers such as Schumpeter, with his doctrine of creative destruction, were of course well aware that ideas and the state of technical knowledge were also relevant, and indeed that economic growth comes about only through new thinking that shows people new ways to use resources. But as professional economics developed after the Second World War from a largely abstract discipline into one in which calculation was used to draw concrete conclusions about real-life national economies, the crucial role of new ideas in economic life was rather lost sight of. Formal economics tended to imply that all possible goods and services were in principle available at all times, and the role of economic forces was merely to settle what selections of them would be realised in particular circumstances. A satisfactory economic analysis should predict, for instance, that the quantity of television sets manufactured at any time in the nineteenth century would be zero.

Beginning in the 1990s, economists such as Paul Romer argued that this approach was misleading. Just as important as the land/labour/capital categories are the contrasting categories of things and ideas (or 'atoms' versus 'bits'). Technological knowledge is itself a category of good produced through the economic process, and it needs to be given a central role in economists' equations. It was nonsense to envisage the set of possible goods as a fixed spectrum of possibilities, with the quantities of some of them set to zero up until the historical point when they were invented: the range of goods and services that human beings have invented or ever will invent is tiny relative to the endless possibilities that no-one will ever happen to think of.

Even if this is true, it sounds like a purely abstract, philosophical consideration; but it is far more. It makes large differences to the concrete recommendations that economic theory yields. Thus, Romer (1994) argued that failure to incorporate the possibility of innovation into economic equations had caused economists to grossly underestimate the adverse impact on underdeveloped countries of government interference with free trade. A key practical issue for economics is why the 'South' is so much poorer than the 'North' and shows few signs of catching up. An important reason, according to Romer, is that traditional economic theory encouraged governments to introduce trade regimes that the revised theory, giving its proper place to intangibles, predicts to be very damaging to third-world societies. The chain of mathematical reasoning is too arcane to rehearse here, but the conclusion is easy for any of us to understand.

So this new style of conceptualising economic issues has major implications outside the academic ivory tower. It was very much a product of information technology. In principle, the approach was valid before the computer was invented, but only the rise of IT has made it obvious that intangibles are more than just an oddity at the margin of economic life. Paul Romer's specific examples, for instance, are standardly drawn from the domain of computing. In reality, intangibles are central to any economy, and they always have been, even though before the age of computers economists had difficulty in seeing it.

(For an accessible survey of the new approach to economic thinking, see Warsh 2006.)

## ECONOMY OF ABUNDANCE

Economics has traditionally been about how to manage scarce resources. Thanks to the ease of reproducing intangible goods, though, an economy based on them tends to be an economy of abundance, which again interferes with many longstanding assumptions. One of the words frequently associated with 'information' nowadays is 'overload' (whereas we do not hear about 'clothes overloads' or 'car overloads'). In the physical economy, many consumers could consume, without being especially greedy, more than they can get; in much of the intangible economy, consumers can easily get far more than they could possibly consume.

One consequence is that the intangible area of the economy is becoming a casino economy. Bringing an intangible product to market can be more like entering a lottery than earning a predictable return from a day's labour. Goldfinger quotes the case of Hollywood film-making, where out of every 100 'scenarios' under development only one is turned into a completed film, and out of every six films released only one returns a profit – but, with luck, that one returns enough profit to cover the other five films and all the work that led nowhere. Or consider the pharmaceutical industry – where the products themselves are tangible, but the share of scientific research and similar intangibles among the inputs to production is so large that this might best be seen as part of the intangible economy. Only one in 4000 synthesised pharmaceutical compounds becomes a marketed product, and only about a third of those earn back the costs of their development; so the industry as a whole can keep going only if some of those rare successes are very profitable indeed.

Goldfinger argues that in these circumstances the goal for management is not to increase the chances of success for individual products – if companies do that, they are like spectators all standing on tiptoe to see over one another's heads – but to capitalise on the rare successes they achieve: 'to transform hits into megahits'. Thus, Disney makes two or three times as much revenue from spin-off products associated with a successful film (videotapes, computer games, toys, etc.) as is generated directly by people buying tickets to see the film.

It is an interesting explanation for the phenomenon of media-related merchandising, although the logic of Goldfinger's argument is not totally clear. However low the probability of a hit, arithmetically it seems that working to raise that probability by *N* per cent should be as effective a way of maximising profits as working to increase the revenue from hits achieved by *N* per cent. Perhaps the tacit assumption is that doing the second is easier than doing the first – though that does not follow merely from the fact that the former figure is low.

## REWEIGHTING THE VALUE CHAIN

Another consequence of the shift from scarcity to abundance, according to Goldfinger, is that the weight of influence over value chains is shifting towards the consumer's end. Goldfinger quotes the management expert Peter Drucker as saying in 1992 'Power in the economy of developed countries is rapidly shifting from manufacturers to distributors and retailers.'

This is clearly true for industries supplying basic needs such as food and clothing. In recent years farmers and garment manufacturers have had to dance to the tune of retailers such as Tesco and Marks & Spencer in an unprecedented manner. Goldfinger gives other examples from higher-tech domains. In the early twentieth century, he says, the lion's share of power in the market lay with the company that assembled components into a complete product: Renault and Citroën were in a stronger position than, say, Michelin – the tyre company did more than the car-makers to foster the early development of motoring in France, through installing road signs and publishing maps and guides, but no-one makes car-purchase decisions by reference to choice of tyres. With personal computers, on the other hand, Intel and Microsoft are in a stronger position than companies that assemble and market the finished machines.

Again, though, it is not clear whether Goldfinger's analysis is as logical as it might be. He presents these various developments as instances of the same trend defined by Drucker – but are they? Marks & Spencer is nearer on the value chain than its garment suppliers to consumers; but a chip manufacturer such as Intel is surely further away from consumers on the PC value chain than the company that assembles and markets machines incorporating that chip. In terms of position on value chains, Intel and Dell (say) correspond to Michelin and Renault, respectively, not the other way round. The powerful position of chip and software producers surely relates less to position on the value chain than to performance and branding. For users, it makes much more difference what software their machines are running and what chips they are running on than who put the box together, whereas motorists' overall experience of their cars depends more on the marque than on the contribution of any one component supplier.

So, although Goldfinger has raised a range of important issues relating to the intangible economy, there remains room for debate about some of his conclusions.

## MASSIVELY MULTI-PLAYER ONLINE GAMES

So far in this chapter we have seen that some of the goods bought and sold in an economy are intangible, and some of the capital assets on which a business relies in order to carry out its work are intangible. The logical extreme is that the entire economic framework and everything in it might be intangible.

This seeming absurdity is now a reality, in the form of massively multi-player online role-playing games, such as *EverQuest, Second Life* and *World of Warcraft.* Within very few years these have changed from a geeky hobby into a social phenomenon incorporated in significant ways into the business plans of major companies in the conventional economy.[2]

In an MMO, people are not merely producing and consuming goods that happen to be intangible while inhabiting a tangible environment: during the time they spend in an MMO, so far as their conscious awareness is concerned the participants are living in a wholly intangible world.

MMOs are such a strange phenomenon, by traditional standards, that it is not possible to discuss them briefly – the discussion would scarcely be meaningful. This book must either ignore MMOs, or devote more pages to them than their current business significance warrants. I have opted to do the second. From my experience as a computing teacher, I know that many members of the intended readership of the book are intensely interested in this topic; and business interest in them has come from nowhere in a very short time. If that trend continues, the coverage in the following pages may look less excessive in the near future than it perhaps does now.

---

[2] The term 'massively multi-player online role-playing game' is cumbersome, and it gets abbreviated in different ways: MMPORG, MMORPG, MMOG, MMO. Some commentators prefer the simpler term 'virtual world' – but that is too vague, since there are many things at the artificial-intelligence end of computing that might be described as virtual worlds but are nothing to do with what we are considering here. I shall use the abbreviation MMO, for simplicity and also because the concept of massive numbers of participants interacting online is really more central than the 'game' concept. An MMO that focuses mainly on battles, where an avatar can 'win' or be defeated and 'die', is appropriately described as a 'game', but the term scarcely applies to MMOs (such as *Second Life*) which are more oriented to socialising and developing virtual communities – and these are the MMOs that are most interesting from a business point of view.

## HOW MMOS WORK

MMOs grew out of the Dungeons and Dragons type of electronic adventure games created on a hobby basis by enthusiasts. (The first 'multi-user dungeon' was programmed by an Essex University undergraduate, Roy Trubshaw, in 1978.) But, beginning with *Ultima Online* in 1997, they have moved up to a different plane of subtlety and complexity.

In an MMO (for readers unfamiliar with the concept), a participant controls a figure representing him- or herself (an *avatar*), which moves about and interacts with the avatars of other participants, as well as with figures that are essentially robots under the control of software. Through their computer screen, the participant sees what their avatar sees. If my avatar meets your avatar, I may be sitting at a computer in Brighton while you are in Düsseldorf or Shanghai, but you will see my avatar through the eyes of yours at the same time as I see your avatar through the eyes of mine. We can talk, via text messages displayed in speech bubbles. Our surroundings will be the same for both of us, and they will endure independently of individual participants' computer sessions.

The nature of the world inhabited by the avatars is decided by the MMO developers, normally a commercial company that charges participants a monthly subscription fee; the software underpinning a worthwhile MMO is a large (at least seven-figure) investment. Many MMOs offer a Tolkienesque pastiche of the Middle Ages; some cater to other kinds of fantasy. Within the fantasy world, complicated actions and initiatives are possible and indeed necessary for survival. An avatar needs equipment – for instance armour, if this is a warlike MMO – some of which it may be able to make, but other elements of which it will need to obtain by trading. An avatar can create a trading stock by making goods, or by 'harvesting' items that the MMO software causes to grow in particular locations; it sells its goods, or services (perhaps the avatar is a wizard with special skills at healing wounds), in exchange for the MMO's internal medium of exchange, which might be 'gold pieces' or 'doubloons', and with those it buys the things it needs. The physical look of an MMO is somewhat cartoonish (it is beyond current technology to maintain and deliver to users in real time a level of visual detail comparable with the real world); it turns out that participants are happy to accept this and immerse themselves mentally in the MMO, provided their interactions with other MMO inhabitants have the rich complexity of human interactions – and they have, because behind each avatar there is a human being.

## GROWING POPULATIONS

Many people are spending significant amounts of time participating in MMOs. A successful MMO may have hundreds of thousands, or millions, of participants, and any one participant will be active in the MMO for several hours a day on average (the complexity of MMO life is such that lower levels of engagement would probably be pointless, just as one could not lead much of a real-world life if one were awake for only minutes each day). By now there are dozens of MMOs. Total active subscriptions to all MMOs were estimated in mid-2006 at over 12 million, and growing fast.

Participants' emotional commitment to their MMO is often very great. In a 2001 survey of participants in the US-based *EverQuest*, Edward Castronova (2001) found that one in five regarded themselves as actually living in its virtual world, and returning to the real world only as visitors (see also Castronova 2005a).

One response, by people to whom MMOs are a closed book, is to think it very sad that grown people should want to leave real life behind for the sake of 'silly games'. This may be unfair. For decades, many people have been spending hours a day watching television. Which is less sad: slumping passively in front of a television set, or being actively inventive and social at a computer that is functioning as a gateway to an MMO? Still, it could well be that the flourishing of MMOs is telling us something uncomfortable about the kinds of society we have created in the twenty-first century. The appeal of the mock-mediaeval theme is perhaps because a sorcerer, or a knight of the Round Table, is seen as having a degree of influence over his own destiny, for better or for worse, that is unavailable in any present-day walk of life. The game developer David Rickey describes MMOs as 'provid[ing] a vacation from the pointlessness of life's rat race'.[3] It is interesting to note that although MMOs are popular in the English-speaking world, they are proportionately much more popular still in East Asia. The country with the highest density of MMO participants is believed to be South Korea. The MMO with most participants, as I write, is *World of Warcraft*: many of those are in the USA, but far more are in China – remarkable, surely, given the less advanced IT infrastructure of that country.

For present purposes, though, the implied criticism of twenty-first-century society – even if valid – is scarcely relevant. What matters is that large numbers of people are in fact participating in MMOs.

## MMOS AS BUSINESS LOCATIONS

For the companies that develop them, MMOs are a lucrative new type of business. But their real significance for us lies in the business activities taking place *within* MMOs, rather than in the business of developing and running MMOs.

Notice, first, that although the contents of an MMO are entirely 'unreal', its economy is as real as any other. MMO participants put real effort – lots of effort – into making or harvesting virtual goods, and they trade in them not just within the MMO, for virtual gold pieces (or whatever), but in the

---

[3] Contribution to 'Online worlds roundtable #7, part 1', RPG Vault, 2003, Rickey03.notlong.com

real world, for pounds, dollars, Korean won, etc. In 2005, annual trade in virtual goods for real-world money was estimated at $30 million in the USA, via eBay, and over $100 million in Asia. (Total trade for virtual money was estimated at $1 billion for 2005.)

If people transfer to one another things that they have put effort into making or acquiring in exchange for real money, then that is real trading, whether the things are turnips, songs or virtual coats of elfish armour. What's more, the gold pieces and other MMO-internal currencies are themselves real money – they are money as much as pounds sterling or US dollars are. The gold pieces are intangible, but then, money nowadays usually is intangible. Much of it exists only as numbers in computers; even when a sum of money is embodied in a banknote, this is not valued for its physical properties as an oblong of printed paper. Like pound notes, *EverQuest* gold pieces are valued because they can be used to buy things that many people want. MMO currencies, as well as MMO goods, are regularly bought and sold for real-world money. In theory, a new MMO participant can work up from nothing to possession of a satisfying range of gear and virtual bank balance purely by activities within the MMO, but to do that takes hard work and luck over a long period – many participants prefer to use real-world assets to give themselves a head start. Since MMO currencies are traded against real-world currencies, they have specific exchange rates against sterling or the US dollar.

## REAL ECONOMIES IN VIRTUAL WORLDS

Because MMO money is translatable into real-world money, one can quantify the size of an MMO economy in real-world terms. In his 2001 report, Edward Castronova estimated that the gross national product of the *EverQuest* MMO was then about US $135 million – dividing this by the number of participants gave GNP per capita of $2266, about the same as Russia.

If the average is as high as that, one would expect plenty of people to want to engage in MMO economic activities as a paying proposition, not just for fun: and they do. Highly specialised economic niches have emerged; a South Korean firm runs a web portal, NetMarble, 'which does a good business selling everything from virtual hats and handbags to virtual plastic surgery for computer avatars'.[4] (Plenty of MMO participants are female – and many others are men pretending to be women.) In the third world, where real-world wage rates are low, working in an MMO can be attractive as a full-time job. China has been developing 'gold farms', where groups of young men

---

[4] *The Economist*, 13 December 2003.

> ... play games like World of Warcraft and Lineage at the highest levels, amassing booty and building avatars with lots of desirable characteristics. These are then sold on eBay to the highest bidder... [Reportedly] there are more than 2,000 gold farms in China and more than 200,000 gold farmers.
>
> (Seybold 2006: 372)

One Chinese gold farmer commented:

> For 12 hours a day, 7 days a week, my colleagues and I are killing monsters [to steal the treasure they guard]... I make about $250 a month, which is pretty good compared with the other jobs I've had.[5]

A few people are making first-world incomes from full-time work within MMOs. Chris Mead of Norwich used to be a factory worker; he has built up a craft business within *Second Life* by creating animations for couples. When two avatars click on the animation icon, they dance or cuddle. It takes Chris up to a month's work to develop one of these animations, and he sells copies for about 50p; they are so popular that in 2006 he was making about £1000 a week. Real-world tax authorities have understandably taken a while to get their minds round the MMO phenomenon, but in May 2007 an American congressional committee was reported as preparing a recommendation on how to tax *Second Life*'s Linden dollars – South Korea actually began taxing MMO incomes in July 2007.

The situation has been summarised by Tim Harford (2006):

> ... these games, where players contribute considerable labor in exchange for things they value, are not merely like real economies, they *are* real economies.

An entirely intangible world can form the basis of a wholly real economy.

## VIRTUAL MARKETING

Accepting that these fantasy worlds contain genuine trading, why would real-world businesspeople be interested?

The most obvious reason is that MMOs create new kinds of marketing opportunity. As Castronova (2005b) puts it, 'Marketing must go where the people are, and so virtual worlds are the logical next frontier.' If a lot of your target customers are choosing to spend much of their waking time

---

[5] *New York Times* 9 December 2005, quoted in Dibbell (2006: 293).

within MMOs, then you want your brands and products to be visible in those MMOs.

That is starting to happen. Levi Strauss has promoted a new style of jeans by selling virtual versions to avatars in the MMO *There* at a price premium to the generic jeans otherwise available. In October 2006, Starwood, which owns Sheraton Hotels and other hotel and resort chains, opened within *Second Life* the first example of a new style of hotel, hoping in that way to glean customer reactions before committing themselves to the much larger financial commitment of building real-life examples. Reuben Steiger has founded a consultancy company, Millions of Us, in order to help real-world firms exploit the marketing and brand-building possibilities in *Second Life*. He quotes the cost of a good campaign as about $200,000, the bulk of which pays for people to design virtual goods that simulate or relate to the client's real products.

Marketing within MMOs involves novel considerations. People spend time in MMOs in order to escape from the humdrum real world into a fantasy existence: they can be expected to react very negatively to anything that breaks the fantasy. Quoting Edward Castronova (2005b) again:

> … in a synthetic world based on a 1940s [film] noir, Inspector Malone can quaff a Coke, so long as it's in a 1940s-style Coke bottle. But in King Arthur's Camelot, no one would want to see a Coke …

And the nature of MMOs means that disaffected participants could easily punish brands whose presence they object to very severely indeed. On one occasion, *Ultima Online* participants expressed dissatisfaction with their king by visiting the throne room en masse, stripping off their avatar clothes and virtual-vomiting over everything. For, say, an upmarket restaurant chain hoping to use an MMO to develop its brand image, this would truly be a nightmare scenario – and one that could scarcely be paralleled in the real world (at least, one would like to think not).

## TURNING CUSTOMERS INTO CO-DESIGNERS

MMOs, then, offer business novel marketing opportunities but also novel risks; if enough people take to spending time in MMOs, then companies will have to learn how to use the opportunities and avoid the risks. But 'marketing' in the normal sense is a largely one-way activity: a company has brands and products, and it sets out to win potential customers' allegiance to them. More interesting than MMOs as forums for marketing is the possibility of using MMOs to make product development a two-way process, in which potential customers have much more input into product design than they used to have.

Quite apart from the special issue of MMOs, it has become a cliché of recent business thinking that the internet has brought companies closer to their client base and made it easier for companies to 'hear' what their potential customers really want. Patricia Seybold (2006: 4) describes the traditional approach to product development as:

> our ... experts invent and design innovative new products to meet needs customers may not have even realized they have. Then our marketing and advertising departments make prospective customers aware of those needs, wrap a brand experience around our innovative products ... and bring them to market.

In the twenty-first century, she argues, companies cannot succeed that way any longer: they need to turn customers into *co-designers*:

> ... many customers *can* be innovative; they can envision what they'd like to be able to do and help you co-design ways to help them achieve your mutual goals. It's also true that there will always be scientific and technical breakthroughs ... that your customers can't foresee. Yet ... there are an equal number of business innovations and business process breakthroughs that have emerged from customers' desires to do things differently. You can only tap this customer creativity if you're working shoulder to shoulder with customers ...
>
> (Seybold 2006: 6)

For many businesses, MMOs represent ideal laboratories in which to carry out this shoulder-to-shoulder co-design activity. Toyota has developed virtual versions of its Scion car marque, which it began by giving away and since October 2006 has been selling for a modest price to *Second Life* inhabitants. Toyota's hope is that avatars will customise the cars and sell them on, thus creating a buzz of interest in the brand of a kind that would be much harder to achieve in the real world (because it is easier to make interesting modifications to cars made of bits than to cars made of steel). If patterns and trends appear in avatars' customisation, these can feed in to the decisions Toyota's engineers make in developing their next generation of real-world cars.

In the Scion case, the initiative still originated on the company side. But that will not always be so. Second Lifers are routinely creating artefacts to please themselves, independently of any commercial considerations; for a savvy company, this could often act as a trigger showing the company how to please its market by translating trends in avatar creations into real-world products. At least one firm is now manufacturing real-world furniture based on the designs of virtual 'furni' created by *Second Life* inhabitants.

The point is not to gain a free ride by eliminating the expense of in-company design. Once a company spotted a virtual trend that looked worth turning into real-world product lines, it would want to co-opt the trendsetting avatars into its design process and reward them properly for their contributions. That would be simple good business – not just because stealing ideas is unethical, but because that is a way in which MMO participants would learn that company *X* is actively involved in helping to realise trends that they are enthusiastic about, so that new product lines from company *X* will be worth looking out for in real-world existence. The point is, rather, that at present in-house product designers have to *forecast* (broadly speaking, to guess) which direction their customers want to move in; in an MMO, they can *see*.

Commercial marketing and product development are by no means the only ways in which MMOs can serve real-world goals. *Second Life*, in particular, is beginning to act as a laboratory for all kinds of non-commercial but humanly important developments. To take one example, autistic children are being helped to learn how to interpret and give out non-verbal social signals using avatars, because, for someone who lacks those skills, *Second Life* is a safer place to practise than the real world. And, now there is pressure to reduce air travel because of global warming, IBM has been experimenting with the alternative of holding virtual international meetings on private islands in *Second Life*. Applications such as these are outside the scope of this book, but they are many and diverse; indeed, an MMO that became too narrowly commercially oriented would be quite unattractive to participants. Nevertheless, it seems likely that MMOs will become valuable to businesses that learn how to work with them sensitively and respectfully. At the time I write, this movement is only just getting off the ground.

## ECONOMICS AS AN EXPERIMENTAL SCIENCE

Looking beyond the use of MMOs for marketing and product design, a wider and more abstract implication for business is that they seem to offer the possibility of turning economics into an experimental science.

Standardly, economics is seen as a science rather like astronomy – one can observe, but one cannot carry out controlled experiments. If we contemplate demand and supply schedules for a good (like the schedules shown in Figure 2.4 on p. 22), we can observe where the lines cross – that is, the price at which the good in question is actually offered, and the quantity actually produced – but we can only infer the other parts of the curves, as a matter of theoretical hypothesis: logically we know that such curves must exist, but we have no way of plotting their precise shapes numerically.

People have been using computers for some time now to create simulations of economic life (e.g. see Epstein and Axtell 1996). But although these simulations can be of considerable interest to theoretical economists, they are necessarily so simplified that their impact outside academic economics is small – certainly they have little consequence for business life. When economic agents are part of a computer simulation, their patterns of motivation and propensities to act in various circumstances will have so little of the rich, unpredictable complexity of real human behaviour that they can be only caricatures of real economic agents. In an MMO, by contrast, the economic agents possess all of that complexity, because they are human beings; but the circumstances within which they interact economically are controlled by the MMO developers, and in consequences they are both simpler than real life and open to experimental variation. Some of that experimentation could be highly relevant to the business world.

People often find it difficult to warm to economics as an academic discipline, because the considerations that give it its intellectual fascination are hard to perceive behind the humdrum realities of everyday commercial activity. That intellectual fascination relates in large part to the manner in which societies find their way towards allocations of available resources to uses that maximise value. Societies arrive through spontaneous self-organisation at complex structures of relationships, like those hinted at in Figure 2.5 (on p. 26), which succeed in fulfilling their inhabitants' needs via multi-step value chains in which the goods existing at any step could in principle have been produced in many different ways and could in principle be allocated to many alternative uses: and somehow this immensely subtle organisation is achieved through the signalling system provided by prices alone, with no central coordinating machinery.

To those with the imagination to see it, this is a truly remarkable phenomenon, but seeing it is not easy. Most of us directly perceive only the final steps of value chains, which serve up the ultimate consumer goods; or perhaps, through employment, we become familiar with one tiny intermediate segment of a single raw-materials-to-consumer supply chain, without getting much sense of the larger context within which it is embedded or the alternatives that might have existed. Prices seem to us like fixed givens rather than like a system of signals by means of which a society feels its way towards optimal solutions.

MMOs seem to dispel some of this difficulty of perception. If an economy is built up from scratch within a pristine Garden of Eden, then it is relatively easy for an individual participant to grasp its workings. As Julian Dibbell writes, discussing his work as a wholesale supplier of magic suits of armour to a retailer within the *Ultima Online* MMO:

> It was a supply chain, [and] … I was right in the middle of it, where I could see it whole, from end to end. You businesspeople, who live your days in this same, central region of the economy, do you realize what a foreign place it is to the rest of us? … I could see now just how
> *(Continued)*

*(Continued)*

> incomplete the consumer's perspective on economic existence is – how infantile it is, really, to go through life expecting products always magically to arrive on the shelves, never seeing … the enormous social machinery that connects the jobs we do to the things we buy.
>
> (Dibbell 2006: 144)

The price-signalling system changed from a theoretical abstraction in Dibbell's mind to a matter of direct observation:

> The childlike, magical thinking of the consumer mind looks at price tags and bar codes and imagines – I don't know – some celestial database containing the One True Price of every product under heaven. But from where I sat now I saw that things were otherwise. For any given good, there is no single price. There is, instead, a chaos of them – hundreds or thousands or millions of price points at which the market's various players would be willing to trade at any given moment …
>
> (Dibbell 2006: 152)

And, because the properties of an MMO are chosen by the developers, it is possible to change particular features and watch how the economic arrangements of the MMO adapt to the change. MMO developers do this quite often. Because the number of participants who can be accommodated on a given server is limited, they create copies of their virtual world on a series of separate servers; and often they vary aspects of the copies, in order to discover which setting of some parameter makes the MMO most attractive to participants, or to cater to participants with different tastes. Developers reduce or increase the supply of some 'raw material', or of virtual currency, in order to maintain and enhance the appeal of their MMO. These things are exercises in experimental economics, and the environments in which they occur share enough of the features of real-world economies that their outcomes are likely to contain lessons of interest to hard-nosed, real-world business people.

## ARE MMOS BEING OVER-HYPED?

Some observers make very large claims indeed about the potential impact of MMOs on real-world economic and business life. Edward Castronova even foresees a possible future in which so much economic activity has migrated into MMOs that real-world economies become permanently depressed areas, rather like the old mill towns of northern England now that textile production has shifted to the third world.

This seems implausible. After all, even if a proportion of MMO participants *think* of themselves as living in their virtual world and returning to real life only as 'visitors', that is merely part of their fantasy. MMO-ers have bodies that must regularly eat real-world food and that need real-life accommodation – housing, a bed and so forth. Like anyone else's, their bodies from time to time have medical needs, which have to be served by real-world facilities and real-world personnel who have undergone a great deal of real-world training. This is not at all comparable to the mill-town situation: if people can get cotton cheaply from East Asia, or can use artificial fabrics instead, then they truly no longer need cotton woven in Lancashire.

Furthermore, one should beware of over-generous assumptions about how far developments within MMOs can potentially serve as signposts towards real-world business developments. For instance, one of the most vibrant areas of activity in many MMOs relates to avatar clothes and fashions. Many virtual businesses market distinctive lines of avatar garments; there are even online magazines devoted to discussing trends in MMO fashion, such as *Second Life*'s *Second Style* (www.secondstyle.com). Innovating stylistically must be quicker and easier with virtual clothes than with real ones, so there might seem to be scope for the real-world garment industry to profit by looking at which way avatar style is moving and translating those trends into next season's high-street lines. In practice, that will probably never happen. Fashion trends in real life are driven not by the population as a whole but by a few highly creative young people, and they are among the last people who are likely to get involved with MMOs – their real lives are too fulfilling to want to escape into computer screens. Indeed, the fashion industry currently makes strikingly little use of IT even for mundane purposes such as business communication. Fashion and technology evidently appeal to largely disjoint groups of people. Toyota's use of *Second Life* for marketing and gathering design ideas may be a more plausible initiative: cars are themselves technological products.

It is also possible to question the whole idea that MMOs constitute real economies based in virtual worlds. In a hard-hitting blog article, Randolph Harrison (2007) argues that *Second Life* – the MMO commonly seen as the 'realest' virtual economy of them all – is in truth better understood as a kind of pyramid scheme. The founders of a pyramid scheme make significant money by pulling in large numbers of gullible people, who hope that they in turn will have opportunities to profit; but in practice they never do, because the pyramid can expand only so far. Harrison complains that the advertised exchange rate between *Second Life*'s Linden dollar and the US dollar works fine for exchanging trivial sums, but that if one finds a way to make a worthwhile profit and tries to turn it into real-world money, the exchange rate promptly moves against one so that the profit largely evaporates. Harrison paints a dark picture of a world in which many participants are scraping a small virtual income through sordid activities such as selling cybersex while they wait for a breakthrough in a legitimate enterprise such as making virtual jewellery, not realising that the world is structured economically in a way that makes that breakthrough unlikely to happen.

In fairness, though, the many comments on Harrison's blog included a number from people who claimed that they were in fact drawing a useful real-world income from unsordid activities within *Second Life*. In a domain as full of 'smoke and mirrors' as MMOs, it is hard for an outsider to judge where truth lies. And even if Harrison's criticisms were valid, that would not necessarily contradict the idea that MMOs are 'real economies'. After all, scenarios like those he describes are not very rare in the real-life economy.

## INTANGIBLES HERE TO STAY

The reader might well conclude that the MMO phenomenon is just too weird to take seriously. So many major real-world companies are now deciding to embark on involvement of one kind or another with MMOs, though, that this conclusion could turn out to be seriously misguided.

And whatever the eventual fate of these entirely intangible economies may be, the large and growing significance of intangible elements in the real-world economy is not open to question.

# 8 Enterprise Resource Planning

## BLURRED DEFINITIONS

Among business applications of IT, the largest single area is *enterprise resource planning* (ERP). Back in 2001, ERP accounted for slightly over half of all enterprise application spending in Europe. More recently (for reasons discussed in the next paragraph) it has become difficult to separate out figures for ERP spending from spending on other application areas; if we could do that, the ERP proportion would probably be somewhat lower now, but not because ERP is an obsolete technology – rather, because the ERP market is now mature, so that fewer companies are coming forward to adopt it for the first time than in the case of some newer applications.

There is a problem about describing ERP and other enterprise applications, which is that over recent years the boundaries between different applications have been blurring. The ERP market leader internationally is the German company SAP. It originally offered systems that focused specifically on the area traditionally called 'enterprise resource planning', but later it broadened the scope of its systems so that, for instance, they now include *customer relationship management* (CRM) – traditionally a function sharply distinct from ERP. Oracle grew to prominence as a relational-database company, but in January 2005 it bought SAP's ERP competitor PeopleSoft, and in January 2006 it bought the leading CRM company Siebel; for some time now Oracle has been offering an 'E-Business Suite', which integrates all the main enterprise applications into a single system. Similar things have been happening with other companies.

The supplier companies have no motive to maintain sharp definitional boundaries between the various functions covered by their systems; they would naturally like their clients to think of their offerings in as broad a way as possible. So a term like 'ERP' is coming to be stretched into such vagueness that it risks losing its descriptive value.

For the student of e-business this is unfortunate. Even if integrated e-business software suites are available, a newcomer cannot get to grips with everything at once. It is necessary to break down the field of enterprise software into manageable sub-areas in order to explain them.

The solution adopted here is to describe the field in slightly old-fashioned terms, using terminology such as 'ERP' in the narrower sense that was usual when certain companies supplied ERP systems, certain other companies supplied CRM systems and yet further companies supplied other enterprise applications, and the various functions were both commercially and conceptually separate. This is still the best way in to an understanding of the field.

The trend towards integration is itself a development with significant implications for business and economics. We shall look at that trend in the later part of this chapter, before moving on to studying CRM and other specialised enterprise applications in subsequent chapters.

## THE VISION

A vision of what we now call ERP was expressed in the 1980s by Sir John Harvey-Jones, the legendary chairman of ICI who after retiring in 1987 made a second career as BBC Television's 'Troubleshooter'. In his book about industrial leadership, *Making It Happen*, Sir John wrote:

> It saddens me that when people look at the impact of information technology they think so frequently in terms of organizing business in the ways that we have in the past. The enormous powers that are now within our grasp are used merely, so to speak, to mechanize what we have done rather imperfectly before. I see the advent of information technology in a rather different way... We have already got all the knowledge and information available to operate a system where an industrial purchaser will order automatically, through his computer system, from an industrial supplier. The computers at the supplier's end will order up the raw materials, program the production, make out the invoices and the records, almost certainly ensure automatic payment of the raw materials supplier, while collecting from the customer ... what is needed is a totally different relationship between the customer and the supplier. They will have to work together to achieve the enormous savings and the greater efficiencies that will come from such systems, and this means increasingly that the customer/supplier relationship will become more and more like a partnership ...
>
> (Harvey-Jones 1988: 328–9)

This is a fair description of enterprise resource planning, before the thing itself existed. Twenty years later, it is perhaps surprising to read that Sir John expected ERP to produce 'more choice, more freedom, and more self-determination': he seems to have envisaged e-business as liberating the employee almost in the way that twentieth-century technology liberated women from heavy housework. To date things have not worked out like that. In other respects, though, Sir John was accurate in anticipating that computers were destined to do more for business than merely mechanise what was currently done by hand.

## THE CORE ERP FUNCTIONS

The historical origin of what we have come to know as ERP software lay in what were then called 'material requirements planning' systems designed by IBM and the American tractor manufacturer J.I. Case in the 1960s. As that term suggests, these systems deployed computers to monitor and systematise the ordering, delivery and warehousing of physical supplies into the manufacture process, replacing the chaotic manual systems used previously. In the 1970s this was extended to automate related functions such as production scheduling (which entails forecasting materials requirements) and planning inventory holdings to match them with future distribution needs. It is this history that lies behind the word 'resource' in ERP.

But, from the late 1980s onwards, the descendants of these systems broadened to cover adjacent business activities that do not fit easily under the phrase 'resource planning'. Even before the recent blurring of boundaries, the term ERP was a historical hangover, used conventionally for a set of functions wider than the name suggests.

As used since the 1990s, ERP denotes centralised, company-wide software systems that handle in a unified way a large proportion of what one might call the mechanical aspects of keeping a business running, including at least the 'upstream' functions connected with ordering from suppliers and managing the inventory of supplies received, as well as managing the inventory of products awaiting distribution. For several years now, 'downstream' functions such as processing orders received from customers and sending out invoices have standardly been integrated into the same systems. And the upstream ERP functions have often spread beyond the boundaries of individual companies: a large company that has adopted ERP may seek even greater efficiency by giving its key suppliers access to its network, so that routine aspects of the ongoing supply process can be handled with minimal human intervention.

All of these functions might be called 'mechanical', because they involve little or no human judgement. If a customer has ordered 1000 widgets at a quoted price and the widgets have been shipped, there is no need to debate whether the customer should be invoiced. Customer relationship management, on the other hand, is connected to the winning of orders, and so it is an area of business where human judgements are central and IT can function only in a supporting role.

Since its introduction in 1992, the market-leading ERP system has been SAP's R/3; more recently SAP has been encouraging clients to migrate from R/3 to MySAP, introduced in 1999. SAP, based at Walldorf near Heidelberg, is Europe's largest software company. The name stands for *System-Analyse und Programmentwicklung*, German for 'systems analysis and program development'. SAP was founded in 1972 by five German former IBM employees: their first client was the German subsidiary of ICI – the story goes that IBM declined to take on a contract to develop production-planning software for that company, and so the systems analysts resigned from IBM in order to take on the job themselves.

The chief competitor for SAP is Oracle, which since 2005 has incorporated the previously independent ERP vendors PeopleSoft and J.D. Edwards. Microsoft has recently made a move into the ERP area, with its 'Dynamics' line.

## LINKING INFORMATION ISLANDS

The chief motive for a company to adopt ERP is not merely that it automates previously manual functions. By the beginning of the twenty-first century, a firm will probably have been carrying out most of the individual functions automatically for years already. It has more to do with integrating different functions across separate departments.

In the first place, this gives managers more detailed and up-to-date knowledge of what is happening in their company and hence more ability to control it. Ravi Kalakota's standard e-business textbook quoted a manager in a large company:

> You can't manage what you don't know. Before our ERP implementation, it was four to six weeks after the close of the month before we had information reconciled, and we still weren't sure of the accuracy.
>
> (Kalakota and Robinson 2001: 245)

This issue is vital even for a firm that is not expanding its sphere of activities. But also, globalisation means that the information and control problem for managers in many companies is taking on new levels of difficulty. Keeping tabs on what is happening at a separate site or indeed in a separate building is always much harder than keeping abreast of what is going on under a single roof. The chatting in corridors or coffee lounges, which superficially looks trivial or time-wasting, in reality serves vital communicative purposes. Monitoring activities on the other side of the world introduces a higher dimension of difficulty, and not just because of physical distance and time-zone differences: language, currency and tax regime differences add to the manager's problems. ERP is seen as a large part of the answer to these.

Then, the very fact that many individual business processes were automated years or decades ago means that the systems will often be creaky, perhaps full of patches installed as business needs and processes evolved. It might not seem worthwhile to replace an individual application that still just about does its job with a newer package serving just that function, but ERP represents an opportunity to make a clean sweep and replace many separate legacy systems.

The largest single selling point for ERP, though, is the prospect of linking 'information islands' into an integrated continent of information spanning a company from side to side. As Kalakota and Robinson (2001: 246) put it:

> ... most large enterprises find themselves contending with a hodgepodge of disparate, disjointed applications, creating an environment of confusion, misunderstanding, errors, and limited use of corporate information assets.

By linking up the parts of a business electronically, furthermore, ERP speeds up the flow of work through a company, and this in itself is a large benefit. Not least, it reduces inventory, corresponding to capital tied up unproductively. Thomas Davenport (2000: 7) quotes the firm Autodesk, which

> ... used to require two weeks on average to ship to customers, [whereas] 98 percent of products are now shipped within twenty-four hours. Financial closing times were cut in half, from twelve days to six. Autodesk calculates that it has saved more on reduced inventory alone than its SAP system cost to install.

## BMW HAMS HALL

As a case study, consider the introduction of SAP R/3 at the BMW Group's Hams Hall car-engine plant outside Birmingham, regarded at the time and perhaps still now as 'the most modern engine factory in the world'.

Hams Hall opened in 2001 to manufacture four-cylinder petrol engines, currently used in BMW 3 Series, 1 Series and Z4 cars. It came into being shortly after a complicated passage of company history. In 1994 BMW had bought Rover (previously the state-owned British Leyland Motor Company, which earlier still resulted from a merger between Austin, Morris, the lorry manufacturer Leyland, and other companies); then in 2000 it sold Land Rover to Ford and sold the Rover and MG marques to a management buy-out (which later collapsed). In consequence, the workforce at the new Hams Hall site had diverse backgrounds, with a high proportion having been BMW employees for only a few years. Furthermore, the difficulties besetting British car manufacture in the late twentieth century meant that BMW's inheritance from Rover included a history of IT underinvestment; and the various Rover divisions, and BMW, used different systems – causing isolation of one part of the current company from another, unnecessary waste of human time and computing resources, and, perhaps most seriously, the danger of unintended variation in data as it migrated between systems.

The fact of Hams Hall being a new facility on a new site made it a favourable opportunity to draw a line under the past and adopt a new IT infrastructure. The features of SAP that appealed most to BMW were that it is modular, yet network-based so that any particular datum is entered or updated once and then available wherever needed; a clear upgrade path was foreseeable, with the possibility for instance of extending coverage out beyond Hams Hall or BMW to embrace some of its suppliers; and that as the years went by, data entries would cumulate into an efficient 'corporate memory', instead of records of diverse kinds being distributed across many different locations in the company, making efficient information retrieval very difficult.

See for instance Figure 8.1, a screenshot of an engineering change report relating to a modification to the specs of a particular screw at one particular location in the engine, with knock-on implications both for the screw supplier's tooling and production process, and for other areas of the BMW Group that use the same screw in other engines or vehicles. (Parts of Figure 8.1 are blanked out for reasons of commercial confidentiality.) Via the 'traffic lights' at the foot of the screen, the sign-off status with respect to various responsible parties can be checked at any time, by anyone in the

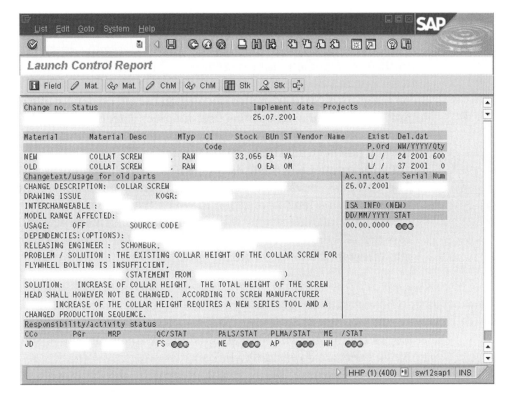

FIGURE 8.1

company with appropriate access privileges; after the issue is resolved, the history of this event (together with countless others like it) becomes part of a comprehensive electronic archive, which can be consulted efficiently whenever someone involved in BMW's global activities needs to do so.

## CHANGING COMPANY CULTURE

It is easy to see why BMW saw benefits to be gained by adopting electronic ERP. But it was a large undertaking. As a BMW engineer put it to me, it represented a 'massive culture change'. An extensive and costly training programme was required. Each worker was given two and a half days training in 'SAP culture', in addition to training in the specific SAP module(s) relevant to his or her work, and 'key SAP users' were designated to provide one-to-one follow-up tuition as individuals required it. Apart from this, sensitive industrial relations issues were created. Workers who previously used pen-and-paper methods often saw computer data entry not as a new and better way of doing their existing job, but as an additional responsibility, of a kind that ought to attract extra pay.

Discovering how to achieve the culture shift was itself a learning process. Often, workers did not understand the power of the system they were interacting with and hence failed to exploit the value that was in principle available. And, like any complex IT system, SAP's software was itself evolving, making learning all the more challenging. So long as the old systems were available alongside, it was too tempting for staff to revert to them to complete immediate tasks, which was all right in the short term but meant that the intended corporate memory was not getting off the ground. So BMW pulled the plug on the old systems, while making SAP more palatable by creating user-interface screens that emulated the previous systems, and incorporating temporary fixes within SAP to cater to work habits formed under the old systems.

Two years after beginning operations, Hams Hall saw SAP as a success. The company envisaged starting to integrate its suppliers into the network, with a long-term vision in which the value chain from BMW's component manufacturers through to the consumers who drive its cars are all connected into a skein of electronic communication that allows instant feedback on quality issues.

## THE OTHER SIDE OF THE PICTURE

Not all companies who have adopted ERP systems have fared so well as BMW. There are downsides to ERP.

Precisely because ERP is so comprehensive, the decision to adopt it carries large risks. It is possible to implement just an individual module of a modular ERP system, but the benefits that the technology offers will not accrue if one just dips a toe in the water: one must go the whole hog. Jim Prevo, chief information officer of the Vermont company Green Mountain Coffee, commented in 1998:

> An ERP implementation is like the corporate equivalent of a brain transplant. We pulled the plug on every company application and moved to PeopleSoft software. The risk was certainly disruption of business, because if you do not do ERP properly, you can kill your company, guaranteed.[1]

Kalakota and Robinson quoted a case of another American company, FoxMeyer Drugs (a pharmaceutical wholesaler), which claimed that it was indeed killed by trying to implement ERP. After beginning a SAP implementation in 1993, FoxMeyer filed for protection against its creditors under US bankruptcy law in 1996 (and was eventually taken over by a competitor). Rightly or wrongly, FoxMeyer blamed its collapse on the ERP software; it sued SAP's American subsidiary, and its implementation partner Andersen Consulting.

## USABILITY AND EXPENSE

Leaving aside the risk of triggering company collapse (which is no doubt rare), two more general downside issues with ERP are that it has a reputation for being difficult to use and that it is very expensive.

The usability issue was examined by the analysts Forrester in 2003; they tested software from 11 ERP vendors for ease of completing three routine tasks. The conclusion was that the poor reputation is merited. According to Forrester's research director Laurie Orlov, 'Overall, the usability of these products is not acceptable for the amount they cost.'[2]

This may be a curable problem. SAP believes (and others agree) that user difficulties with their own software relate not to the functionality that it provides but to the way in which that functionality was delivered by the R/3 system. Their newer product MySAP, which is gradually taking over as their flagship ERP package, has a more user-friendly web-based interface.

The expense issue is harder to challenge. These systems are some of the most complex software in use nowadays for any purpose; the costs of developing them were large, and the charges to users are correspondingly high.

---

[1] Quoted by April Jacobs, 'Business process software pays off', *Computerworld* 31 August 1998.

[2] Quoted by Gareth Morgan, 'Poor usability forces up ERP training cost', *IT Week* 20 January 2003.

The analysts Ovum found in 2003 that the cost of implementing SAP or PeopleSoft systems was ranging up to £60,000 per seat.

This was not all, or mostly, the up-front cost of buying the software licence from the supplier; implementing ERP involves large further costs. Typically, only a fifth of the cost for installing R/3 is for hardware and software:

> ... the vast majority of the investment is for consultants to customize the software, to redesign organizational processes, and to train the staff in the use of the new system ...
>
> (Brynjolfsson *et al.* 2002)

With figures like these, only large companies could consider investing in ERP systems. Furthermore, because these are complex systems designed for use at sites with numerous staff, even large companies have often found themselves unable to introduce the systems in their small branch offices or subsidiary companies. Dennis Keeling, chief executive of the British-based Business Application Software Developers' Association, commented in 2003 that 'The original dream was to implement ERP from wall to wall, but in many cases, this just isn't practical.'[3] The branch operations are given different, smaller-scale systems from suppliers such as Sage – negating the aim of linking information islands seamlessly into a single information continent. (A report in January 2008 from the interconnectivity company Citrix found that IT, instead of 'annihilating distance', is actually tending to reduce the availability of data to branch-office staff relative to the level of access enjoyed at companies' headquarters.)

By now, though, the large-company ERP market is fairly saturated (and many large companies that SAP hoped would migrate from R/3 to MySAP have proved reluctant to do so). To continue growing their market, ERP suppliers have needed to develop offerings aimed at medium-sized or small firms and sites. Attempts by SAP to cut R/3 down to a lightweight version did not get far; but in 2003 it launched a separate product, Business One, with pricing comparable to Sage, which was based on software acquired from an Israeli company but adapted to be compatible with R/3. By 2006 SAP was advertising via the general press and television commercials (which would have been irrelevant channels for marketing a system as heavyweight as R/3); an advertisement in December 2006 showed a small-businessman asking in surprise 'An SAP solution on our budget?' (In mid-2007 the SAP website seems rather cagey about how much traction Business One has so far achieved.)

---

[3] Quoted by Cath Everett, 'How can you get more from your ERP package?', *Computing* 20 November 2003.

NetSuite introduced an ERP product for smaller companies under the software-as-a-service model in June 2007, and SAP is due to launch its own SaaS version of ERP for smaller companies, A1S, in 2008. Given current trends, the move to SaaS seems inevitable, though some observers feel that it is going to be challenging to deliver the complex functionality of ERP that way.

## REFORMING BUSINESS PRACTICES

The implementation issue is not only about money but also about the impact on a company's business practices.

An ERP implementation embodies a set of business processes and rules. Companies such as SAP sell versions of their systems tailored to particular market sectors, e.g. Insurance or Apparel & Footwear; but a particular firm will typically have its own procedures, which will not be exactly the same as those of other firms in the same sector. The firm will be attached to its own ways of doing things, and often with good reason – its distinctive procedures may provide part of its competitive edge.

With ERP, either the firm pays to have the software customised to fit its procedures, or it must change the procedures to fit the off-the-shelf package. But significant customisation of a large ERP system is a hugely expensive undertaking, and it is the kind of software project that can easily fail. So adopting ERP may mean operating more efficiently, but it also means agreeing to operate in ways that a firm has not chosen for itself.

One can see this in a positive light. Inherited business processes may be out-of-date processes; ERP suppliers aim to make their software embody best current practice from the relevant industrial or commercial sector. The clean sweep of old processes required when ERP is installed may be a blessing in disguise, enabling senior managers to push through, as a technological necessity, working reforms that they lacked the political clout to push through as desirable in their own right. From this point of view, customising ERP to fit the company may be not just too expensive but actually undesirable, because it preserves bad old ways and makes it harder to replace them with good new ways.

Kalakota and Robinson pointed out that a successful ERP implementation begins by analysing a firm's business processes (which may have been understood tacitly without ever being systematically written down), and then rationalises them, making them simpler overall and cutting out anything that does not add value. Only after a firm's business processes are rationalised should they be crystallised into ERP software: 'Automation without simplification only immortalizes ineffective processes' (Kalakota and Robinson 2001: 262). Kalakota and Robinson were bullish about the positive impact on firms' operations implied by adopting ERP. But they are cheerleaders for the new technology. If one accepts their axioms uncritically, they seem to imply that no firm has worked effectively before ERP. Doubtless any organisation has room for improvement, but a generalisation as blunt as that seems self-evidently exaggerated.

## POLITICAL PROBLEMS

Another issue is the political resistance that is unavoidable with a culture-changing phenomenon such as ERP.

Kalakota and Robinson, in their cheerleading role, presented this as little more than instinctive hostility to any change: 'Never underestimate the reluctance to change processes.' That conservative instinct is indeed a powerful force in any human organisation, but if that were the only human problem there would be ways to address it – Kalakota and Robinson suggest sensible approaches, such as finding ways of sharing the vision motivating the change with the staff who will be asked to operate the new system, and giving them small pieces of the system to play with at an early date so as to dissolve their fear of the unknown.

There are weightier reasons than that for staff to resist ERP, though. Thomas Davenport (1998) explained that, because ERP links together what were previously islands of information, managers use it

> ... as a lever for exerting more management control and imposing more-uniform processes on freewheeling, highly entrepreneurial cultures. An executive at a semiconductor company, for example, says, 'We plan to use SAP as a battering ram to make our culture less autonomous.'

People do not enjoy finding themselves on the wrong end of a battering ram.

Ben Worthen, in the course of an enlightening case study of Nestlé's SAP implementation (cf. p. 4), which proved difficult and long drawn out, quoted Nestlé USA's chief information officer Jeri Dunn:

> When you move to SAP, you are ... challenging [people's] principles, their beliefs and the way they have done things for many, many years.[4]

## THE DANGER OF OVER-CENTRALISATION

It is far from clear that resistance to centralisation will in fact be against the interests of the company. Kalakota and Robinson assumed that it is

---

[4] Ben Worthen, 'Nestlé's ERP odyssey', *CIO Magazine* 15 May 2002.

'unhealthy' for local managers to strive to maintain their autonomy. But a great deal of thinking from outside the IT sphere suggests that it may be very healthy.

The point is made concisely in the same book by Sir John Harvey-Jones with which we began the chapter:

> Vast amounts of human effort have been made in large organizations to coordinate and optimize, so to speak, at the centre of the wheel ... it is perfectly possible for all those at the rim of the wheel to self-optimize... The reality of life is that they are the only people who can optimize, and so much of past management theory has been to try to find ways in which they can be encouraged to do so.
>
> (Harvey-Jones 1988: 329–30)

It seems ironic that Sir John in 1988 saw IT as helping the people 'at the rim of the wheel' to optimise their local activities in the light of their detailed local knowledge. Some aspects of business IT may have this effect, but not ERP.

There is a weight of opinion about business and social issues that would side with Sir John in saying that over-centralisation of the affairs of any organisation cannot lead to good outcomes. From this point of view, what should be seen as 'unhealthy' is perhaps not the local autonomy that ERP batters into submission, but the natural inclination of people at the top to micro-manage their subordinates, which ERP tends to encourage.

Apart from centralisation of control, the recent trend towards extending ERP systems into comprehensive 'integrated suites' also raises issues about standardisation of business processes. We turn to that topic now.

## Integrated suite v. best of breed

In May 2000 Oracle released the first version of its E-Business Suite, which aimed to provide ERP, together with various other business IT functions that we shall be looking at in later chapters (under headings such as 'customer relationship management' and 'supply chain management'), in a single integrated system of software.

That first version of Oracle's E-Business Suite was widely scorned as bug-ridden and unusable; but the bugs were progressively eliminated, and the functionality of the suite extended. According to Matthew Symonds (2003: 420), already by 2002 the world's largest steelmaker (the Korean firm Posco) was claiming to achieve annual cost savings of $600 million by using it.

Meanwhile, other software vendors have been extending their own offerings to cover larger portions of the e-business spectrum. SAP has added CRM capabilities, among other things, to recent versions of its ERP systems. Microsoft has been extending its office productivity suite to include enterprise application elements. Companies that continue to focus on specialised e-business niches (such as i2 and Ariba, to be discussed in Chapter 11) have sometimes looked vulnerable; and although these two companies continue as independent entities, various other specialised enterprise application vendors have been swallowed up by larger players.

Since about 2002–3, 'integrated suite' versus 'best of breed', as alternative strategies for companies to use in sourcing their business software, has been a hot issue. 'Best of breed' refers to the idea that a company chooses the most suitable ERP package for its purposes, the most suitable CRM package, and the best available offerings under other application headings (which may each be supplied by a separate vendor), and then uses so-called *middleware* to stitch them together into a collection of systems that succeed in talking to one another electronically.

The best-of-breed strategy is championed by IBM, which nowadays makes much of its income by providing consultants who integrate different business applications by deploying middleware that enables the applications to cooperate. The most outspoken champion of the integrated-suite strategy is Larry Ellison, chief executive of Oracle. According to Ellison:

> If Detroit ran like Silicon Valley, nobody would sell cars – just parts. Customers would have to figure out which were the 'best' parts – a Honda engine, a Ford transmission, a BMW chassis, GM electrical system – and buy them and try to assemble them into a working car. Good luck.
>
> (Symonds 2003: 6)

Instead, the way forward (according to Ellison) must be to invest in a single suite from one vendor that is pre-integrated and already does everything you need.[5]

## ORACLE ADVANCES AND RETREATS

The integrated-suite versus best-of-breed issue has a significance that reaches well beyond relative cost-effectiveness. Depending on which way the business world goes, we may see large consequences for the general economic environment, and possibly even for the future political complexion of societies.

The term 'best of breed' implies that systems designed to execute individual business functions will carry out those functions better than

---

[5] The remainder of this chapter is adapted from Sampson (2006).

the relevant components within an integrated suite. Although that is clearly not a logical truism, many observers confirm that in practice it is a reliable generalisation. According to Esteban Kolsky of the analysts Gartner:

> The broader you go with a suite, the less functional you become. You can always get a better solution with a specialized tool.[6]

On the other hand the best-of-breed approach can create large management problems. Even David Mavashev, chief executive of a firm (Nastel) that supports middleware solutions, comments:

> ... best-of-breed solutions can rapidly become somewhat unmanageable... While each vendor component may be a best-of-breed choice, most closely matching the specific requirements of the relevant area of operations, the issue is that company performance will depend on end-to-end business operations encompassing potentially all of the individual vendor components. For example, a performance problem with one middleware component will affect the entire business process.[7]

Larry Ellison himself accepts that Oracle's integrated suite lacks some features relative to best-of-breed solutions; however, he says that it

> ... may not have one hundred percent of what you want, but it has a hundred percent of what you need. The advantages of out-of-the-box integration more than make up for a few missing nice but not necessary to have features.
>
> (Symonds 2003: 37)

As the initial shortcomings of Oracle's offering were overcome, many managers were converted over the years to the message that integrated-suite business software is the way of the future – both because of the large saving in implementation costs when an individual company does not need to pay for customised software links between separate best-of-breed systems, and because great efficiency

---

[6] Quoted by Erika Morphy, 'On-demand grapples with best of breed', *CRM Daily* 24 March 2005.

[7] 'Thoughts from the Integration Consortium: the problem with best-of-breed integration solutions', *DM Review* March 2005.

gains and improved managerial control are possible if a company's operating data is held in one database accessible company-wide rather than dispersed among separate databases.

The initial appeal of the integrated-suite approach was predominantly to smaller firms:

> In general, small and medium-sized businesses have shown the greatest propensity for going with unified product stacks, valuing the simplicity of the stack over any fears of lock-in [to a single supplier who might exploit that situation in terms of pricing, etc.], while larger enterprises have generally valued functionality over simplicity and have gone with a 'best-of-breed' approach.[8]

But, by about 2003, the consensus was that the integrated suite was destined to prevail everywhere. Developments by companies such as SAP and Microsoft imply that they take broadly the same view as Larry Ellison, without being so vocal about it.

Against that background, it came as quite a surprise when, at the annual Oracle user conference in San Diego in January 2004, Ellison and his company president Chuck Phillips announced that the latest version of their E-Business Suite would contain features (notably, the 'customer data hub') that help customers to link Oracle applications to home-grown or third-party applications – that is, which facilitate a best-of-breed approach. After the vehemence with which Ellison had attacked best of breed, this looked like an admission of defeat by the chief advocates of integrated suite. It was widely reported as such. By 2007 Dave Chaffey (2007: 126) feels that the best-of-breed strategy is unavoidable: 'there is not, and probably never can be, a single solution of components from a single supplier'.

## FREEZING BUSINESS EVOLUTION

Most commentators discuss these developments purely in terms of reducing the costs of business operations and increasing their efficiency. In the opening years of the new century, when many companies were finding themselves focusing on survival more than on the long-term future, that was inevitable. But their significance goes far further. Automating business processes, and particularly the seamless upstream-to-downstream, uncustomised automation represented by the integrated-suite approach,

---

[8] Tom Berquist, 'Oracle Corp. (ORCL): short-term integration risks outweigh long-term opportunity', research report, Citigroup/Smith Barney, 14 February 2005.

implies suspending the ordinary incremental evolution of processes that occurs in the absence of automation.

That becomes very clear from the literature introducing managers to the ERP concept, which repeatedly stresses that a company must put effort into optimising its business processes before automating them. Recall Ravi Kalakota's comment (p. 139) about ERP systems immortalising business processes. What business processes are most effective is a question whose answer constantly changes as the business environment changes, and if automating processes 'immortalizes' them then it is obvious that a company will do well to bring its processes as up to date as it can before taking that step. But the business environment will not cease to change just because a company has automated its processes. The corollary of Kalakota and Robinson's recommendation is that adopting ERP will make it difficult for a company to continue adapting to future changes.

Indeed, ERP may make it impossible to optimise business processes even for the current environment. One common criticism, according to Davenport (2000: 16), is that

> many times companies end up doing business in a way that they don't really want just because the system requires it.

Markets engender a continuing process of discovering how to create more value from available resources, as new experiments prove profitable and spread, causing older ways of doing things to be discarded. But the tendency of business process automation must be to moderate Schumpeter's gale of creative destruction.

This is especially clear in the philosophy promulgated by Oracle. Symonds (2003: 52) quotes Larry Ellison as

> ... want[ing] customers to change their processes to take maximum advantage of the Internet-based best practice captured by the software. Ellison said, 'Don't tell us how you've been running your business... It's a classic business mistake to say, "This is how we do business; change your software so we can automate it."'

Ellison's vision has been one in which companies give up their individual, distinctive business processes in favour of the economy and robustness associated with a standard, uncustomised software system that covers all aspects of business operation. Even a disinterested observer such as Thomas Davenport (2000: 21) accepts that, in future, 'One company's processes are likely to be similar to another's'. Comparing the integrated-suite approach with the best-of-breed approach, Ellison commented: 'Why do people use heavily customized, one-of-a-kind business systems? Because they had no other choice' (Symonds 2003: 44).

It may be true that customers for enterprise application software had no alternative to individually tailored systems before Oracle's E-Business Suite, but logically it does not follow that they can have no reason to continue with the individually tailored approach. One reason (which might or might not be valid in a particular case) would be that a company's competitive advantage depends on distinctive business processes that have to be given up as the price for adopting standard software. The more business process automation eliminates individual companies' distinctive competitive advantages, the less possible it becomes for market forces to bring about valuable innovations.

## THE EVIDENCE OF BUSINESS PROCESS PATENTS

This is not to say that suspending the evolution of business processes would eliminate all valuable innovation. Plainly, it would not. The same internal business processes can be used to produce different outputs in terms of products or services. Product innovation could continue even if processes did not alter at all.

But the socially beneficial effects of a market economy have not traditionally related only (or, perhaps, mainly) to product innovation. A commercial enterprise produces its outputs by applying some pattern of processes to some range of inputs of scarce resources (human labour, data, raw materials and components, and other things); industrial advances are often associated with finding methods to produce equivalent outputs from fewer or cheaper inputs, leaving more resources free to benefit members of society in other ways. One demonstration of how crucial distinctive business processes are to firms' competitive advantage is the recent explosion in business process patents (p. 67 above). The effort firms are putting into securing and enforcing these patents is clear evidence that successful methods are crucial to competitive advantage.

Thus, the standardisation and freezing of business processes associated with enterprise application software must tend to damp down the beneficial effects of competition.

## A SHIFT TO PUNCTUATED EQUILIBRIA?

Business process automation tends to reduce competition in another way also. Companies are beginning to extend the reach of their enterprise application networks beyond their own boundaries to include favoured suppliers within 'extranets'. In consequence, Frances Cairncross (2002: 15) comments, 'Companies build deeper links with fewer suppliers.' Even if processes within a single company are slow to change, rearranging supply relationships among a wide range of companies with different modes of operation is another way that the overall pattern of productive activity in a society can adapt rapidly to permit more value to be squeezed out of fewer resources in a changing world. The more that companies move towards fixed relationships with narrow ranges of suppliers, the less room this mechanism has to yield beneficial innovation.

So, for society as a whole, the spread of business process automation poses real long-term risks. Yet, for individual companies, the medium-term gains in terms of operating-cost reduction and operating efficiency may often be too attractive to turn down. And the style of business process automation that claims to offer the largest medium-term gains (uncustomised, comprehensive suites) is just the style that poses the greatest threat to the 'creatively destructive' action of the free market.

Even if integrated e-business suites were to become a standard component of the industrial landscape, would that mean the end of innovation in the activities that they perform? That seems unlikely. If there are large enough gains to be made by changing some aspect of a company's methods, then the point will surely come eventually when it is worth adapting one's software system accordingly. But we can expect the cost of change to be much higher than it used to be. Before IT, a manager who saw a better way to organise things had only natural human inertia and misunderstanding to overcome. Those hurdles are not trivial, but in future there would be the extra barriers of replacing a fully automatic with a partially manual system, or paying the considerable costs of programming custom-designed software components.

The effect might be that an industrial ecology of continuous incremental evolution would be replaced by one of 'punctuated equilibria', to borrow a metaphor from evolutionary biology. Business processes would remain fossilised in the form of standard enterprise application software for long periods, until the potential gains from innovation build up to the point where the pressure is irresistible, and the current software is abandoned in favour of a burst of innovations.

## POLITICAL FALLOUT

In democratic societies, changes of this order to the complexion of the industrial landscape might have political consequences.

A free market produces winners and losers, and winning or losing is not correlated with players' moral worth or likeability. Voters' natural sympathy for those who lose through no fault of their own make a statist form of society look attractive to many: people would like governments to intervene in the economy sufficiently to make everyone a modest winner. Where free markets exist, they do so because enough voters are persuaded by the argument that excessive state intervention to achieve equality would destroy the socially beneficial operation of the market: even the poor gain from a free-market economy, because a rising tide lifts all boats.

If voters perceived that industrial innovation was being stifled, and economic competition between companies was ceasing to be an engine of innovation and turning into a mere jostling for commercial advantage within a zero-sum game, this argument would lose its force. Consequently, widespread adoption of standardised business process software could push the politics of industrially advanced societies in a leftward direction.

Thus, medium-term cost-effectiveness for companies is really a minor aspect of the overall implications of the integrated-suite versus best-of-breed issue. It may be that integrated suite versus best of breed should be seen as setting the interests of individual firms, and of society as a whole, against one another, in the sense that the integrated-suite strategy offers firms financial benefits that they cannot individually afford to turn down, while widespread adoption of that strategy tends to negate the advantages that society reaps from competition.

## A TEMPORARY TRUCE

Since Oracle seems now to have resolved the conflict in favour of the status quo – that is, in favour of the multi-vendor business applications environment which had evolved in an unplanned way, before Oracle began to push for its alternative vision – there might seem to be little reason to spend time thinking about the hypothetical consequences of realising that vision.

But the 2004 'truce' is not a permanent settlement. The 2004 version of Oracle's E-Business Suite is the way it is because current trading conditions forced Oracle to move that way – not because Oracle has changed its mind about the vision. Ellison and his colleagues were explicit about this. Ellison 'conceded that a different approach was necessary for companies battling too many legacy systems and third-party applications'; however, at the same time he said:

> We are not giving up on what we said before, but not everyone in the world wanted to go that way... People said they wanted to live in a heterogeneous world.[9]

According to Oracle spokeswoman Karen Tillman:

---

[9] Quoted by Mark Street, 'Oracle improves integration for a multi-vendor world', *Computing* 4 February 2004.

> The [customer data hub] provides another option for customers, we
> still think that the overall E-Business Suite on the single platform is
> your best strategy, the best information below its cost.[10]

After the PeopleSoft acquisition at the end of 2004, Oracle announced a
plan called Project Fusion; one interpretation of the Project Fusion publicity
is that Oracle aims by 2008 to meld its own existing systems together with
the PeopleSoft and J.D. Edwards systems and, now, Siebel's CRM software
in order to create an even more comprehensive integrated suite.

As the SaaS or 'hosted' model of enterprise computing begins to spread,
Erika Morphy notes that the same integrated-suite v. best-of-breed issue
is starting to crop up within that model.[11] Morphy says that as yet 'there
are few comprehensive hosted suites on the market', so that companies
opting for SaaS have been forced to stick to the best-of-breed strategy.
But as such suites begin to appear (Morphy cites several systems,
e.g. NetSuite, which contain broad enough functionality to approach the
integrated-suite category), she questions whether the best-of-breed
approach will survive in the SaaS model.

Furthermore, the new regulatory pressures that are beginning to impact
on business (things such as the Sarbanes–Oxley Act) may well increase the
attractiveness of the integrated-suite approach in future. It seems likely that
integrated business software systems centred on single company-wide
databases would make compliance with audit requirements easier, whether
or not they are desirable in terms of long-run business profitability.

So the integrated-suite versus best-of-breed debate remains a very live
and unresolved issue. Its resolution is likely to affect all of us, whether or
not we work in e-business.

---

[10] Quoted by Jim Wagner, 'Oracle comes full circle in enterprise', *internetnews.com*
30 January 2004.
[11] 'On-demand grapples with best of breed', *CRM Daily* 24 March 2005.

# 9 Marketing and Customer Relationships

Marketing is the activity of planning how to sell and promoting a company's products to customers. The distinction between marketing and the actual selling activity is colourfully expressed by Robert Cringeley:

> Marketing is the creation of long-term demand, while sales is execution of marketing strategies. Marketing is buying the land, choosing what crop to grow, planting the crop, fertilizing it, and then deciding when to harvest. Sales is harvesting the crop.
>
> (Cringeley 1996: 204)

In the context of this book, an important fact about marketing is that much of what there is to say about it is not affected greatly by whether a company is involved in new or old technology. It is always important, but it is especially important in connection with marketing, to stress that an e-business is a business. The principles laid down in standard business textbooks, such as David Needle's *Business in Context* (Needle 2004), are as relevant to e-companies as they are to any other kind.

At the same time, IT has introduced new considerations into the picture. In particular, customer relationship management (CRM) systems are, after ERP, by most reckonings the second most important enterprise application category.

## LIKE IT OR NOT

One thing to be said about marketing is that, to many people, it seems the least admirable side of business. Particularly at the B2C level, advertising is often seen as persuading people to buy things they don't need, and it is blamed for creating an excessively materialist tone in present-day societies.

On the other hand, defenders point out that marketing fulfils essential functions, giving consumers (and business purchasers) product information that they need in order to exercise choice intelligently, and obtaining information about their wishes and preferences that business needs in order to serve them better. There have been societies in the recent past, for instance Eastern Europe during the Cold War decades, where individuals were not subjected to the endless bombardment of selling messages that are such an irritating feature of our time. That made for a certain dignity in everyday life, which arguably we have lost; but the reason for it was that producers had no motive to attract custom. The goods and services available were few and often of poor quality; purchasers had to take what they could get.

We cannot have it both ways. Many feel that the selling messages are a price worth paying in exchange for the styles of life that are made possible by a modern market economy. In any case, within our society as it actually exists marketing is a very necessary function for any business, so we need to learn something about it.

## THE FOUR PS

Space does not permit a comprehensive survey of marketing principles in this book. We shall touch on the subject briefly, by introducing the famous 'four Ps', before moving on to examine the various special contributions made by IT.

Standardly, a marketing strategy is broken down under four headings:

- *Product* (its nature and design)
- *Price*
- *Promotion*
- *Place* (channels of distribution)

The fourth P refers to the channels by which a supplier's goods physically reach the buyer, and to decisions about whether and how to use intermediaries. We have considered the issue of intermediaries in e-commerce in Chapter 3, and we shall not revisit that topic here. The other three Ps are considered in turn below.

### Product

It might seem that a product is what it is, and the marketing function must simply accept that. But a manufactured product or commercial service is designed with a market or markets in mind. Deciding to introduce a new product is an investment decision, made after studying whether the investment is likely to pay off.

Furthermore, in many business sectors, what a company brings to the market is typically not a single product but a product line. When a car manufacturer creates a new model, it will be sold in a base version and various higher-level or specialised variants, and similar differentiation occurs with other goods. Differentiating between separate variants of a product is expensive, and deciding how far the potential market calls for such differentiation is itself a marketing function.

Also, even physical goods are in many cases not simply sold as such in isolation. Often, they are bundled with associated services: free delivery, routine after-sales servicing, guarantees lasting beyond the legally required period, and so on. Again it is a marketing decision as to what elements of this sort to include and which to omit or to offer as options for additional payment.

## Price

In economics textbooks, prices are determined as the crossing points of smooth supply and demand curves such as those of Figure 2.4 (see Chapter 2). Real life is more complicated. Supply and demand may be represented accurately by smooth curves in the case of agricultural products, say; but with manufactures, these are only an idealized approximation.

For one thing, to consumers price is not a featureless linear scale. Logically, the difference between £93 and £98 is identical to the difference between £98 and £103, but – for consumers who pay in pounds – the latter jump breaches the two-figure barrier.

This can influence economic behaviour in two directions. Often, market research will show that people shopping for *X* will typically be unwilling to pay more than £*Y*: instead of being a smooth curve, the demand schedule has a kink at the £*Y* mark. This may then feed back into the product design process, via *target costing*: the price of a future product is set first, and then the product is designed so as to be sellable at that price.

Robin Cooper and Bruce Chew (1996) have argued that globalization and the internet-speed economy make target costing more important than it used to be. In the past, a company that marketed a novel product had a de facto monopoly for a while. It took competitors some time to catch up, even though no legal monopoly barred them from supplying similar products. In present circumstances, innovators get so brief a free run before imitators begin to compete that products have to be sold on price rather than on unique qualities from day one. (Research by Proctor & Gamble shows that the average lifecycle of American consumer goods fell by as much as half just in the 10 years to 2002, before the full impact of the internet had been felt.[1])

The other side of the picture, though, is that where high quality or luxury status is part of a product's attraction, setting a higher price (within reason) can actually reinforce this image. Rather than falling steadily from north-west to south-east, the demand schedule may level out or even turn upwards a little way. In its home market of Belgium, Stella Artois is a cheap beer, but when the company began selling in the USA it chose to position it as a luxury brand:

[1] See 'Revving Up', *The Economist* 13 October 2007.

> ... the company restricted distribution to the hippest bars in New York ... and charged far more than it does in its home country. Consumers were soon convinced that it must be good ...
>
> (Bonabeau 2004)

When a company decides a product price, manufacturing cost and the competition set a floor and a ceiling respectively. A company that sells its output for less than cost cannot keep going indefinitely (though, if investors are sufficiently optimistic about the company's future, it may survive for quite a while – as in the case of Amazon and many other internet retailers). Likewise, a company that sells things identical to what a competitor sells but at a higher price will lose its customers – although this is a less clear-cut barrier: the products supplied by different companies are rarely quite identical. If customers see the differences as important, then a company's pricing may be less constrained by that of its competitors.

Even if the floor and ceiling are fixed, a great deal of thought goes into where to set prices between those limits. For maximum profit, points near the ceiling are indicated. But a company may be more interested in building market share than in immediate profit – in which case, it will choose to set its prices lower. And, in the B2B domain, whatever a company's overall strategy may be, it will sell at lower prices to favoured (usually large) customers – a supermarket chain will get better prices than a corner shop from the same supplier, because 20 per cent profit on £100 is far less worth having than 5 per cent on £100,000.

## Promotion

Promotion covers the obvious cases of advertising and direct marketing (e.g. mailshots, leaflets delivered house-to-house, telephone selling) but also sales promotion techniques such as point-of-sale displays in super-markets, free samples given away by company representatives seconded to stores, cheap off-peak fare offers, and many similar techniques. Needle (2004: 484) tells us that more than 70 per cent of all spending under the 'promotion' heading relates to sales promotion rather than advertising or direct marketing.

Online advertising and related activities have become a complex subject in their own right. We shall look at that subject in Chapter 10. In this chapter we shall focus on more central aspects of marketing.

Another promotional activity is seeking to place stories about a company or its products in the media: independent news stories or features carry much more weight with readers than paid advertising. One advantage for e-commerce startups in the early years was that journalists were so keen to produce stories about this new phenomenon, and at the same time knew so little about it, that they would often print dotcom press releases more or less word for word – any marketing manager's dream.

Products are also promoted via the individual relationships that suppliers' representatives are often able to cultivate with buyers, particularly in the B2B world. The importance of these is demonstrated by the way companies structure their marketing efforts. Any company selling a wide range of product lines to a diverse spectrum of buyers has a choice between structuring its selling around its product lines or around the different industry sectors to which customers belong. The more complex the products, the more appropriate it might seem to opt for the former choice, so that supplier representatives can develop fuller expertise about what they are selling. But in practice IT companies usually structure marketing the second way, so that their representatives have a better chance to forge close relationships with buyers.

It is natural for the IT enthusiast to assume that for a company to make its detailed product information available on the web is an obvious promotion technique that could hardly fail to be beneficial. With respect to the B2B world, at least, that would be a naively simple view of the marketing process. Trailer and Dickie (2006: 50) quote the case of a plastics manufacturer that posted over 10,000 pages of product information on the web and then found its business tailing off. It turned out that many prospects 'felt so well informed by the online information, they didn't see the need for an in-person or phone meeting with a company rep' – so those prospects were never registered as leads to be followed up, and sales representatives never had the chance to make their pitch to them.

## MULTINATIONAL MARKETING

Traditionally, business saw marketing for export as a separate area from marketing for home sales: products may be adapted to suit foreign preferences, cultural assumptions or legal constraints, and pricing policy may be different in different countries. On the World Wide Web it becomes hard to maintain this distinction. The global reach of the web looks like an advantage from the seller's point of view, making it as cheap and easy to communicate with customers on other continents as at home. But if essentially the same product line has been priced differently in separate national markets, perhaps because it is marketed as a luxury in one country but as a good-value purchase in another, then the web may give customers a new ability to compare prices internationally, leading to resentment in countries where people see themselves as overcharged.

The problems of marketing to a multinational audience go much deeper than issues about price structure. Cultural differences between nations mean that, standardly, one cannot sell things the same way in different countries. Needle (2004: 510–11) describes some of the differences. Germans stress 'product development and careful targeting'. Americans stress active promotion and selling. In Japan, competition focuses on product differentiation and service rather than on price. Such cultural differences can require large differences in the way the same product is marketed to different national audiences. The resort chain Club Med succeeded in Europe by promoting an image of laid-back hedonism; a similar campaign in Japan fell flat, and the emphasis had to switch to self-improvement, for instance by drawing attention to facilities for organised sports.

One might imagine that these cultural differences are a hangover from a past age, and that globalisation of the media and trade – and the internet itself – will soon make them entirely irrelevant. As a statement about the world as a whole, this view looks naive since the 9/11 atrocities. Even as between the richer Western nations, there is plenty of evidence that cultural differences still matter and need to be reckoned with in business.

In 1997 the American supermarket chain Wal-Mart opened a series of stores in Germany. Assuming that German shoppers would appreciate the same courtesies from shop assistants as American shoppers expect, they taught staff to smile at customers and help with packing their shopping.

> Wal-Mart discovered that many Germans regard shop-assistants who try to help them with suspicion and flee the premises to avoid buying anything from them.[2]

In 2006 Wal-Mart gave up and sold its German shops to a local competitor.

What is fundamentally the same product may need to be packaged up differently for different national markets. Amazon uses tight specifications for the colour scheme of its web pages to help define its brand, but it has to deviate from this scheme for its Japanese site, because the Japanese colour sense is too different from ours. Clotaire Rapaille (2006) claims that the US telecommunications firm AT&T once had a shipment of cables that had been ordered by Nippon Telegraph and Telephone rejected because they were ugly, although they met all the technical specifications (and were destined to be buried underground where no-one would see them).

## CUSTOMER RELATIONSHIP MANAGEMENT

Customer relationship management (CRM) software provides automated support for acquiring new customers and encouraging customers, once acquired, to remain loyal. (The latter is an especially important issue, because it is a marketing cliché that the costs of making further sales to an existing customer are many times less than those of acquiring a new customer; Jim Sterne (2001: 15) suggests a ratio of five or ten times less.)

Automating relationships with customers might sound like the worst kind of dehumanising computer application. A more realistic understanding, though, is that in modern circumstances, where much commercial interaction inevitably has to be electronic rather than face-to-face, CRM software

---

[2] 'Trouble at till', *The Economist* 4 November 2006.

helps companies to treat their customers *more* as individuals than would otherwise be possible. Amadeus is an IT vendor specialising in the travel sector; in February 2007 Amadeus's Frédéric Spagnon introduced a report on airline use of CRM by stressing the theme 'humanization of technology'. Most people find air travel either for business or pleasure a wearing activity; according to Spagnon CRM can offer customers a more personalised service, making their experience pleasanter and hence encouraging loyalty.

The essence of CRM is to integrate the various contacts that a company has with a customer or sales lead, so that a coherent history of the company's dealings with that person is available whenever a new interaction occurs. Until it was acquired by Oracle in January 2006, the leading CRM supplier was Siebel Systems. Its website explained the CRM concept this way:

> The challenge is to make it easy for customers to do business with the organization any way they want – at any time, through any channel, in any language or currency – and to make customers feel that they are dealing with a single, unified organization that recognizes them at every touchpoint.

A particular customer may be in contact at different times via a company rep visiting the customer's site, via a phone call to a call centre or to a specific member of company staff, via e-mail or via the web. The company may have separate product ranges produced and marketed by different divisions, and the same customer may buy from separate divisions at different times. A CRM system assembles information that enables whoever deals with the customer on a given occasion, wherever he or she works in the company and whatever the channel of contact, to interact with that customer intelligently and knowledgeably. It cuts out the need for the customer to rehearse much of the background repeatedly in successive calls. It may enable the call centre to route the customer's call efficiently, cutting out the requirement to respond to numerous rounds of 'If you need XYZ, press button 3'. When a past purchaser of the company's equipment telephones for advice or support, CRM should arm the service operative with information about that customer's installation, so the operative can move directly to asking about the problem rather than wasting time establishing the background. The proportion of support queries resolved by a single call increases. CRM is crucial for individualising the material shown to a customer who visits the company website.

A number of commentators on CRM argue that a wise firm deploys the technology principally in order to improve customer experience, rather than to sell more or to reduce costs by employing fewer human sales representatives. Jeffrey Rayport and Bernard Jaworski believe that the actual products sold by most companies are by now so commoditised that

> ... interactions with customers, and the customer experiences that result from those interactions, are, for many businesses, the sole remaining frontier of competitive advantage.
>
> (Rayport and Jaworski 2004: 48)

CRM is part of the potential solution to achieving that kind of competitive advantage.

A less congenial aspect of CRM is that it can help companies to discriminate between customers, for instance by adjusting prices of given purchases. In the retail sphere that sounds shameful – although nobody takes it amiss if a cafe offers a special rate to pensioners. Andrew Odlyzko (2004) believes that the internet may cause the systems of variable discounts that are taken for granted in the B2B world to spread into e-tailing too. That has not happened yet, but for instance American banks' CRM systems have long been alerting call-centre staff about whether the current caller is a valuable client who deserves to have a request to waive a minor charge agreed, or an unprofitable account-holder who should be given no special favours.

## CRM UNDER A CLOUD

The potential value of what CRM promises is obvious, and from the late 1990s onwards business invested heavily.

Only a few years ago, the consensus was that the results of these investments had proved disappointing. *The Economist* in 2003 pronounced that 'Few things in technology have promised so much and delivered so little as CRM software.'[3]

Some problems stem from the fact that the technical challenges CRM has to solve are large. From the user's viewpoint, what CRM aims to deliver sounds simple, but to achieve that the system has to integrate data captured through many different channels, some of which may involve outdated legacy formats; and it has to put all that material together in real time, for instance while a customer introduces him- or herself to a support agent on the phone. CRM systems were seen as unduly expensive, difficult to implement and overly complex to use. The apparent triviality of the task, from the user's viewpoint, led to unrealistic expectations. When software purchasers rated suppliers, the CRM market leader Siebel repeatedly ranked at or near the bottom. Indeed, one did not need to consult user ratings to infer that the technology was not as well worked out as it might have been. On one extraordinary public occasion in 2002, Tom Siebel, founder and chairman of then-independent Siebel Systems, said:

---

[3] 'Banking on the technology cycle', *The Economist Technology Quarterly* 6 September 2003.

> I'm surprised that there's not more outrage on the part of customers...
> I'm surprised that they have not taken their enterprise application
> providers – including Siebel – and just thrown them out.[4]

There have also been large people problems. For sales representatives, the
lists of sales leads they have developed, their personal familiarity with
the individual backgrounds of their company's customers, and so forth
are much of what makes them valuable to their employer; they can easily
envisage CRM as automating their jobs away. Discussing the history of
CRM adoption some years earlier by the New York firm Harris Interactive,
Cotteleer and colleagues (2006: 20) commented:

> Sales agents at Harris still remember having to hand over their files,
> which held all the information about each customer relationship (and
> therefore much of the agents' leverage with their employer).

A survey of CRM problems perceived by managers (Trailer and Dickie
2006) found that the largest single problem area was populating the
systems with data and maintaining the data, but a close second was
winning acceptance by the staff who must use the systems. As we saw
with ERP, it is clear that successful use of CRM depends heavily on how
the reasonable worries of staff are addressed.

## CRM REVIVES

The article in *The Economist* in 2003, quoted above, marked the low point.
Since then the fortunes of CRM have risen. Spending on CRM systems
has been on a sharply rising trend, and senior managers have become
enthusiastic. It is not just that the technology itself has improved, but also
people have gradually been learning how to get the best out of it – for
instance, by using CRM in a focused manner to solve well-defined
problems rather than expecting in a vague fashion that it will transform an
entire business. Also, managers have been using CRM more economically,
by deploying its expensive real-time capabilities only where they are
genuinely needed. In the early years of e-business, a lot of waffle was
heard about companies becoming 'real-time enterprises', but as Darrell
Rigby and Dianne Ledingham say:

> ... few companies need perfect information throughout their
> customer relationship cycles... A hotel manager certainly needs
>
> *(Continued)*

---

[4] Quoted by Douglas Hayward, 'Strategy paper', *Computing* 31 October 2002.

*(Continued)*

real-time data on the availability of rooms but not on the customer's opinion of the carpets and drapes. A cable company needs real-time figures on service outages but not on the profitability of its pay-per-view programs.

(Rigby and Ledingham 2004: 122)

This is all part of the general process whereby business, which initially felt so ignorant and awestruck in face of the new technology that it had no option but to let the techies set the deployment agenda, has slowly been coming to see how to use IT rather than be used by it. Quoting Rigby and Ledingham again:

Managers should not be distracted by what CRM software *can* do; they should concentrate instead on what it *should* do – both for their companies and for their customers.

The same point is valid for enterprise applications in general, not just CRM, and that is the way things are now moving.

Used well, CRM has in some cases done wonders for the quality of companies' customer service. In 1996, Yorkshire Water was rated by one national newspaper as the 'UK's most hated company', and it was at the bottom of Ofwat's customer service league table. To redress this situation, according to Yorkshire Water manager Duncan Bennett,

We established that we needed a single view of all customer contact with our business, as well as a single view of all planned and ongoing work on our water infrastructure that could have an impact on customer service.[5]

The firm installed a customer-centric IT infrastructure, comprising the Amdocs Clarify CRM system, together with ERP from SAP, and a mobile-workforce management system. By 2003, to quote a few statistics, unnecessary field jobs had been cut by 50 per cent, written complaints were down by 40 per cent, and 70 per cent of customer calls were closed on first contact; in that year the company won an award for CRM excellence, and it was second from top in Ofwat's league table. Furthermore, although the IT investment cost over £40 million, it was saving £8.5 million of costs annually – an excellent rate of return on investment.

CRM was the first major enterprise application to be made available under the software-as-a-service model – the pioneer company was Mark

---

[5] Quoted in 'Utility puts the flow back into the business', *Computing* 11 September 2003.

Benioff's Salesforce.com, founded in 1999, and that now has competitors. This is one factor that has made it possible for smaller companies to adopt the technology, and that part of the market has been growing particularly fast – even a Cambridge hairdresser, the Wacky Hair Company, is using CRM to remind clients of appointments, halving the number of missed appointments. Specialised CRM packages are available for particular business sectors, reducing the need for customisation.

## MARKETING TO INDIVIDUALS

Conventional marketing breaks down the universe of potential customers into segments, based on factors such as region, social class, sex, age, lifestyle and (according to Needle 2004: 497) increasingly race. Segmentation may be used to develop variant products to appeal to separate kinds of people, or to promote the same product in different ways to different segments.

Needle (2004: 498) offers striking examples of the success of segment-based marketing. In the 1970s and 1980s, the advertising of Coca-Cola emphasised the concept of 'one world' – some readers might remember commercials based round the pop song 'I'd like to teach the world to sing in perfect harmony'. In 1993 Coca-Cola changed tack. It began to distinguish many different market segments and promoted its product differently to separate segments. Over the following four years, sales rose by 21 per cent.

One claim made for business IT is that it can improve on marketing to demographic segments by marketing instead to individuals. Without IT, it just was not feasible for retailers to amass enough information about most of their customers or potential customers to treat them individually in their marketing activities. Now, it is.

Some of the ways that this is happening, for instance the use of cookie-derived information collected by DoubleClick and its rivals and sold on to firms that can use it, are hard to write about because they are not well publicised – we have looked at the large worries about invasion of privacy in Chapter 4. A case where the facts are much clearer is the use of loyalty-card data by supermarkets. This is by its nature a favourable test-bed for looking at marketing techniques, because supermarkets sell a wide range of products ranging from basic staples to exotic items, individuals have diverse tastes, and most of the population uses supermarkets frequently – thus the data is rich and complex.

In particular, the Tesco Clubcard is an especially instructive case study, not only because it has proved a highly successful IT-based marketing initiative but also because Tesco has allowed the Clubcard experience to be publicised in some detail. Clive Humby, who with his wife Edwina Dunn runs the Dunnhumby consultancy that steered the development and use of Clubcard, has co-authored a book-length account of the initiative, *Scoring Points* (Humby and Hunt 2007).

## THE TESCO CLUBCARD

After trials in a few areas, Tesco launched its Clubcard nationally in 1995. In essence, the bargain it offers shoppers is that in exchange for shoppers allowing Tesco to swipe their cards and thus build up complete item-by-item, trip-by-trip profiles of their individual shopping habits, Tesco gives them a price discount via rebate vouchers mailed out four times a year.

The discount amounts to one penny in the pound, i.e. 1 per cent. To shoppers that might sound like a minor saving – though it has persuaded most of Tesco's customers to sign up. But, to the company, the figure is not at all small. Grocery retailing is a low-margin business. In the 1996 financial year, Tesco's profit margin was 6 per cent (it has sometimes been lower since). In other words, launching Clubcard meant offering to give up about a sixth of current profit (plus the cost of running the scheme), in the hope that the information gained would be more valuable than that. It was quite a gamble.

Loyalty schemes that simply gave regular shoppers rebates or gifts have a long history, and Tesco was not the first British supermarket to experiment with an electronic scheme generating detailed sales data. But enthusiasm for these was waning; it seemed too difficult to use the data in ways that justified the large costs. Safeway was first in the field with its ABC card, but it abandoned it in 2000, saying 'Loyalty cards have lost their lustre'; Safeway complained that analysing the data was 'like drinking from a firehose'. Likewise, Waitrose gave up the idea, saying 'Trying to analyse all the data is madness.'[6]

The quantities of data certainly are colossal. In the first three months after launch, Tesco assembled data about more than five million shoppers making more than 50 million shopping trips and buying more than two billion items. The analytical categories that Tesco uses to register this mountain of information are highly refined. A product is associated with a large set of attributes; for instance a ready meal may have up to 45 attributes: expensive or cheap; own brand or Birds Eye; ethnic or traditional… As for the shoppers, one can tell a lot about people from their postcodes, but Tesco go further – they link in data from the electoral roll, the Land Registry and so on to build up a detailed picture,

> … so [they] can work out the ethnicity of coriander shoppers in South Shields, or whether single white mothers in Hackney prefer Pampers to Huggies.[7]

When the authors of the Clubcard scheme presented the results of their pilot trials to the Tesco board in late 1994, there was a silence, broken by the chairman, Sir Ian MacLaurin:

---

[6] Safeway and Waitrose quotations from Humby and Hunt (2007: 6, 94).
[7] Harry Wallop, 'Big Sister is watching you shop', *Daily Telegraph* 17 June 2006.

> What scares me about this is that you know more about my customers
> in three months than I know in 30 years ...
>
> (Humby and Hunt 2007: 56)

## HOW CLUBCARD DATA IS USED

One key to exploiting this data mountain, according to Humby, is to appreciate that there is no chance of mechanically extracting all the valuable generalisations that in principle are hidden within it. Using the material has to be an art rather than a science; the data will answer the analyst's questions, but the analyst has to think of the questions to ask.

> Trying to achieve perfection with transactional data is next to
> impossible: far better to have a good idea based on experience and
> instinct, then to go looking for the data to prove it, or at least strongly
> support it.
>
> (Humby and Hunt 2007: 92)

So how do Tesco use Clubcard data to expand their business? In many ways – here are a few examples:

One thing that quickly emerged was that the average shopper was visiting only a few of Tesco's departments. Tesco wanted to encourage customers to 'shop the shop'. When it sends out the quarterly mailing, alongside the general vouchers giving a rebate on any future purchase it includes six coupons giving money off specific items or types of item. Four of the six are for things that that shopper has already bought, but two will be for other items. Without Clubcard data, the traditional approach would be to offer money off whatever the firm happens to have in surplus. With the electronic data Tesco can be much subtler about fostering broader shopping habits. The coupons will be for items that are often bought by shoppers whose profiles are otherwise similar to the target, but that the target shopper has not yet bought.

And the data enables Tesco to be subtle about price cuts. Like other supermarkets, to retain market share Tesco must periodically make and publicise price reductions. To lower prices across the board would entail a massive, unacceptable loss of profit, and so the obvious alternative is to focus reductions on a few staples that everyone buys, such as bananas: all shoppers will notice that. However, some shoppers are more price-sensitive than other, more affluent shoppers; a few pence off bananas will not have much impact on the latter. Using Clubcard data, Tesco can identify products that are bought heavily by price-sensitive shoppers and little by non-price-sensitive shoppers – an example is their own-label Value Brand margarine. Price cuts on those products are efficient: they win favour with shoppers who care about price cuts, without wasting cuts on shoppers who do not.

Data on purchasing patterns is used to fine-tune the product range stocked in particular shops. A rise in sales at one store of various pickled vegetables 'may suggest Polish immigrants have moved in, prompting it to stock *barszcz*, meatballs and sauerkraut.'[8]

Tesco sell Clubcard data to their suppliers, who use it for instance to judge whether to introduce new product lines. Drummond Hall, chief executive of Dairy Crest, explained the reasoning behind introducing a branded mild cheddar cheese, Cathedral City Mild. Mild cheddar had commonly been unbranded:

> So are people buying mild because they don't like brands and want a cheaper product, or are they buying it for taste reasons, for your children, say? The Dunnhumby data shows us that mild-cheese shoppers are every bit as brand-prone as mature-cheese shoppers ...[9]

– they choose mild cheese for taste rather than cheapness. That meant that there should be a market for a branded mild cheddar, which proved to sell well.

From the introduction of Clubcard in 1995 to mid-2006 (the most recent date for which I have figures), Tesco's market share grew almost threefold. That is huge growth; and external observers believe that Clubcard is the single most important contributory factor. This case alone, then, establishes the potential significance of marketing to individuals, which only IT makes possible.

---

[8] 'Fresh, but far from easy', *The Economist* 23 June 2007.
[9] Quoted in Elizabeth Rigby, 'Eyes in the till', *FT.com* 11 November 2006.

# 10 Advertising and Web 2.0

## TWO-WAY VERSUS ONE-WAY PUBLICITY

Advertising in the conventional business world is a one-way activity. Companies pump out their messages, and the public absorbs them (or ignores them). IT is modifying this. Even online advertising is tending to involve action by 'advertisees' as well as advertisers; and other methods of publicity are coming along that involve two-way interaction. In this way, marketing online is becoming part of the trend known as 'Web 2.0'.

## ONLINE ADVERTISING

The first thing to say about advertising in general is that for much of the present decade the industry has been in disarray. Total spending on advertising plummeted at the turn of the century; advertising in conventional media no longer seemed to work as it had; and there appeared to be little prospect of the new technology rescuing the situation. Devices such as TiVo were making it easy for television viewers to skip commercials, and a generation of people known to commercial-television executives as the 'Lost Boys' were growing, who were more interested in video games than watching television or reading newspapers.

When the web was first commercialised, people expected that it would function as an advertising medium quite comparable to newspapers and magazines: as you viewed a web page your attention would be caught by an advertising banner on a small area of the screen, and if you clicked on the banner you would view the advertiser's full message. Websites tried to make money from advertising in the way the press does, by charging an advertiser so much per 1000 pairs of eyeballs exposed to the advertiser's banner (cost per mille, CPM). The trouble was, people didn't click. In 1997 the *click-through rate* was only about 1 per cent. (By now it has fallen to a fraction of that.) Already in 1997 the web guru Jakob Nielsen was arguing that 'advertising doesn't work on the Web':

> TV [is] much more suited for the traditional type of advertising which is flashy and promotes superficial qualities of products. While watching TV people approach a vegetable state... [On the web] the user is *actively*
>
> *(Continued)*

164

*(Continued)*

> engaged in determining *where to go* next. The user is usually on the Web for a purpose and is not likely to be distracted from the goal by an advertisement ...[1]

(Nielsen noted that classified advertising works *better* on the web than in newspapers – but small ads are not the kind of 'advertising' we are concerned with here.)

Chaffey (2007: 405) quotes research published in 2003 suggesting that even television advertising had become ineffective. By the end of 2002 *The Economist* was describing the mood in the advertising industry as one of 'panic',[2] and it seemed likely that direct marketing and sales promotion were increasingly destined to achieve more than advertising for companies.

Over the past few years, though, the advertising industry has bounced back. Part of its problems stemmed from the general economic downturn that followed the collapse of the dotcom bubble, and Western economies have moved on now; recently they have been growing very healthily. More interestingly for present purposes, people are finding new ways to use the internet for advertising – ways that do work.

## ADVERTISING VIA SEARCH ENGINES

In 2002, Jakob Nielsen added a PS to his essay quoted above, saying that paid-for listings on search engines such as Google are an exception to the generalisation about web advertising. Since people visit those sites in order to find others to go to, and visitors' search terms provide a basis for deciding which listings may interest them, a well-targeted advert can work.

In the early years, search engines were not the key component of web activity that they have since become. Nowadays, most people reach most of the web destinations they ever visit via Google or another search engine; and search-engine companies are evolving novel and successful business models for advertising.

The classic problem for advertisers was stated in words often attributed to the Philadelphia department-store pioneer John Wanamaker in the 1870s: 'Half the money I spend on advertising is wasted. The trouble is, I don't know which half.'[3] Money spent on displaying adverts to people who are not plausible prospects for your message is money down the drain. But with conventional media it is impossible to be very selective. Space on a hoarding can only be charged for in terms of total numbers of passers-by,

---

[1] Jakob Nielsen, 'Why advertising doesn't work on the Web', 1 September 1997, www.useit.com/alertbox/9709a.html.

[2] 'High hopes in adland', *The Economist* 7 December 2002.

[3] There is controversy about who said this first, but it is a crucial point, whoever said it.

who include anyone and everyone. With a magazine, the advertiser knows not only how many people read it but also something of what kind of people they are – although only in extremely crude terms.

With search engines, the list of paid-for links displayed to a user is made to depend on the search string that the user has input; an advertiser can buy a slot in the paid-for listings displayed in response to search strings containing a specified word or phrase – in other words, the advertiser can target only those individuals who are known to be currently interested in finding out about a given topic. (With Google, the so-called *organic* listings, generated purely through an algorithm that ranks relevance of sites to the search string, are shown on the left of the screen; paid-for or 'sponsored' listings are on the right.) Furthermore, rather than charging by CPM, the search engine can charge by *cost per click*: an advertiser pays only when their listing is clicked on. Now the chargeable events are so selective that each one is seriously valuable to advertisers, who can fine-tune their audience in an unprecedented way.

Google's version of this system is called AdWords. Advertisers bid a fee-per-click they are willing to pay for a given search term, say 'mountain bikes'. A typical figure would be 50 cents, though it depends on the term: an American law firm will pay $100 for 'mesothelioma', the name of an asbestos-related cancer that happens to have been giving rise in the USA to lawsuits that are extremely lucrative for the lawyers involved. Fifty cents corresponds to a CPM of $500; in conventional media, a typical CPM is only about $20.

Advertisers pay for sponsored search-engine listings because they work. In November 2007 *Fortune* magazine quoted a click-through rate of over 5 per cent for Google ads (versus a fifth of 1 per cent for online advertising in general). The search expert John Battelle (2005: 35) quotes research by an investment bank suggesting that the average cost of acquiring a new customer is $70 via direct mailshots, $20 via Yellow Pages listings and $8.50 via search-engine listings.

## INCREASING SELECTIVITY

The selective approach can be taken further still. Once VoIP (voice over internet protocol) telephone calls via computer become widespread, search engines can charge by *cost per call*. One motive for eBay's ill-fated decision to buy Skype in September 2005 was the possibility of selling advertising not in the form of sponsored web links but as Skype buttons that initiate calls to the advertiser's sales staff: the advertiser pays only for the actual calls received (and hence will be willing to pay a lot). And the original inventor of the cost per click model, Bill Gross, is now pursuing the logical conclusion of this refinement process: *cost per sale* (Gross calls it 'cost per action', CPA). Gross's startup company Snap.com offers a search engine with software that enables an airline, say, to pay for inclusion of its link in the sponsored listings just on those occasions when a click leads to a ticket purchase. (In April 2007 Google announced that it was developing its own cost-per-sale system.)

Cost per sale is seen as the Holy Grail of advertising. It totally eliminates the 'Wanamaker waste', which for conventional advertising is far, far more than 'half' – perhaps John Wanamaker was right to think that about half of his adverts achieved nothing at all, but even the worthwhile ones will have affected the buying behaviour of only a fraction of the people who saw them. Cost per sale is technically difficult to implement, but the rewards for getting it right should be large.

The new advertising models are not unproblematic. There is now much concern about *click fraud*: people attacking competitors by arranging for repeated bogus clicks on their listings, draining their advertising budget without producing any extra sales. In 2006 the Atlanta-based company MostChoice.com lost over $100,000 that way. (Another type of click fraud relates to the kind of affiliate programmes discussed on p. 52: someone with an affiliate link to, say, Amazon on their site can arrange for bogus clicks on the link, generating a stream of commission from Amazon without any books being bought.) In 2006 the monitoring service Click Forensic demonstrated that at least 14 per cent of clicks on paid-for listings were fraudulent – corresponding to a huge amount of advertising spending. And Eric Schmidt, Google chief executive, created outrage that year when he seemed to say at a conference that the problem should be ignored. But, faced with legal threats, both Google and Yahoo! have now agreed to set up systems to combat click fraud; as *The Economist* put it, 'Like recalcitrant teenagers, they are grudgingly giving in and doing the homework they should have done ages ago.'[4]

New business models inevitably spawn new kinds of fraud, but there is no reason to suppose that click fraud is uniquely uncontainable.

## ONLINE ADVERTISING BOOMS

It has also emerged that the early pessimism about banner advertising was exaggerated. Adverts on websites do have a measurable impact. Since 2005 Google has offered an additional business model in which it functions like a conventional advertising agency, placing adverts on third-party sites (and charging on a CPM basis if that is what the advertiser prefers).

The consequence of all this is that, although spending on advertising as a whole has been recovering from the low near the beginning of the twenty-first century, spending on internet advertising is rising faster than any other category. (The spending is going overwhelmingly to one

---

[4] 'Truth in advertising', *The Economist* 25 November 2006.

company: in 2006 it is estimated that Google received a quarter of all online advertising revenue.)

Admittedly it is easy for the internet share of advertising to grow, because it started small. In Britain online advertising accounted for only 1 per cent of total advertising spending in 2000. By the end of 2006 the estimated figure was over 13 per cent, and it was overtaking the share of national newspapers. Meanwhile, spending on television advertising, although high, has not been growing.

Increasingly, spending on online advertising is organised by traditional, established advertising agencies, which are beginning to incorporate the internet as one channel into campaigns using a variety of media.

## ETHICAL DILEMMAS FOR GOOGLE

Google's dominant position in online advertising creates ethical dilemmas. Refusing a paid listing does serious damage to an advertiser's business, and yet Google feels bound to impose limits. Not everyone is happy with the way Google does this. Alcohol and tobacco sites are refused; pornography sites are accepted.[5] In February 2004 a non-profit environmental advocacy organisation, Oceana, had its paid-for listing deleted because its site criticised Royal Caribbean Cruise Lines for releasing inadequately treated sewage at sea: Google's policy was that it would not list 'sites that are "anti-" anything'.[6] Perhaps there really is no way to draw these ethical boundaries that everyone would accept as thoroughly principled, but in Google's case a remarkable degree of power rests on one man, Google's co-founder Sergey Brin, who makes these decisions essentially single-handedly.

## HIDDEN PERSUADERS

Now that the population is developing a degree of immunity to conventional advertising such as television commercials, IT is also being used to create novel methods of getting advertisers' messages past people's psychological defences.

There seems to be a long-term shift in social attitudes here. When Vance Packard published his million-selling book *The Hidden Persuaders* in 1957, readers were deeply shocked by concepts such as subliminal advertising, in which a visual message was flashed so quickly that television viewers would be influenced by it without consciously being aware of seeing it. Laws were introduced to limit the ways in which advertisers were allowed to approach their audiences. Some of the things

---

[5] Josh McHugh, 'Google vs. evil', *Wired 11.01*, January 2003.
[6] McHugh, as previous note.

that online advertisers are beginning to do might seem similarly questionable, but comparable reactions are scarcely occurring. Doubtless we have all grown more cynical over half a century.

Since youngsters are tending to abandon television for video games and MMOs, companies are incorporating advertising within the game worlds. Until now this has been simply a matter of reproducing conventional publicity within the game: as players move through city streets, they may see advertising hoardings or vans with real-world company logos on the side. But, according to Jonathan Epstein of Double Fusion, one of the companies organising this kind of advertising, 'the future is intelligent three-dimensional ads [and] ads with behaviour'.

> For instance, [Epstein's] technology will soon allow Coca-Cola to place a Coke can into a game, where it fizzes when a player walks by and might give him certain powers if he picks it up. If a character uses a mobile phone inside a game, the technology can swap the brand and model of the phone depending on which country the player is in.[7]

And there is *viral marketing*, in which material such as a video clip is released to a social networking site in the hope that people who enjoy it will spread it round, while it contains a commercial message, not too obviously, alongside its fun content. In August 2006 a short rap video, 'Tea Partay', was posted on YouTube, parodying New England 'preppy' lifestyle: within two weeks it was viewed half a million times. 'Tea Partay' was commissioned by Smirnoff to publicise a new drink, Raw Tea; but, according to Andrew Keen (2007: 90), 'few consumers realized the extent to which they'd had the wool pulled over their eyes'.

Another new technique that is tending to blur the boundary between content published for its own sake and paid advertising is *in-text advertising*. An advertiser can sponsor a keyword occurring within ordinary editorial matter on a webpage, so that when readers click on the keyword they see a pop-up advert.

> From the user's perspective, it is often not even clear what the association is between the underlined word and the advertisement. But from the advertiser's perspective, as long as they view the ad, it hardly matters.
>
> (Keen 2007: 88)

---

[7] 'The ultimate marketing machine', *The Economist* 8 July 2006.

In March 2007 it emerged that a Google researcher had filed a patent for a scheme that analyses computer gamers' behaviour, so that the in-game advertising displayed to them can be made to depend on whether they are categorised as 'risk-taker', 'non-confrontational', 'dishonest' and so on.

Legitimate? Or sinister? You decide.

## SEARCH ENGINE OPTIMISATION

One can choose to advertise via sponsored search-engine links, but more important is achieving a high ranking in the organic listings. It is well established that web users pay more attention to organic than paid-for listings (even though this difference may function at an unconscious level – a 2005 survey showed that most users are not aware of the distinction). But, if your site is not within the first screenful, it might as well not be there at all.

Since organic search ranking is so crucial, companies naturally try to manipulate it, tuning their site contents to try to improve their rankings – an activity known as *search engine optimisation* (SEO). Google and other search engines keep the details of their ranking algorithms secret, and modify them from time to time to foil site developers' attempts to game the system. (Google's PageRank metric, based on inbound links, is well known – but by now PageRank is only one of over 100 factors taken into account by Google's ranking algorithm.) In Google's case, the algorithm changes happen two or three times a year and are called 'Google Dances', as sites suddenly shift many places up or down the listings returned in response to given search terms. (For a fuller discussion, see Battelle 2005: 153–66.)

Some SEO techniques (such as including numerous 'hot' keywords hidden on a page in lettering the same colour as the background) are regarded as underhand, and by now the search engines have become good at detecting and ignoring, or punishing, 'black-hat' SEO. In February 2006 Google removed the listings of two respected companies, BMW Germany and Ricoh Germany, because of SEO practices regarded as unethical (both companies apologised, changed their sites and were reinstated). Google issues advice to web developers on achieving high rankings, much of which boils down to making their sites useful and interesting to human visitors – if people like a site, the suggestion is that Google's robots will like it too. Undoubtedly there is much truth in that.

Nevertheless, professional SEO is now itself big business. It has a history of tacky practice, using black-hat (or at least grey-hat) techniques and offering meaningless guarantees of getting clients' sites in the top screenful. (If one does not specify search terms, that is an empty promise: searches for a company's own name should certainly return that company's URL at or near the top of the organic listing, but what one needs is a high rank in response to searches on generic terms.)

Nowadays, though, there are plenty of legitimate SEO practitioners who are achieving real benefit for clients. An Oregon investment bank, Pacific Security Capital, stopped spending $50,000 a month on pay-per-click advertising and switched to paying one-tenth that amount to an SEO firm. It now ranks first on several search engines for about 50 search terms.

By 2005, worldwide spending on SEO was $1.25 billion – about a tenth of the figure for internet advertising.

## THE CONCEPT OF VIRTUAL COMMUNITIES

Contrary to the commonsense viewpoint that sees the function of a commercial website as being to publicise and sell a company's wares, as David Siegel saw it in the early years of e-commerce, 'The ultimate goal of many web sites is to create a community' (Siegel 1997: 18).

Many *virtual communities*, of course, have no connection with business (and note that the concept is quite separate from 'virtual company' or 'virtual organisation', discussed in Chapter 2). The virtual community concept was formulated by Howard Rheingold (1993) before the internet was commercialised, as a way of describing a sizeable group of people who form a network of human relationships based on some common interest but mediated by the internet rather than face-to-face interactions. (We looked at Amazon's early attempts to create a virtual community based on its site on p. 39.) After the business consultants John Hagel and Arthur Armstrong published their influential book *Net Gain* (Hagel and Armstrong 1997), many commentators came to believe that these electronically mediated communities of interest had an essential role to play as links between companies and their potential customer base – at the B2C level, and perhaps also at the B2B level.

An extreme expression of this belief was the so-called Cluetrain Manifesto, published by Christopher Locke and others, originally online and later as a book (Levine *et al.* 2000). As the Manifesto writers saw it, the internet was destined shortly to transform the nature of relationships between the business world and the society in which it is embedded.

They set out from the widely shared observation that present-day society has an alienating impact on its individual members: people are made to feel less than fully human in their transactions with large anonymous corporations and bureaucratic government organisations, and in their consumption of mass media. Locke and his co-authors expressed nostalgia for the days when 'commerce' typically meant face-to-face trading at market stalls, where conversation and banter made commercial exchanges a human, social activity as much as a strictly economic one. They argued that the effortless, instant communication facilitated by the internet was about to revive those relationships between sellers and buyers. Modern firms might present a bland, anonymous face to the world, but in reality they are just groups of human beings like you and me, and the internet was making it possible to humanise their interactions with consumers and with one another. Indeed they would *have* to go that way; society would not allow them to get away with the old approach much longer.

The Cluetrain Manifesto dates to the height of the dotcom frenzy – the foreword to Levine *et al.* (2000) was by Thomas Petzinger, whom we saw earlier (p. 15) announcing the abolition of the laws of supply and demand. Like that pronouncement of Petzinger's, the Manifesto is hard to take entirely seriously. The reason why interactions with a company are less personal than with a market stallholder is that a complex modern company comprises many people, not just one, and so its dealings have to be formalised in order to represent the whole company properly. A stallholder can do whatever deal he or she likes with a customer on the spur of the moment; a telephonist for Megastore Ltd obviously cannot. The internet does not change that.

## VIRTUAL COMMUNITIES AS A MARKETING TOOL

Nevertheless, commentators such as Kannan *et al.* (2001) argued in a more restrained style that 'virtual communities' were likely to play a significant role in e-commerce. The key is 'ownership', in the psychological more than the legal sense. A company may set up the infrastructure that allows a virtual community, oriented towards its market sector, to develop; but, to get full value from the existence of the virtual community, Kannan *et al.* argue that the company must let go. The community must become something that exists to serve all its participants; the company needs to be merely one contributor, not the controller. When consumers seek product information or advice by posting queries on virtual community bulletin boards, often the most helpful answers will be from other consumers rather than from company representatives. By raising the shared level of understanding and confidence in the product line, C2C interchanges such as this might do more to support sales than any amount of company advertising.

The literature on business benefits from virtual communities was predominantly hypothetical in tone, though. One of the few concrete examples, referred to by writer after writer, was Parentsplace.com. This was a California-based site that began as an e-tailing initiative: it was intended to be a business selling child-related products to parents, with social features such as chatrooms included in order to support that goal. Parents who joined the community proved to be much more interested in using it for things such as exchanging childrearing advice than in ordering goods from the site; so the site owners changed their business model, abandoning the retail operation and generating a revenue stream instead by selling advertising space to companies marketing the kinds of goods that the site had initially sold.

However, this does not seem to be a good illustration of Hagel and Armstrong's concept, because in this case there was no ongoing business for the community to support. There were cases that matched Hagel and Armstrong's concept better, but, a few years after the Cluetrain Manifesto, 'virtual communities' as a key concept looked like a mistaken prediction about the way e-business would go. When individuals visit an e-commerce site, they come to learn about what the company behind the site has to offer, and perhaps to buy – they do not come in order to interact with other site visitors.

## B2B MARKETPLACES

In particular, the idea of extending the virtual community concept to the B2B level seems to have been definitively abandoned since the dotcom crash. In the first wave of enthusiasm for e-business, it was expected that online *B2B marketplaces* would become important e-business facilities, linking companies active in a given industry sector, some of which would be suppliers for others while some would be one another's competitors.

A well-known example was Covisint, which was created by a consortium of leading American car manufacturers to act as a neutral electronic marketplace within which they could conduct negotiations, including auctions, with parts suppliers, marketplace participants could exchange documentation and suggestions for product improvements, and so forth. By 2002 a great deal of activity was happening in Covisint. But in 2004 Covisint ceased to be a neutral forum; it was bought by a B2B software company, Compuware, and it now offers services to manufacturers as one proprietary supplier competing with others. E-auctions in car manufacturing have migrated to 'private B2B exchanges', owned and run by individual manufacturers that control the range of firms that are allowed to participate.

This seems to have been the general fate of the B2B marketplace concept. For one reason or another, the idea of neutral forums has not flourished at the B2B level. The issue is discussed in detail by Chaffey (2007: 325–30).

## WEB 2.0

At the B2C level, though, the virtual community idea has taken on a new lease of life, in connection with what has come to be called 'Web 2.0'.

This term is an ill-defined buzzword that has come to be used differently by different people.[8] Some use it to mean the multimedia-rich type of websites, comprising music, high-definition photos, videos and so forth, which have come to the fore as broadband has penetrated the online population. But for many people the essence of Web 2.0 is two-way participation. In that sense, Web 1.0 is mainly organisations displaying static material to the public; in Web 2.0 the public gets in on the act, via blogs but also via podcasts, wikis, online social networks, 'mashups' that use other sites as inputs to create novel output on one's own site, and so on. The web becomes less 'publication', more 'conversation'.

In about 2006–7 it became apparent that Web 2.0 technologies such as social network sites, which at first looked to be of interest mainly to teenagers, were developing significant business uses. When in May 2007 the City law firm Allen and Overy banned staff from accessing the social network site Facebook at work, they thought they were simply cutting out a time-wasting non-work distraction; but the edict had to be reversed when staff rebelled, because Facebook was useful in their professional lives. One major business use of social network sites has been in recruitment; they are a good way of spreading the word about interesting vacancies beyond the circle of those actively looking for a new job, to friends of friends who might well be the right choice once they know the opportunity is available. The investment bank Dresdner Kleinwort Wasserstein has experimented with company-internal blogs and wikis as means of helping members of a project to keep up to speed with one another's activities, and they claim to have found measurable productivity gains.

IBM announced a social software platform, Lotus Connections, in January 2007, designed specifically for business uses; the expectation is that this will routinely be bundled with various standard enterprise application packages.

These are cases where Web 2.0 technologies are providing new modes of communication within pre-existing communities, such as the staff of a firm. But Web 2.0 is also being applied in the Cluetrain Manifesto sense, by attempting to create social networks of interest linking a firm with its customers. Some of the attempts have been clunky. Wal-Mart tried launching a networking site for teenagers, the Hub, in July 2006, but the target audience found it so corny that it closed down that October. But in May 2007 Tesco's online operation, Tesco.com, announced that it was going to use Web 2.0 technologies to give its website some of the community aspects of a bricks-and-mortar supermarket. Jon Higgins, Tesco.com's IT director, said:

---

[8] The term was coined in 2003 by Dale Dougherty, co-founder with Tim O'Reilly of the O'Reilly textbook publishers, to refer to the dynamic web pages that are made possible by software such as asynchronous JavaScript. But people soon lost sight of that precise definition.

> The web site is a great selling vehicle, but we want to put more heart into it. Tesco stores have a range of community initiatives, such as notice boards, and we want Tesco.com to be more local.[9]

Higgins hopes in this way to 'make the online experience more closely resemble the in-store experience'.[10] At the time of writing it is too soon to know how much will come of this, but Tesco is such a sure-footed business that we can expect the development to be worth watching.

Web 2.0 techniques are another means, less way out than MMOs, by which Patricia Seybold's vision of customers as co-designers (p. 124) is being realised. It was reported in October 2007, for instance, that Kimberley-Clark's Huggies baby-products division is now building 'crowdsourcing' – interaction with a virtual community – into its product development system, and thereby cutting time to market by 30 per cent. Its liquid baby powder is the result of ideas originating with its customers rather than in-house.

## CORPORATE BLOGGING

To date the most fully developed business use of Web 2.0 technology is corporate blogging, which began to take off in about 2003.

A weblog or 'blog', as many readers will know, is like an individual's diary, posted on the web with the most recent entries nearest the top; commonly (though not invariably) a blog allows readers to post comments on individual entries, so that an ongoing conversation builds up between the blog owner and his or her readership. The relevance to business is that there are many blogs that are written by company employees, mainly about their work, including discussion of their company's products (though there may also be family or other non-work topics mixed in). The best-known example is the blog begun by Robert Scoble at Microsoft as early as 2000, which continued until Scoble left to join a blogging-software startup company in 2006. We shall use the term 'corporate blog' to cover any company-related blogs by employees, whether these are tolerated or even positively encouraged by the employer, or published anonymously in the face of employer disapproval. Robert Scoble analyses the corporate-blogging phenomenon in his book *Naked Conversations* (Scoble and Israel 2006).

Corporate blogging is related closely to the virtual community idea. It gives companies a human face (or faces – in 2006 Microsoft was reported as containing 3000 corporate bloggers), and this may encourage readers to develop a lasting loyalty to a company's products – if a company is

---

[9] Quoted by Dave Friedlos, 'Tesco chases online appeal', *Computing* 31 May 2007.
[10] Quoted by Dave Friedlos, 'Online retailers must keep evolving', *Computing* 28 June 2007.

lucky, it may even 'convert customers into word-spreading evangelists' (Scoble and Israel 2006: 88). And conversely it can be a good way for companies to learn what their customer base really cares about or hopes for from future product development. Furthermore, the audience for company-related blogs may not be only potential customers, but also potential recruits; Gary Flood comments:

> In the UK ... firms are looking at blogging as a way to communicate some of the excitement and recruitment value that otherwise is hard to get through to outsiders.[11]

In another way, blogging is rather different from the virtual community idea. The agenda for discussion is set by the topics that the blogger chooses to raise, whereas 'virtual community' implies that any community member might raise new issues. Corporate bloggers might allow themselves to be guided by points that recur in readers' comments, but the initiative rests with the blogger.

One can see corporate blogging as an alternative, or complement, to the press releases generated by a company's public relations department. Press releases are one-way communication – they do not create a possibility of reader feedback; and they are carefully tailored to give just the positive messages that the company wants the public to read. The sophisticated twenty-first-century public knows that, and discounts their contents accordingly. What PR tell us may not be false, but it is not likely to be the whole truth – nothing in real life is positive through and through. Blogs by company employees are more credible precisely because they cover downsides as well as positives. Scoble and Israel (2006: 183) tell us that:

> Scoble has at times been among the most critical voices of Microsoft, and many people have been surprised that Microsoft did not respond by firing, or at least disciplining, him ...

Instead, Microsoft actually encouraged him to blog in company time. It is generally accepted that the net effect of Scoble's blog has been to improve overall public perception of his company. But, Scoble insists, the advantages of corporate blogging will accrue only if blogs are sincere and independent-minded. If a competitor has a superior product, then the blogger should say so and include a link to the competitor's website.

---

[11] 'Corporate web sites get personal', *Computing* 7 September 2006.

## HOW GENERALISABLE IS MICROSOFT'S APPROACH?

What seems questionable in Scoble's account of the virtues of corporate blogging is the suggestion that many other firms could benefit as Microsoft has. Scoble discusses 'who should not blog', but the answer is essentially just the bad guys – 'companies with cheesy products and disdain or contempt for their customers' (Scoble and Israel 2006: 136, quoting Jackie Huba, co-author of the 'Church of the Customer' marketing blog). But there are surely plenty of companies making good products and having respect for their customers for which blogging would be irrelevant. What could it achieve for a kitchenware manufacturer, for instance? Doubtless, if one is involved closely in the design and manufacture of pots and pans, then there are interesting stories to tell; but how many members of the public, bombarded as we all are by an overload of information on every topic under the sun, are going to become regular readers of a kitchenware blog? A few keen cooks, perhaps. But one point that Scoble stresses repeatedly is that blogging is very time-consuming. If a worker ends up devoting a significant fraction of waking hours producing a blog read by a handful of enthusiasts, then the employer is hardly likely to gain from it.

Microsoft is not an average company. Its product, software, is intricate, intellectually fascinating and constantly evolving, so that many people are interested in reading inside stories about new developments. Furthermore, when Scoble began blogging, Microsoft had a serious image problem (a company that finds itself nicknamed 'the Evil Empire' clearly needs any humanising factors it can come up with), while it did not need to worry much about negative comments in blogs reducing its market share, because in practice it had something close to a monopoly position. Demonstrating that Microsoft had an open enough culture to tolerate intelligent criticism from within was probably much more important than allowing people to see that insiders shared some of the public's misgivings about Microsoft products.

None of these things applies to the average company. If a blog about kitchenware company A gave reasons why company B's pots and pans are better, with a link to company B, then presumably many readers would think 'Thanks for the tip', follow the link, and forget about buying A's products. Few customers care about the internal 'culture' of a kitchenware company.

Even among technology companies, not all are as friendly as Microsoft is to employee blogging. Apple and Google both discourage it. It poses obvious dangers. These relate less to the possibility of negative comments by readers (if the comments are unmerited, then, Scoble argues, one can rely on other readers to contradict them) than to things the bloggers might include. A blogger might release inside information that is intended to be confidential because it is useful to a competitor, or might make incautious remarks that lead to adverse legal consequences. Some companies that tolerate blogging try to minimise these dangers by publishing guidelines (Microsoft just says 'Blog smart', but other companies are more prescriptive). The only way to eliminate the dangers altogether, though, would be to require blogs to be cleared officially before release – and that would destroy the spontaneity that gives them their credibility.

At present there is a wave of enthusiasm for the potential of corporate blogging. But ultimately the strongest reason for companies to accept blogging may be one expressed by Jeff Mann of the business analysts Gartner: 'If you do not support blogging or try to prevent it users are just going to route around you and do it anyway.'[12]

How far corporate blogging and other business uses of Web 2.0 correspond to the original 'virtual community' concept is another question. Tim O'Reilly is sceptical:

> I always hated the word 'community', it is one of those words people use so they don't have to think about what really matters.[13]

O'Reilly believes that some of the most successful so-called 'community' websites actually function with an internal dynamic quite different from the standard, 'all in this together' implications of the word in everyday English. But there evidently is a significant new set of business tools becoming available – whatever words we choose to describe them with.

## E-MARKETING IS MARKETING

This and the previous chapter have examined various aspects of marketing for e-business. To sum up, let me repeat the point made at the beginning of Chapter 9: an e-business is a business. Marketing in the online world is not radically different from marketing in conventional business. IT gives us new tools; some are more useful than others. Some may be double-edged.

[12] Quoted by Gary Flood, 'Corporate web sites get personal', *Computing* 7 September 2006.
[13] Quoted in 'A brave new world wide web', *Computing* 3 May 2007.

# 11 Diverse Enterprise Applications

## FURTHER APPLICATION GENRES

ERP systems, which relate mainly to internal and 'upstream' (supplier-facing) activities, and CRM systems, which face 'downstream' (towards customers), are the two leading genres of enterprise software application. There are quite a number of others. In this chapter we shall look at some of the most important remaining enterprise application genres, under five main headings:

- business intelligence
- workflow management
- supply chain management
- use of RFID data
- e-procurement.

(RFID is an odd one out here, because it is not a genre of software application but a new source of data for various applications. But we shall see that this topic fits well alongside supply chain management.)

## BUSINESS INTELLIGENCE

Business intelligence (BI) is like military 'intelligence' – it does not mean cleverness but, rather, keeping track of what is happening. The phrase has been used for 20 years or more, but only since 2003 or so has BI software matured to the point where it is delivering useful results to a wide range of firms.

Some leading BI supplier companies include Cognos, Business Objects, SAS and Information Builders. And they are now having to compete with much larger firms that are adding BI capabilities to more general enterprise software systems. Oracle, SAP and IBM are all taking that route, while from the desktop direction Microsoft is beginning to incorporate BI features into new versions of its Office suite. (In late 2007, Cognos and Business Objects were taken over by IBM and by SAP respectively.)

Although BI is fairly new as a significant enterprise application genre, it is currently very 'hot'. A report in February 2007 showed that BI is now firms' top choice for new software investments.

At the same time, the phrase has its full share, or more than its share, of the obscurity that infects much business-IT terminology and that sometimes seems to be positively encouraged by suppliers. Stephen Gallagher of Accenture calls business intelligence 'a catch-all phrase'.[1]

---

[1] Quoted by Jason Compton, 'Is this business tool ready to pass intelligence test?', *Computing* 23 February 2006.

The IT journalist Phil Muncaster sees BI vendors as 'among the worst for deliberate obfuscation, truth-bending and generally talking in riddles'.[2] The present discussion will endeavour to clarify the realities underlying the obfuscation, but one can achieve only so much: if the jargon of the profession is genuinely ambiguous, then one cannot pretend that it is precise. A survey of British and Irish IT managers released by Oracle in April 2006 showed, among other things, that a majority believed that BI was an important tool used by their senior managers, while a large majority believed that their organisation had no BI systems. They cannot all have been right both times!

One way to explain BI is to contrast it with ERP and CRM. These latter applications keep track of individual transactions, whether internal, with suppliers, or with customers; it is not their job to aggregate separate transactions into overall statistics, to show how well or poorly the company is executing its various functions. BI carries out this analytic task, taking numerous individual data and digesting them into performance indicators.

## HISTORICAL *v.* REAL-TIME ANALYSIS

The analyses may be output in the form of reports on performance in successive periods, which managers can use to monitor how well their strategies have succeeded or where something needs attention. Raw data for a given month or year is extracted from the company's data warehouse, cleaned up to eliminate inconsistencies (if, say, a branch name is abbreviated one way in one set of records and another way in a separate set, then the contradiction has to be resolved before the full dataset can yield meaningful figures) and fed into analytical algorithms to produce the report.

Increasingly, though, this historically oriented approach to BI is being supplemented or overshadowed by systems that analyse business performance in real time, allowing managers to monitor the current health of various functions for which they are responsible, and even extrapolating from present data to make predictions about the future. The terms 'dashboard' and 'scorecard' (as opposed to 'report') are used in connection with this present-time-oriented type of BI system. Managers are offered 'dashboards' that show the current state of sales, inventory or whatever statistics they need, in the same way that a car dashboard shows current speed, fuel quantity and so on. A 'scorecard' shows how functions are performing measured against set targets; scorecards may relate to the work of individual employees, for instance sales representatives.

For a few years after the turn of the century another term, *business performance management* (BPM), came into vogue for this kind of present-oriented analytical system. But by about 2005–6 the historically oriented and the real-time approaches were merging into single systems,

---

[2] Phil Muncaster, 'Blogwatch', *IT Week* 5 February 2007.

and the term 'business intelligence' is now usual for these. There are quite enough abbreviations in business IT, so this book will not use the term 'BPM'.

BI systems often use sophisticated visualisation techniques to present analytical results in a way that humans can understand. Kevin Quinn, a vice-president at Information Builders, comments:

> The amount of data in most organisations is now so large that it is impossible to look at it in any depth without visualisation tools.[3]

One example is the way that the state of Louisiana is using Information Builders' software to detect shops that fraudulently accept food stamps (issued to poor people as a welfare measure) in exchange for non-food goods. Previously, administrators had to search through massive text files line by line looking for anomalies. Now, they can throw up a map of the state with dots coloured to show how far on average food-stamp recipients are travelling to particular shops. A dot showing people coming a long way to a shop, surrounded by other dots representing closer shops, raises a suspicion of fraud; detection rates have climbed accordingly. Welfare law enforcement is not 'business', and so strictly this example falls outside our purview – but it illustrates how visualisation techniques enable people to extract meaning from large datasets, including business datasets.

## DATA-MINING

Some BI algorithms are subtle and computationally challenging. The term 'data-mining' is used for statistical algorithms that discover unexpected patterns or generalisations in mountains of data, such as those found nowadays in firms' data warehouses. Data-mining applied to business is part of what the term BI covers. (Some people see BI as little more than a new name for data-mining, though BI normally also covers other, simpler analytical techniques as well as visualisation tools – data-mining is about analysing rather than about presenting the results of analysis.) For an introduction to data-mining, see, for example, Larose (2005).

The example of data-mining that almost everyone has heard about is the nappy/beer case. In 1992, a chain of American drugstores called Osco analysed the make-up of 1,200,000 market baskets (sets of items that one individual bought at one time). They found a significant statistical tendency for people shopping between 5 p.m. and 7 p.m. to buy both disposable nappies and beer.[4]

---

[3] Quoted in James Murray, 'Maps and charts point way to BI gold', *IT Week* 20 November 2006.
[4] This finding is often discussed as if it were no more than an 'urban myth'. For the facts, see Daniel J. Power, 'Ask Dan!', *DSS News* 10 November 2002.

Once the correlation has been discovered, it is not too hard to come up with an explanation. The favoured story seems to be that people who buy both items are young fathers sent out to buy nappies at an hour when, in recent bachelor days, they would have been sinking a pint with their friends in a pub (or American equivalent) – they take home cans of beer as the nearest they can get to those carefree years. That may be right or wrong – it scarcely matters; but notice how implausible it is that anyone would have guessed at a link between these two particular items, *before* data-mining showed the link to exist. If Tesco's Clubcard analysts limited themselves to using their data to answer questions that they thought of without mechanical help, as Clive Humby suggests (p. 162), they would hardly have thought to check this particular combination.

Yet the knowledge was potentially valuable. Store managers could have arranged to shelve beer close to the nappies, so that a young dad on a nappy quest would be more likely to pick up a pack of beer at the same time. (In fact, Osco never made any use of this particular finding – though *The Economist* claims that Tesco does exploit a similar linkage between baby wipes and beer by sending out Clubcard discount coupons for both together.[5]) Data-mining is motivated by the expectation that data warehouses will contain many pieces of unguessable knowledge, some of which, once uncovered, will have large commercial value.

## CONSTRAINTS ON DATA-MINING DEPLOYMENT

Although data-mining may be able to uncover useful knowledge without human prompting, the statistical algorithms it uses to do so are extremely processing-intensive. A typical procedure is to find 'natural groupings' among a large number of entities – for instance, a retailer will want to divide its customers into classes whose members tend to act alike in their buying behaviour. There is a range of 'clustering' algorithms for achieving this, but the quantity of processing that they require grows much more than linearly with the size of the dataset – it might grow as the square, or even faster. That means that with the really huge datasets that are now common, even current technology is strained to the limit. Thomas Davenport (2006: 106) mentions that the data-mining group at one consumer products firm 'went so far as to build its own supercomputer because it felt that commercially available models were inadequate'. This is one area of business IT that really does need the power of 64-bit processing. And the mathematical subtlety of the algorithms means that availability of competent staff is a serious constraint.

The computing demands of BI, and the shortage of qualified staff, make it an expensive enterprise application genre, and until recently only large organisations could consider it. But there have recently been moves to produce cheaper, easier-to-use BI packages. And accessibility is being

---

[5] 'Fresh, but far from easy', *The Economist* 23 June 2007.

promoted also by developing special-purpose BI systems tailored to specific business sectors, reducing the need for client firms to customise the systems extensively.

## KNOWLEDGE MANAGEMENT

A concept that was much discussed a few years ago and is related closely to BI is *knowledge management*. (The phrases 'information management' and 'group memory' are also used in much the same way – some people probably draw distinctions between these concepts, but I doubt whether different people draw the distinctions the same way.) The idea behind knowledge management was that the collective knowledge embodied in a firm is so crucial to its activity that it needs to be captured electronically.

The suggestion that companies are based on diffused knowledge is not in itself controversial. In the eyes of some economists, the very essence of a business firm is that it forms 'a repository of productive knowledge' (Winter 1993: 185) – an institution whose function is collectively to store and apply knowledge of how to execute some complex range of useful economic processes. No one individual in a firm, including its managing director, possesses more than a fraction of this knowledge, which resides rather in the firm as a whole – 'it is the firms, not the people who work for the firms, that know how to make gasoline, automobiles, and computers'. Some of this knowledge is formal and explicit, but much is transmitted through fleeting interactions between staff.

The 'group memory' vision was that electronic systems might enable what was of lasting value in these interactions to be systematically recorded and preserved, reducing the inefficiencies that stem from facts and ideas getting lost from sight as work moves forward.

The original inspiration for group memory software lay in the successful *groupware* program Lotus Notes, which supports collaborative work by colleagues who interact via e-mail, making it easy for them to keep systematic records of how their thinking and discussion on particular topics, and the documents they jointly put together, develop over time. Many companies aimed to build on this general concept to create systems that would maintain corporate memory in some grander sense.

But little came of the idea, partly because it seemed too vague. Attempts that were made to implement it often yielded few bankable benefits in practice; the initial enthusiasm for purpose-built groupware diminished after web technology made it easy to achieve some of the same goals via company intranets. More than one speaker at the future-of-computing conference mentioned on p. 12 argued that 'knowledge management' is a mirage, because knowledge is not something that can be managed.

BI might perhaps be seen as reviving what was worthwhile in the knowledge management concept, but in a more focused and hence more practical way – not attempting to capture any and every kind of knowledge that resides somewhere in a firm's filing cabinets or in the heads of employees, but rather organising and analysing certain especially important and well-defined subsets of all that information.

## USES OF BUSINESS INTELLIGENCE

For a company that can afford the costs of BI, potential applications are very diverse.

ITV uses it to monitor the profitability of its drama programmes, gathering data held on a variety of legacy systems about costs of everything from the concept stage to production, and about audience figures and income from commercial breaks, and digesting them into a measure of profitability within minutes rather than the two months it took before BI.

Some pub chains are changing the prices of drinks from day to day, using data from the impact of 'happy hour' discounts on sales volume for particular drinks in order to estimate optimal price points for the following day. Jim Goodnight of SAS explained:

> There are a lot of firms out there that still have the same price for a product all the time... The technology is now there to change that price every hour if need be... Retailers have wanted to have the ability to optimise prices for decades, but it really is very difficult to do effectively and needs analytical software to automate it.[6]

One major use of BI is protection of credit-card holders by detecting patterns of usage that depart from the individual's norm. I was grateful for BI when my card issuer phoned to ask if I had just been making a series of expensive purchases in Spain (which indeed I had not).

Yorkshire Water uses BI to predict places where water mains or sewers are likely to fail, dealing with many problems before they arise rather than waiting for unhappy householders to call them out.

A February 2007 report from AMR Research found that, without BI, a retailer needs an average five weeks to detect a change in demand and another five days to do something about it (by which time, demand patterns may have changed again); BI should be able to eliminate that delay almost completely.

And retail demand can be analysed in subtler ways. According to Richard Neale of Business Objects, one supermarket chain found that sales of an expensive French cheese were too low to justify continuing to stock it – until BI showed that the few people who did buy the cheese were

---

[6] Quoted by James Murray, 'Industry-specific business intelligence', *IT Week* 18 September 2006.

some of the supermarket's most profitable customers, and so it was worth keeping on despite the disappointing level of sales.

As with other enterprise applications, a further pressure pushing companies into using BI is the need to achieve compliance with new legal regulations. For instance, it was reported in 2004 that all 10 of the leading banks in Europe were using Cognos software for this reason.

## WEB ANALYTICS

Another area that, logically speaking, might be described as a branch of BI is *web analytics*: applying analytic algorithms to a company's web logs to extract commercially valuable knowledge. In practice, web analytics is commonly seen as a separate topic from BI. This may be because techniques are available in the former that do not apply to the latter. Websites lend themselves to experimentation. Pfeffer and Sutton (2006: 73) quote Yahoo!'s chief data officer, Usama Fayyad, as explaining

> … the home page gets millions of hits an hour, so Yahoo can conduct rigorous experiments that yield results in an hour or less – randomly assigning, say, a couple hundred thousand visitors to the experimental group and several million to the control group. Yahoo typically has 20 or so experiments running at any time, manipulating site features like colors, placement of advertisements, and location of text and buttons. These little experiments can have big effects. For instance, an experiment by data-mining researcher Nitin Sharma revealed that simply moving the search box from the side to the center of the home page would produce enough additional 'click throughs' to bring in millions more dollars in advertising revenue a year.

Experimental data as rich as this is harder to come by in other business areas. But the idea of applying analytic algorithms to files containing millions of records is essentially the same idea, whether the records correspond to the contents of shopping baskets or to hits on web pages. The web analytics firm Omniture integrates weblog data with other kinds of marketing data standardly treated under the 'BI' heading.

## WORKFLOW MANAGEMENT

Workflow management is a good example of a business function that seems an obvious candidate for computerisation, and where various systems have been marketed for a long time; yet a comment made by Peter Gloor (2000: 112) at the turn of the century, 'the great breakthrough has not yet happened', still holds true.

The concept of workflow management is easy to explain. Many businesses involve paperwork in standard formats passing from office to office along standard routes. Gloor's example is a health insurance company. When a client applies for a policy, the company collects data from the client. On the basis of the data, the company decides whether a medical examination is required. If so, the client's details are passed to a health centre allied with the insurance company, and an invitation to attend is printed out and posted. When the client arrives, a receptionist registers their attendance, and the doctor adds medical data to their file. On the basis of the accumulated data, an insurance risk factor is worked out, and the file is passed back to the insurance company, where a decision is made on whether an individual premium must be calculated by an expert, or whether the case is routine enough for automatic calculation to suffice – as it will for clients not asked to undergo an examination. Either via the expert or directly, the file then arrives at a point where a policy and invoice are printed out and posted to the client.

Traditionally, what will have moved from client to office to office, perhaps crossing from insurance company to health centre and back again, will have been paper documents – forms in which data is progressively entered into the spaces. Nowadays, some of the data exchanges might happen via e-mail; but it is not yet usual for the flow of documentation in moderately complex scenarios like the one just sketched to be entirely electronic. Sometimes, data will be transferred manually from paper into a computer system more than once during the overall process.

Often, a complex document is transmitted from one point to another as a PDF file, which has to be downloaded and printed out before being filled in and sent on by post. Bruce Chizen, chief executive of Adobe (owner of the PDF technology), agreed in 2002 that this way of working is absurdly inefficient, but he pointed out that with documentation such as insurance papers 'presentation is critical, not least because of the laws and regulations concerning the information within the documents.'[7]

Adobe is a leading company that has been developing solutions to automating the workflow function. The PDF format defines a document in terms of its visual appearance, for human consumption, and does not in itself provide any means for computers to identify and process specific items of information contained in the document. But Adobe's 'intelligent document architecture', launched in 2003, integrates PDF with the markup language XML (to be discussed in Chapter 12) in order to allow documents to comprise information both in the manner required by human eyeballs and as required for computer processing. For instance, a document can contain machine-readable routing information, or a worker can OK a document by adding an element that will be recognised automatically when the signoffs are checked at the end of the workflow. If a client has

---

[7] Quoted by Rod Newing, 'Time to break our paper chains', *IT Week* 21 October 2002.

moved, then the difference in address can be detected automatically and the document routed to wherever in the organisation address records are updated, without a human being having to search tediously for address discrepancies.

What is more, the machine-usable version of the information can be represented not only electronically but as a visible barcode, so that even if a complex workflow route requires a document to move as hard copy at some point (perhaps because a consumer has no computer), on receipt it need only be scanned, not retyped, in order to reconstruct the entire electronic file as it last emerged from a machine.

Workflow functionality is an obvious direction for office productivity software to evolve, and Microsoft's Office 2007 incorporates a number of workflow features. Other companies, too, have been moving in a similar direction for some time.

## SLOW PENETRATION

Efficient workflow systems would be a major productivity boon. One might have supposed that by now the IT world would have cracked this one, and the fully paperless office would be a reality. In most organisations, it is not.

Part of the problem is a human factors issue. In many ways paper is easier and less stressful for people to work with than a shiny monitor with an ever-winking cursor. (Rather than new processors or operating systems, one of the biggest genuine improvements to computer technology would surely be displays that functioned by reflected rather than transmitted light, so that they were as restful to look at as the other contents of an office.) But we have not yet got the software right either.

This is an area that has been beset by alternative standards. Since the early 1990s standards-developing efforts have been divided between the Workflow and Reengineering Internet Association (WARIA) and the Workflow Management Coalition (WfMC).[8]

A legal wrangle with Adobe prevented Microsoft from including PDF support with the Office 2007 suite. In March 2006 a consortium including IBM, Sun, Oracle and many other companies jointly established an OpenDocument Format (ODF) Alliance to sponsor a single XML-based

---

[8] In 2006, WARIA merged with Enix Consulting under the new name BPM-Focus. BPM stands here for 'business process management', another piece of terminology that is not easy to distinguish from 'workflow management'. Some writers tend to use 'workflow' for early systems where almost all the active work was done by people and the machines only moved documents around, while they use 'business process management' for newer cases where decisions resulting in modifications to document content are often made automatically. But this is not an absolute difference; Derek Miers (2005: 23) of Enix writes 'All that has really changed are the terms. Now it's called Business Process Management (BPM) rather than workflow.' Both in order to avoid multiplying terminology, and because business *process* management is not the same as business *performance* management – cf. p. 180 – this book will avoid these terms.

standard file format for office documents, but in January 2007 Microsoft asked ISO (the International Organization for Standardization) to accept its own Office Open XML as a competing standard – the ODF Alliance objected. Until standards are universally agreed, it seems unlikely that workflow technology could develop beyond, at best, processes strictly confined within single organisations.

And the other problem is that the task is more challenging than it looks. Those of us who are not administrators often think of that type of work as tediously static, but the truth is that organisational routines frequently change. More awkward still, business processes often contain unstructured components mixed in with the structured aspects. Peter Gloor's example is that approval of a new product will involve a well-defined signoff process up a company hierarchy, but it may well also involve 'informal soundings' among colleagues. The unstructured elements can scarcely be integrated into an automated workflow system; but, if that means they get squeezed out, the company might lose more than it gains through efficient exchange of electronic 'paperwork'.

## SUPPLY CHAIN MANAGEMENT

In an ideal business world, goods flow smoothly down the many paths from the raw-material stage at one extreme, through the numerous stages where parts are assembled into wholes or less finished items are processed into more finished items, towards the ultimate point where business sells goods to consumers. The items move quickly and cheaply from one firm to the next and, within a given firm, through the different departments that need to deal with them. No pathway ever dries up, so that the next stage has to wait idly for supply to resume; but at the same time paths never become clogged with items arriving faster than they can be processed at a given stage – in business terms, a bottleneck like that would mean at best that the company that owns the goods piling up at the bottleneck is losing money because its investment in the goods is not yielding an immediate return, but it might well also mean that the goods have to be written off or sold at knock-down prices, because many economic goods lose value rapidly with age.

Real life is not like that. Within a firm, one department finds that it needs to hold a buffer of input materials to guard against interruption of supply from the department or departments upstream; totalled over the entire company, these buffers add up to a lot of unproductive inventory at any time. The needs of the client firms change in unpredictable ways, but the company cannot change the pace of its throughput to match changing demand overnight. Suppliers' output may reduce, for a host of reasons – in the worst cases, a factory fire or a bankruptcy ends output abruptly, and it may not be easy to locate an alternative source quickly.

Fires and bankruptcies are extreme events, but, such things apart, it might seem that the little hitches to perfectly smooth flow should average themselves out and represent only a minor nuisance. The actual pattern of the movement of raw materials to consumer goods would be fairly constantly a few percentage points short of the ideal, and that would be just a fact of business life that everyone took for granted. But the situation is not as favourable as this. There are branches of mathematics, such as queuing theory, that explain in abstract terms what businesspeople know from practical experience: the natural tendency of trivial supply chain glitches is often not to even themselves out, but to escalate into major calamities.

## THE BULLWHIP EFFECT

For instance, there is the *bullwhip effect*, by which small blips in demand at one point in a supply chain become amplified into larger swings further upstream. According to *The Economist*, the effect was first discovered by Procter & Gamble, which

> ... noticed an odd thing about Pampers, its well-known brand of disposable nappies: although the number of babies and the demand for nappies remained relatively stable, orders for Pampers fluctuated dramatically. This was because information about consumer demand can become increasingly distorted as it moves along the supply chain. For instance, a retailer may see a slight increase in demand for nappies, so he orders more from a wholesaler. The wholesaler than boosts his own sales forecast, causing the manufacturer to scale up production. But when the increase in demand turns out to have been only a blip, the supply chain is left with too much stock and orders are cut back.[9]

The deleterious consequences of the bullwhip effect can be massive. Cisco Systems, which makes networking equipment, was the world's most valuable company for a while in 2000; in 2001 it had to write off $2.2 billion worth of unsold production, and it reported its first quarterly loss since going public. The bursting of the dotcom bubble naturally led to a drop in demand, but it was the bullwhip effect that caused such a large mismatch between Cisco's output and what the end users of the equipment actually required.

## QUEUING THEORY

Then there is the relationship between capacity utilisation and waiting times. Think of a bus stop where buses arrive at regular intervals, and people show up to wait for a bus at a given average rate, but at irregular times

---

[9] 'Shining examples', *The Economist survey of logistics,* 17 June 2006.

varying round that average. If the capacity of the buses is much greater than the rate at which people come to the stop, then average waiting time is short because everyone can always get on the first bus to arrive. If the flow of people to the stop is closer to the capacity of the stream of buses, then some people may have to wait for a second or third bus before they reach the head of the queue and can board it: average waiting time goes up. But this increase will not be linear. As the flow of people approaches bus capacity, queuing theory shows that for a while the waiting time will increase slowly, and then suddenly it will shoot up (see Figure 11.1). The more irregular the flow of people arriving at the stop, the further to the left will be the point where the graph bends sharply upwards.

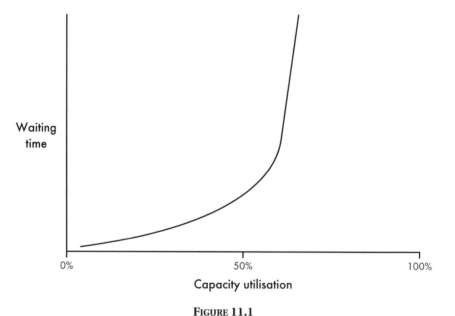

FIGURE 11.1

Now think of the passengers as a firm's clients (whether consumers or other firms). Even if the average rate at which they put in orders is stable, in most businesses the actual flow of orders will vary irregularly around that stable mean. The capacity of the buses (seats per hour) corresponds to the maximum rate at which the firm can produce output. If orders are very irregular (the bend in the graph is well over to the left), then some clients will face long delays before their order is fulfilled, unless the firm's capacity is far higher than the *average* rate of sales. Clients who find that a given supplier can rarely be relied on to deliver promptly will take their custom elsewhere. But adding extra capacity means expensive investment in larger premises, more equipment and staff and so on, much of which will often be underused. It is a difficult balancing act.

So there is plenty of scope for managing supply chains to bring them as close as possible to the ideal smooth-flowing scenario. That ideal can never be completely attained, but the financial implications of getting as close as practically possible rather than standing back and 'letting it all happen' can be huge.

## HUMAN *V.* AUTOMATIC SUPPLY-CHAIN OPTIMISATION

Many steps that can be taken to optimise supply chains could not be automated. These can range from things as basic as reducing the risk of interruptions to supply by developing relationships with more than one vendor of any essential component, to ensuring that the structure of incentives for different nodes in a supply chain tends to promote success of the chain as a whole. Narayanan and Raman (2004) comment:

> Companies often complain … that their supply chain partners don't seem to want to do what is in everyone's best interests, even when it's obvious what's best for the supply chain.

They explain that this is a frequent effect of misaligned incentives. For instance:

> In the late 1980s, Campbell Soup offered distributors discounts several times every year, hoping that the savings would be passed on to retailers. However, distributors bought more units than they sold to retailers, so Campbell's sales fluctuated wildly. For instance, the company sold 40% of its chicken noodle soup each of those years during six-week promotional periods. The uptick put a lot of pressure on the company's supply chain. When Campbell realized that it gathered data on distributors' purchases but not on their sales, it invested in information technology systems that could track both. Then, by giving the distributors discounts on sales but not on purchases, Campbell eliminated the incentive to forward-buy large quantities.

No-one suggests that business can turn over the task of formulating contracts or incentives to computers. Nevertheless, supply chain management, or supply chain planning (both phrases are used – the former seems more frequent, often abbreviated SCM, and we shall use this variant) is a recognised area of business IT. A survey in 2005 by the consultants Bain found that SCM systems are one of the genres of enterprise software with which users are most satisfied. Some leading vendors include i2, Manugistics and Retek. (As part of the recent wave of consolidation, Retek was acquired by Oracle in 2005 and Manugistics by JDA Software in 2006.)

However, this is not an area where a firm will typically acquire a single SCM system, implement it and job done. The situation is rather as described by David Taylor:

> Although supply chain management software forms a tidy category on industry analysts' charts, in reality, it's an odd conglomeration of packages from a variety of vendors, few of which are large and stable players.[10]

According to Taylor:

> The mainstay application is the advanced planning and scheduling (APS) system, which offers a mix of design and planning tools that use mathematical techniques to optimize the flow of goods across the chain. It generally includes separate planning modules for managing demand, distribution, production, material requirements, purchasing and fulfilment, all of which have some overlap with the modules of enterprise resource planning systems. Linking an APS system to an ERP system, although simple in principle, is a major integration project.

ERP is about things happening within one organisation, or at the interface between that organisation and its immediate suppliers, while SCM looks at longer segments of the overall chain; and ERP is about monitoring the transactions that actually occur, while SCM is about optimising the pattern of transactions, and about enabling managers to ask 'What if?' questions – how could the company guard itself cost-effectively against the risks of various unexpected changes in supply or demand? But we have seen that the various genres of enterprise application are tending to blend in to one another, and according to Taylor the distinction between ERP and SCM is dissolving as flagship ERP systems are extended in the SCM direction.

## EXTENDING INFLUENCE ALONG THE SUPPLY CHAIN

Optimising a many-step supply-chain segment clearly requires knowledge of and a degree of influence over distant steps, which will not always be the case. Hau Lee (2004: 106) describes how the clothing companies Zara and H&M order fabrics, based on rough sketches of new lines, as soon as their designers spot possible trends.

> That gives them a head start over competitors because fabric suppliers require the longest lead times. However, the companies finalize designs and manufacture garments only after they get reliable data from stores. That allows them to make products that meet consumer tastes and reduces the number of items they must sell at a discount.

---

[10] David A. Taylor, 'Supply chain vs. supply chain', *Computerworld* 10 November 2003.

A retailer that did not make its own garments, as Zara does, could achieve this only if its relationship with manufacturers was trusting enough for the latter to be willing to commit to purchases of fabrics destined to be made up into not-yet-finalised designs. SCM software can help a company to optimise those aspects of its supply chain that it can influence, but acquiring the influence is human work. Some commentators, though, feel that the benefits of optimised supply chains are so great that firms will be forced to collaborate in using common SCM systems that cross their organisational boundaries, in order to remain competitive. Already, Narayanan and Raman (2004) note that 'some organisations have made real-time sales data available throughout supply chains – and that was unimaginable five years ago'.

(Some business commentators have even taken to claiming that we are entering a world in which competition will be between supply chain and supply chain, rather than between individual firms. Although this may sound impressive, it is not altogether clear what it means – Rice and Hoppe (2001) suggest that it may not mean very much.)

## LEAN MANUFACTURING

At present, the fashion in business is for 'lean manufacturing': to minimise unproductive uses of capital, by squeezing inventory out of one's system, and by operating with the least capacity one can get away with. As the delivery of goods has become increasingly efficient and reliable, some firms have taken inventory reduction to the point where they

> carry no stock themselves but use the lorries and aircraft of firms like UPS and FedEx as warehouses on the road and in the sky.[11]

For a company that enjoys a strong bargaining position with its suppliers, it can be tempting to reduce its own inventory unilaterally by insisting that the suppliers deliver on a just-in-time basis; but that simply shifts the inventory buffer a stage upstream, forcing the suppliers to raise their prices. As Antti Wre of Nokia puts it:

> There's no point transferring your inventory to your suppliers, because they'll then have the inventory costs, and you'll see them showing up in your component prices. But if you can reduce the whole chain's inventory, then you will be very competitive.[12]

---

[11] 'Chain reaction', *The Economist* 17 June 2006.
[12] Quoted by Rob Rodin, 'Payback time for supply chains', *Optimize* December 2001.

If a multi-member supply chain is willing to cooperate to become competitive in this way, SCM tools are what allow them to adjust their mutual interactions to achieve that. And the leaner and hence more fragile the system is, the more need there is for risk-reducing SCM technology. Although Britain is at present behind some other large European countries in this area, business nowadays seems to be embracing that logic.

## EXPLOITING RFID DATA

We considered RFID technology in Chapter 4, in the context of consumer fears about loss of privacy. But although RFID has been in the news mainly in connection with the retail domain, that is not the leading area for RFID deployment. RFID is appropriately discussed at this point in the book, because its most important use to date has been in managing supply chains – both the paths linking company to company, and the paths along which items move upstream to downstream within a company.

RFID usage has not taken off as rapidly as expected. Nevertheless, the potential gains are clear. RFID tagging should make the distribution process more efficient; enable stock to be monitored with little human labour; combat pilferage; reduce inventory buffers; enable downstream businesses to accept accountability for the provenance of everything they handle (so that, for instance, a supermarket can identify the ultimate sources of each ingredient of a ready meal) ... the list goes on and on.

One problem has been cost. The tags have fallen in price dramatically (from about £1 each in 1999 to 6p or so in 2007), but although this is low enough for some applications it is still too high to attach tags routinely to individual low-value retail goods. There have also been problems about standards. For *closed-loop* applications, meaning that items are tracked only within a company, standards are irrelevant; but much of the benefit of the technology is expected to come from the ability to track goods all the way down company-to-company supply chains, which often extend across the globe, and the standards needed for that have taken longer to develop than anyone expected. And, in the hurly-burly of factory or warehouse environments, the technology does not yet work perfectly: in principle an RFID tag can be scanned at a distance without needing line-of-sight, but in practice a small percentage of scans fail, for instance because metal disturbs the signals. (One day, warehouses may routinely be built in an RFID-friendly way, but the technology is too new for that yet.)

Nevertheless, already RFID tags are coming into use in many ways – so far, more often (for cost reasons) at the level of tagging cases and pallets of goods than tagging the individual items they contain. By July 2006 a survey by Forrester Research showed that almost half the companies surveyed were using RFID to manage inventory in their warehouses. Those will mostly be closed-loop examples, but open-loop deployments are also beginning. In 2003 both the giant American retailer Wal-Mart and the

US Department of Defense decided to require their main suppliers to RFID-tag all deliveries – for Wal-Mart this went operational in January 2005. By some estimates, using RFID data to avoid 'stock-outs' (where a branch runs out of a given item) could add 3–4 per cent to Wal-Mart sales.

## RFID FOR MANAGING ASSETS

RFID tagging is being used not only to track trade goods moving down supply chains but also to manage business assets.

Airbus and Boeing have begun to use RFID to keep track of the maintenance history of their planes: any component that needs to be checked or replaced at set dates has a tag, and this is updated as the part's service history develops.

Tube Lines, the organisation that provides maintenance services for the London Underground, uses RFID tags to keep records on every maintainable element of the underground system – individual railway sleepers have tags showing when they were laid, when repaired and so forth. (In applications such as these, it is not necessary for the information to be stored on the RFID tag itself; in some cases it will be more efficient to keep the detailed records on a central database, indexed with a code number, which is all the tag contains.)

The budget airline Flybe is experimenting with the use of handheld RFID readers to speed up aircraft turnaround on the ground (a crucial issue for airline profitability) through faster checking that items such as lifejackets and safety manuals remain on board, as required by regulation.

In April 2005 the toolmaker Bosch began marketing tools with embedded RFID tags, together with readers and software to track where the tools are used – it adds a few percentage points to the price of the tools, but the worldwide construction industry is estimated to lose £550 million worth of tools to theft annually.

## AN AVALANCHE OF DATA

It might seem that discussing RFID applications is taking us some way away from computer science into the physical details of business operations. But the advance of RFID technology has important computing consequences. As RFID tags become widespread, and move from pallet-level to item-level usage, they will be generating torrents of data for which at present we have no real precedent. We saw that processing data from supermarket loyalty cards is like 'drinking from a firehose'. Imagine the situation once any carton of orange juice on a supermarket shelf has a tag that not merely identifies it as a carton of orange juice but also provides a detailed schedule showing when and on what farm the oranges were harvested, summarises the processing and transport history, identifies each additive, and so on. Dealing with data on this scale will be like drinking from Victoria Falls.

Much technical work currently is aimed at enabling RFID data to flow into enterprise applications. At the March 2006 annual RFID World event in Dallas, Sun announced a new version of Java System RFID Software that is integrated with SAP's Auto-ID Infrastructure technology, so that an ERP system can accept RFID data, and that is minimised in terms of code footprint, so that RFID data can be processed by devices such as handheld scanners (rather than having to be sent raw for processing centrally, clogging up networks). Meanwhile, Tesco as a leading early adopter has been shifting all its enterprise software onto a common platform, 'Tesco in a Box', designed in part to make integration of RFID data with existing applications more straightforward. But these moves are only the beginning. They direct Victoria Falls towards the drinking glasses, as it were. Developing good ways of abstracting usable information out of the torrents of data will be a continuing process over many decades.

## RFID IN THE RETAIL ARENA

At the retail level, RFID potentially offers much more than just control of shoplifting and automatic calculation of bills at the checkout. BT's Retail Enterprise division has a demonstration 'store of the future' in which shelves detect what products they are filled with and display details and prices to shoppers automatically, transmitting a replenishment request when needed. Zygmunt Mierdorf, chief information officer with the German-based Metro (a chain of more than 2500 department stores in 30 countries) comments:

> The vision isn't only for logistics and inventory management, it's about taking the technology deeper towards the customer, even after the sale, into warranty claims. It's about having the ability to track returns and trace merchandise to comply with regulatory issues, and product recalls and safety.[13]

In July 2007 the adventure park Alton Towers launched a new 'YourDay in the Park' service: visitors wear RFID-chipped bracelets that trigger cameras to record them on the rides and other attractions, which by the time they leave have been automatically compiled into a personalised souvenir record of the visit on DVD.

Retail applications that might be seen as more intrusive are being developed too, despite the history of consumer disquiet. Zeeshan-ul-hassan

---

[13] Quoted by Laurie Sullivan, 'European retailers take RFID further', *Computing* 17 March 2005.

Usmani of Princeton University is developing an RFID-based system for supermarkets that aims to exploit the herd instinct: people like to do what they know other people are doing. RFID data transmitted from the items in shoppers' trolleys are compiled into displays on the shelves showing how many people currently in the shop have picked a given item – where the number is high, others may be encouraged to buy on impulse. With interest from both Wal-Mart and Tesco, tests got under way in spring 2007. And an (unnamed) British retailer has been experimenting with CCTV cameras interacting with RFID tags, not to detect potential shoplifters but to monitor what items shoppers pick up and then put back, and what paths they take through the shop, with a view to optimising the layout of shelves and positioning of products.

## E-PROCUREMENT

A firm does not need to buy in only the raw materials or parts that it processes into the finished products that it sells. To do its job, it also needs to buy many other kinds of thing, ranging from capital equipment such as heavy machinery to maintenance and repair supplies, office furniture, stationery, travel and so on. Buying these things is called *procurement*, and it is normally treated as a separate business issue from buying the materials that go into the products. Procurement activity will typically be more dispersed across a company, and less regular, than purchasing of production supplies; and until recently, optimising the procurement process has not typically been seen as a business priority.

Nevertheless, procurement costs represent a large share of a firm's outgoings, so there is considerable scope for increasing profitability by using *e-procurement* systems to reduce those costs. A leading supplier is Ariba.

The essence of an e-procurement system is an application running on the terminal of any employee authorised to make purchases, giving access to the catalogues of approved suppliers, and offering a simple mechanism for placing orders.

Nobody suggests that this is an especially subtle use of IT. But, for companies that use e-procurement, it can be a valuable one. Traditionally, procurement has been an inefficient aspect of business operations, based on complex paper systems that use up large quantities of salaried staff time for transactions that, individually, can sometimes be for tiny amounts: just the kind of scenario for which IT is made. Furthermore, e-procurement makes it easy for managers to analyse overall company spending patterns; with distributed procurement it is quite difficult to work out where money is draining away. Steve Singleton is senior manager of the consultant Accenture's supply-chain practice; in 2007 he commented:

> As procurement professionals you need to know where you spend your money to support the business at a more strategic level. Many large companies still can't push a button and find out who is buying what against which contracts.[14]

When British Airways adopted Ariba procurement software in 2003, it cut £300 million off its annual procurement budget of £4 billion. The University of Edinburgh, astonishingly, reduced its overall purchasing costs by 25 per cent via e-procurement by 2006.

## ONLINE B2B AUCTIONS

In about 2000–1, Ariba began to move beyond straightforward fixed-price purchasing support into the field of B2B auctions, offering a 'Dynamic Trading' system that aimed to increase liquidity in the market by making it easy for companies to bargain with one another, not only on the price of goods but also on non-price features such as exact specifications, delivery dates and so forth.

After the dotcom bubble burst, B2B online auctions lost impetus for a while. But, from an economist's point of view, auctions make a lot of sense: they are an efficient, rapid way to discover the point where the vendors' supply schedule crosses buyers' demand schedule. Later in the decade, e-auctions revived; in 2003 eBay launched a B2B version, eBay Business. By now, online auctions are a major feature of B2B trading. Many variants are possible: auctions can be *public* (a company advertises its intention to purchase goods or services on a public website appropriate to its industry sector) or *private* (a large company invites bids only from its preferred group of suppliers); and they can be *forward* auctions in which suppliers invite bids from buyers, or *reverse* auctions in which buyers invite tenders from suppliers. In the early days of online B2B auctions, they were used mainly for low-value goods such as stationery; but, in principle, anything traded between organisations may be traded via auction, and online techniques can make the process much simpler.

Some organisations are making impressive savings. Cancer Research UK reported in July 2006 that after its first 12 months of buying office supplies and lab equipment via e-auctions it had saved £2.5 million out of its total purchasing budget of £130 million; over the next few years it expected the saving to increase to 10 per cent of total budget, and it was considering extending the same online system to acquire temporary office staff. The agency that acquires IT and communications systems on behalf of the Ministry of Defence was reported in March 2005 to have cut

---

[14] Quoted by Linda More, 'Buying the best', *Computing* 28 June 2007.

£4.2 million off a planned spend of £12.5 million over 31 months by means of online auctions.

Organisations gain not only by paying lower prices but by reducing the time and effort needed for traditional procurement. In February 2005 BP reported an average cost saving of 4 per cent, but a 25 per cent saving of admin time, by using e-auctions. And although commonly an e-auction relates to 'commodity' goods that are specified in precise detail, so that the only question is who will offer the lowest price, they can be used in more subtle ways. In 2005 British Airways announced an auction to choose a firm to provide its European public relations. PR firms vary in many important respects other than their fees; but, by using an e-auction, BA could discover each firm's best and final offer on fees, and use that information along with many other considerations to pick the company it would go with.

It might seem that e-auctions are good for buyers but bad for sellers – they just drive prices down. Probably there is more for the buyers to gain, but it is claimed that there are advantages for sellers too. Traditional procurement often involved an element of favouritism: company buyers might develop relationships with a few trusted supplier representatives, so that it was hard for a newcomer to break in even with good-value offers. And buyers tended to be economical with the truth as they tried to play off competing suppliers against one another; suppliers sometimes prefer the transparency and honesty of online auctions.

## TOO MANY GENRES TO LIST

There are further genres of enterprise software application that we have not examined. *Product lifecycle management* systems (two suppliers were MatrixOne and Dassault Systèmes, which merged in March 2006) support managers through the equipment and financial consequences of bringing a new product to market and later winding down in favour of a next-generation replacement. *Strategic management* software, such as the applications supplied by Clarity Systems, has been the most widely used single genre of enterprise application for many years; an April 2005 survey by the consultants Bain showed that managers are more satisfied with their strategic management systems than with any other genre. And one could go on. But we have now seen a fair spectrum of the kinds of application in the marketplace, and this has been enough to provide an understanding of the ways in which business activity is being modified by the advent of IT.

There would be little to gain by listing every category that some vendor identifies as a distinct application. Particularly in view of the movement towards blending diverse applications into integrated suites, which we examined in Chapter 8, this kind of categorisation is becoming less meaningful.

# 12 Web Services

## A NEW BUZZWORD

Since about 2002, *web services* has become one of the hottest buzzwords in the e-business vocabulary, and it was joined slightly later by the related phrase *service-oriented architecture* (SOA). As so often happens, once these phrases became fashionable they began to be attached to almost anything and everything that some IT vendor was trying to promote, so that they risked being drained of any clear meaning.

Yet behind the hype there is a real, significant new concept here, which is being translated into valuable business activity more slowly and uncertainly than originally expected, but which is gradually becoming a reality. A decade or so from now, it could well look like the most significant development in e-business since the creation of the World Wide Web.

The best way to explain the fundamental concept behind 'web services' is in fact by analogy with the creation of the web.

What the World Wide Web offers, in essence, is a way by which anyone connected to the internet can display documents in straightforwardly readable form to anyone else connected to the internet, without prior arrangement, and can help readers (via links) to find other documents. Before the web with its file format (hypertext markup language, HTML) and transmission protocol (hypertext transmission protocol, HTTP) had been invented, an IT expert who was told by some prophet that a system for doing these things was on the way might well have answered that it was not needed: these things had been possible for years. Data files had been exchanged since the beginnings of the internet. Text documents and graphics are represented electronically simply as long streams of bits, and anyone aware of the format used to encode a given document into bits could readily apply the appropriate software to decode it back into a human-friendly text or picture. To include internet addresses in documents is trivial. 'What would this "web" give us that we haven't already got?', the 1980s IT expert might have asked.

I remember hearing a talk explaining the World Wide Web in about 1991, and thinking that it sounded mildly interesting, without having any conception of just how large an innovation it was destined to be. All the things it does could in a sense be done already; but they were technically complex things, which IT experts needed skill to execute, and between any pair of individuals wanting to exchange documents there needed to be an understanding about things such as which particular formats would be used for encoding.

The big differences now we have the web are that, in the first place, strangers can exchange documents 'without having been introduced', as we might put it in terms of a social metaphor – no prior agreements at all are needed with the people or organisations from whom one downloads webpages; and also, no skill or time-consuming activity are needed to read material on the web. Doing so is as quick and easy as clicking a mouse button, and another click lets you follow a link without examining the URL to which the link points. Even putting one's own material on the web, though it is slightly more challenging, is one of the easiest IT techniques for non-technical people to master.

As a result, a channel of communication that in practice was limited to partners who were technically competent and had some relationship with one another – they had 'been introduced' – is now routinely used for communication between arbitrary strangers. In 1991 I did not foresee the significance of that, because computers were for technical people; it was beyond my imagining that the average family home would one day contain a computer connected to the internet. Largely because of the web, nowadays they do.

## LIMITATIONS OF ELECTRONIC DATA INTERCHANGE

All this is about people providing human-usable inputs (documents) to other people. 'Web services' is about computers providing inputs to software running on other, distant computers. (The name 'web services' is not well-chosen – the technology is separate from the World Wide Web, and it applies to trade in goods as well as services.) It happens now – between computers that have 'been introduced', and with some time and effort on the part of competent IT staff to set the arrangement up. The web services vision – which is starting to become more than a vision – is that an innovation analogous to the web will allow such things to happen routinely, with no time, human effort or prior arrangements required.

In business, computers provide input to software on distant computers for instance via *electronic data interchange* (EDI). A company orders goods from a supplier, say, via an electronic purchase order in a standardised coded format, rather than via a sheet of paper designed to be read by a human. The data is moved by so-called *value-added network* companies over privately owned wide area networks (WANs).

In most business sectors the shift to EDI is itself recent and incomplete. Robert Johnston *et al.* (2001: 236) still presented as a currently ongoing 'paradigm shift' the change in perception

> … from the earlier vision of computers as intelligent logic engines (to be applied to problem solving and planning), to a view of computers as a medium for communication and co-ordination between parties and business transactions.

For many small companies, moving from manual to EDI systems would involve costs that are difficult for them to afford, even if they would like to make the transition.

EDI is very much a going concern. But it is starting to look like an evolutionary dead end. There are two problems about it. One is that using proprietary networks is expensive, when the internet is available as a cheap alternative communication channel. The deeper problem is that the system of holding data in individual company file formats and translating between these and various industry standard formats is inherently inflexible and unrobust, and EDI presupposes a prior agreement between specific pairs of organisations to use EDI in defined ways. In these respects EDI is like exchanging human-readable documentation over the internet, before the web.

## A WEB-SERVICE EXAMPLE

What would become possible, with a computer-to-computer analogue of the web, that has not been practically possible until now? An early writer on the topic of web services, William Oellermann (2001), invited us to imagine a specific scenario: a businessman returning to the airport to get home after a work trip. Because of traffic hold-ups, he realises that he will miss his flight. If he carries on regardless, perhaps there will be a later flight; but perhaps the next flight is tomorrow morning, and he should instead focus on finding a room for the night. If so, he would have various special requirements – say, he would need a data line for his work, and he would want a room that is set aside for non-smokers. Sorting all this out would take a number of separate phone calls – or website visits, assuming he has wireless internet access. Meanwhile, what should he say to the taxi driver?

How much simpler if he could visit just one website and let its systems sort everything out, with the airline's site negotiating with hotel sites as required.

In theory, that has been possible for a long time – but only in the sense that person-to-person document exchange was possible before the web. In practice, it didn't happen. Oellermann described how, at the turn of the century, he found himself puzzling why he was not seeing an explosive rush to B2B automation, comparable to the rush to build company websites that had already occurred.

One barrier was technical. As already said, web technology is simple to master; B2B automation requires business expertise, to grasp the detailed logic of the transactions to be automated, and also IT expertise, to implement systems in an environment where there were few high-level standards, so every detail had to be decided ad hoc.

But the other, very significant barrier was political. Even when partner organisations are on an equal footing, achieving detailed collaboration and agreement between people working at different sites for separate employers is always massively harder and more time-consuming than when the individuals concerned work in a face-to-face situation; that is just a fact of life. In this case, perhaps more importantly, the technology was making it hard for B2B partners to relate to one another equally even if they wanted to.

## WHY NOT JUST USE THE WEB?

One might think that active collaboration should not be necessary in order to use web communication infrastructure for providing input to software. The web does not physically require agents accessing it to be human beings. Nothing prevents someone setting up a program that downloads web pages and uses the information contained in them as software inputs. Nothing, except that it would not work. Web pages are fluid. Their design and contents are frequently changed, to make them more appealing or more useful, and they rely on visitors' human understanding to interpret the graphically rendered HTML files and pick out the wanted information from a page that may have altered since the last visit. As Oellermann put it, a program designed to extract data from an airline's website might well find, after the next tweak to the site, that it was receiving information on a flight departing at b>07 rather than 0748.

So it will not work to treat a website set up for presenting information in human-usable form as a source of software input. Of course, an airline website could help visitors to find hotel rooms by treating hotel websites as they are designed to be treated: that is, by including links on the airline website that take the visitor to the hotels' sites. But that would not be very satisfactory either for the airline (no company wants to encourage visitors to its site to leave for other sites) or for the visitor – in Oellermann's scenario he would still be making the web-equivalent of separate phone calls, though with the minor advantage of having each calling partner 'dial the next number' for him. Suppose tomorrow's flight is delayed for some reason: the airline will have no way of sending a message to the traveller's hotel to tell him that he can take longer than planned over breakfast – the airline has no way of knowing whether one of the hotel website links it offered led to a room booking.

The airline could collaborate with a range of local hotels to develop a jointly owned website. This might solve these problems, but in a way that the companies would find unappealing. Within such a consortium it is inevitable that content relating to one company's business will often have to reside on a server owned or physically controlled by another consortium member, so the companies will see themselves as surrendering ultimate control over core aspects of their own businesses. And an arrangement like this would be inflexible. Adding another hotel to the airline's offerings could happen only after successful completion of negotiations to admit the new member to the consortium. Contrast that with a case where an airline offers benighted travellers a printed list of local hotels: a new hotel advertises its details to all comers, and if the airline wants to add it to the list it just does so, with no hassle. (In practice, an airline might well make a deal with hotels that want to be included on its list – but it does not need to.)

## MACHINE SHALL SPEAK UNTO MACHINE

What web services offers is an approach to integrating different organisations' applications that exploits those aspects of web technology that remain relevant to the new goal (the communication channel linking unrelated agents, and the concept of a universally accepted file format), but marries them to new technologies to handle aspects of the new tasks that go beyond exchanging documentation.

In the web-services model, organisations have a standardised way to 'expose' software interfaces that they choose to allow outsiders to provide input to, and a standardised format playing the role that HTML plays for the web, in which one organisation's software can encode output to be used as input to a 'stranger' organisation's software.

It would not be appropriate in this non-technical book to go into details of the various conventions and formats involved in defining the web services environment, but one of the central components is XML (eXtensible Markup Language). Like HTML, XML is a markup language allowing the logical structure of a data file to be explicitly specified; but whereas HTML permits markup in terms of units such as 'paragraph', 'heading', 'image' and so forth, relevant for defining the structure of a human-readable document, XML allows user communities to define their own logical units – so they can be business-relevant categories such as 'order', 'invoice', 'part number', 'cost per unit', 'delivery address' and so on. And, with XML, a file specifies the grammar of the class of data files of which it is an instance, so that corruptions in transmission can be detected automatically – a corruption in transmission will normally cause a file no longer to fit the *document type definition* it claims to instantiate, so the receiving machine can ignore it rather than attempting to use it as input. If the HTML code defining a webpage is corrupted, then someone trying to use a browser to read the page will see a mess that, to a human, makes little sense, so human judgement can be used to ignore the page. Computers lack judgement, and if they tried to run corrupted inputs mayhem would ensue. XML compensates for machines' lack of judgement by providing a mechanical way to check that incoming files 'make sense'.

Thus, in the near future, the traveller will visit the airline website and discover that his next available flight is on the following day. The site will offer a hotspot labelled <u>Find me a hotel room</u>; clicking on this will not cause the traveller's browser to move to a hotel's website – instead, it will cause software on the airline's server to exchange XML files over the internet with various hotel servers. After asking the traveller about his specific requirements, the airline server will look for a suitable vacancy, make a reservation when one is found and report back to the traveller accordingly. Airline and hotel both know about the transaction; if the next day's flight is delayed, it is a simple matter for the airline's system to ask the hotel's system to pass a message to the traveller. When a new hotel opens for business, it will add details about its web-based reservation system to the public web services register. Airlines will be free to add it to the list of sites that their site negotiates with, when someone clicks the Find me a room button.

Or consider a rather more complex scenario from B2B trading suggested by *The Economist*:

> Imagine ... that a company receives an electronic order. The software application that takes these orders must first ensure that the customer has an adequate credit history. It therefore consults a directory of Web services, finds an application from an independent firm that checks credit ratings, contacts this application and finds out that the customer is a reliable debtor. Next, the software consults the directory again, this time to find an internal application that keeps track of inventory in the warehouse, and finds that the product is in store. Now it goes back to the directory and looks for an external billing service, and so forth until the entire transaction is closed.[1]

(The term 'service-oriented architecture', or SOA, is used in a rather vague way to refer to a computing environment centred on web services like these. The business analyst company Gartner defines SOA as a way of designing software so that applications are decomposed into separate services.[2] The textbook author David Whiteley (2004: 254) prefers to define SOA as referring to the combination of a web-service requester machine, a web-service provider machine and a service registry. To my mind the term 'SOA' adds nothing to the concept 'web services', and I shall stick to the latter terminology.)

In the software-as-a-service model discussed in Chapter 6, software is run on one site in order for its results to be used at another site, but normally that use will involve human intervention. Some commentators are beginning to suggest that SaaS should be seen as an intermediate step away from traditional on-premises client/server IT towards a widespread deployment of web services.

## LOOSE COUPLINGS

One advantage of the web services model, as originally envisaged, was that it should lead to much more flexibility in forming and re-forming trading

---

[1] 'If in doubt, farm it out', *The Economist* 30 October 2004.
[2] Douglas Hayward, 'Software design finds a fresh path to follow', *Computing* 4 September 2003.

partnerships between firms in response to changing circumstances and needs. We have seen that one consequence of IT for B2B commerce has been to change the industrial landscape from one of separate companies like walled cities, set far apart and communicating sparingly, to a situation where companies frequently collaborate almost as intimately as work-groups within a single company. That has economic advantages, but it also has disadvantages. It tends to tie in companies to their existing partnerships, even when more value could be created by breaking some current links and forming other links with new partners. When partnerships are forged by human beings, they take a great deal of time and effort to put in place. If machines can find suitable partner machines across the internet, without human involvement, links can quickly and easily be formed and dissolved in response to the needs of the moment.

In the paper that introduced the business world to web services technology, John Hagel III and John Seely Brown (2001) anticipated that

> With the Web services architecture, tight couplings will be replaced with loose couplings. Because everyone will share the same standards for data description and connection protocols, applications will be able to talk freely with other applications, without costly reprogramming. This will make it much easier for companies to shift operations and partnerships in response to market or competitive stimuli.

They concluded:

> Over time, the location of particular capabilities – whether inside or outside the walls of any given company – will become less important than the ability to discover and orchestrate distinctive capabilities across enterprises in order to deliver greater value to customers.

Bruce Harreld, IBM's senior vice-president of strategy, commented in 2003 that 'About 42 per cent of a typical IT budget goes towards integration. Yet still there is a lack of integration.'[3] Web services promises to make integrating separate computer systems far easier and cheaper.

## WHAT IS HAPPENING NOW

The airline/hotel scenario and *The Economist*'s scenario are only examples, but it hardly makes sense to ask in general what range of tasks web services could be used to address. That would be like asking what a computer can be programmed to do: the answer is 'anything that can be stated

---

[3] Quoted by Brian Glick, 'The next era of IT will be based upon integration', *ITWeek* 26 June 2003.

as a well-defined algorithm'. What can be done is to indicate a few ways in which web services are already being used.

Since 2002, Amazon has exposed some of its software, such as the system for searching its product databases, so that developers of other sites can use the data to generate content on their own sites. They take the Amazon data about product details, what other customers have bought, and so forth, and digest it into some form directly relevant to their own site; if display of this material leads to a sale, Amazon pays the other site a commission.

Again since 2002, the packaging manufacturer Rexam has been exposing its ordering, fulfilment, invoicing and payments systems internally to one another and also, where relevant, externally to its customers, cutting out a large amount of paperwork and rekeying.

By 2005, British Airways had incorporated links to third-party businesses such as hotels and car hire into its site in something like the way envisaged by Oellermann.

In June 2007, Google agreed to provide web services to Salesforce's online CRM clients. A Salesforce user will be able to sign up, on the Salesforce site, to buy sponsored Google listings in response to particular keywords in search strings, and when a Google user clicks on their sponsored listing, the Salesforce software will set about gathering information from the Google user to pass to the advertiser's sales team for them to follow up.

## UNSOLVED PROBLEMS

These and other existing examples by no means add up yet to the scenario originally envisaged, though. One reason why web services have been slow to take off is that the various standards needed in order to ensure that unrelated companies' machines can talk to each other successfully have been slow to jell. The World Wide Web needed only HTML and HTTP. For web services, we have had XML for a decade, and by now we have a fairly well-worked-out version of the Web Services Description Language (WSDL) that enables the technical and contractual aspects of a web service to be specified in machine-readable form – version 2.0 was finalised in mid-2007; but web services need further protocols relating to security, transaction certification and so on. For a while it began to look as though rival sets of conventions might evolve. That risk was addressed seriously only in 2003, when IBM and Microsoft jointly announced a range of protocols (subsequently nicknamed 'WS splat') that they would be using, and lesser players have consequently accepted.

It is also true, though, that the examples that have emerged so far are not really typical of the possibilities anticipated in the original vision. The issue of universally agreed protocols has largely been solved, but the idea of web service connections happening between arbitrary machines – computers that 'haven't been introduced' – is barely happening yet. To date most use of web services is internal to single organisations. Adding a defined universal interface to diverse systems is often a relatively painless way for an organisation to get a complex range of software, including old-fashioned but functional Cobol programs, to interact with one another. The real-life examples quoted above do mostly cross company boundaries, but they do not link stranger companies; these examples were (or will be) put in place after negotiations between staff of specific companies.

The extract in *The Economist* referred to a computer consulting a 'directory of Web services' to locate providers of the services it needed. Clearly, the 'stranger to stranger' type of web-services links cannot happen without some way for would-be service-user machines to find suitable suppliers in cyberspace, just as human users of the web need search engines to locate the information they are looking for. An industry-wide consortium called UDDI (Universal Description, Discovery and Integration) was launched in 2001 to develop such a directory, but to date the UDDI register has not evolved in the way initially intended. (In March 2007 an individual firm, Iona Technologies, released its own attempt to provide the software framework for a web-services registry, under the name Artix – the fact that Iona felt it worth offering its system demonstrates that UDDI has not panned out.)

Even if the registry problem can be solved, another large barrier to stranger-to-stranger web services is security. This scarcely needs spelling out. Putting it bluntly, if unrelated organisations' computers are going to be interacting and running each other's software with their own inputs, then who knows what they may be saying or doing to one another? Ronald Schmelzer, senior analyst at ZapThink, comments:

> XML and Web services cut through firewalls and email-based filters like a hot knife through butter. Existing routers do not inspect the content at the level necessary to deal with XML-based virus and content-based attacks ...[4]

## AN OPTIMISTIC CONSENSUS

It might seem that the security issue is so worrying that it will prevent the web services vision from ever being realised. That is not the consensus. Few sectors are as obsessive about security as banking. Alan Jebson was (before retirement in 2006) chief operating officer for the HSBC banking group, and no pushover for technology hype, and yet in 2002 he commented:

---

[4] Quoted by Jason Compton, 'Web services builds a case for usability and reliability', *Computing* 26 May 2005.

> I'm a technology cynic. I've been in this business long enough to
> have watched it over-promise and under-deliver for ... years, so
> I immediately treat any hype as just that. [Nevertheless,] The last great
> technology breakthrough was the relational database, but web
> services could be in the same category. I really do believe it will be
> revolutionary.[5]

(Readers who understand the role of the relational database in business
computing will appreciate how strong a statement Jebson was making.)
By 2005 the reasons for caution about expecting rapid and comprehensive
web-services deployments were well understood, but in June of that year
the analysts AMR Research saw the ERP market as entering

> ... a major technology-transition phase in which service-oriented
> architectures are likely to transform the technology as much as the
> emergence of client–server systems did in the 1990s.[6]

If that is right, then not only the technology but also the nature of typical
computing careers will be affected. I have already suggested that, in future,
computing jobs are likely to involve less coding and more involvement with
management issues and orchestration of pre-existing packages. It is the
move to web services above all that is set to bring about this change.

## EVOLUTIONARY COMPUTING MEETS E-BUSINESS

There was an extreme version of the original web services vision that
perhaps no-one believes in any more. A clear example was an initiative by
Hewlett-Packard at the end of the 1990s, which they called 'e-Services'.
This drew on an artificial intelligence technique known as *evolutionary
computing*. Software to achieve tasks that may be too complex for human
beings to program successfully is instead *evolved* through a Darwinian
process in which populations of simple programs mutate randomly and
are weeded out, or multiply, depending on how far they develop features
approximating to the desired target. Hewlett-Packard's e-Services might
be described as 'evolutionary computing meets e-business'.

A useful commercial service is a complex structure that can be logically
decomposed into a number of simple, generic services and electronic
resources marshalled together in a specific way. An e-service was an
electronic agent that represented one of those modular elements, and that
could describe itself over the internet, using a language Hewlett-Packard

---

[5] Quoted in *Computing*, 12 September 2002.
[6] 'Major change ahead for ERP', *Computing* 23 June 2005.

called e-Speak, to other such agents in other ownership. It could advertise itself, discover complementary services or resources supplied by others, and agree bargains on behalf of its owner.

A human might assemble a group of e-services together manually into a structure capable of delivering a human-level, complex service. But, excitingly, the e-services could band together of their own accord to offer complex services, perhaps services different from anything a human had yet thought of. Peter Gloor (2000: 129) noted that 'HP hopes that entire ecosystems of e-services will grow and change dynamically as new e-services advertise their capabilities over the Net.' The internet might become not merely an arena where people can implement their business ideas, but an active participant generating new business ideas of its own. One could perhaps draw an analogy with biological life forms gradually emerging from a 'primaeval soup' of simple chemical building blocks.

## LEVELS OF PRIOR AGREEMENT

Hewlett-Packard eventually ceased pursuing e-Services as a proprietary initiative and handed over the work already carried out to an industry-wide consortium developing the web services concept, largely in a less science-fiction style. The dream exemplified by e-Services continued to motivate some of the effort devoted to this area, though. The reason why it seems unlikely ever to be more than a dream was explained by Andrew McAfee (2005).

McAfee points out that there are different levels of prior agreement needed before the internet can be used for business interactions. If (1) the agents linked by the internet are human beings, then only a low level of agreement is needed, because human intellectual flexibility and intuition can fill in the higher levels on the fly:

> As soon as the Web's engineers finalized its transport protocols, the rest of us quickly began using it to send messages to each other and browse Web sites. We didn't need to sit down in advance and agree on whether sentences in e-mails would always begin with capital letters or on whether all e-commerce sites would include shopping carts and personalized recommendations.

But if (2) the agents are machines, lacking human understanding, then prior agreement is needed about message structures and contents; and if (3) the machine–machine interactions consist of more than a single step, then further prior agreement is needed about business-process parameters. McAfee says that existing technologies used for web services, such as XML, offer only the lowest level of agreement:

> … just as HTML doesn't predetermine what kind of pictures or text
> should go on a page (Level 2) or in what order pages should be viewed
> (Level 3), XML doesn't predefine the set of valid e-documents (Level 2)
> or business processes (Level 3).

That does not mean that these higher levels of agreement might not be created in future. A large consortium of technology companies, RosettaNet, has been working since 1998 to define a standard, non-proprietary framework for processing business transactions between companies electronically – a framework that would cover McAfee's Levels 2 and 3. For a given business sector, RosettaNet defines a master 'dictionary' specifying properties that characterise products, trading partners and transaction types, cutting through the confusion that can arise from companies using idiosyncratic terminology. It also defines a standard range of *Partner Interface Processes* (PIPs), so that the kinds of interaction that occur between companies can be specified and understood the same way at both ends. In an early version, for instance, PIP2A2 was 'Query Product Information'; this, and any other PIP, specifies a business document with the vocabulary of the message dialogue, and a business process with its 'choreography'. Using the standard battery of PIPs, interactions that previously had to be executed manually can be automated: the 'choreography' lays down which moves are expected from the respective partners at which stage, so the dance can proceed with neither partner stepping electronically on the other's toes. (Microsoft's 'BizTalk' is a proprietary attempt to achieve somewhat similar goals.)

Whether developments like RosettaNet and BizTalk will eventually lead to the kind of stranger-to-stranger web-services scenario originally envisaged depends both on solving technical problems and on the business benefits achievable. McAfee uses a case study to argue that even if the technical problems could be solved, stranger-to-stranger web services will not happen: the technology will in practice be restricted to company-internal applications, or to 'hierarchical' situations in which a large company has sufficient clout to persuade its trading partners to put effort into collaborating on web services.

> Why not invest only in tools to facilitate human–human and human–application interactions, which are cheaper, much easier and faster to put in place, very flexible and clearly helpful?
>
> Web-services advocates often suggest that anyone asking these questions 'just doesn't get it,' but in many cases unenthusiastic companies actually *do* get it. They've evaluated the costs and benefits
> *(Continued)*

*(Continued)*

(both current and potential) of the new technologies and have concluded that they aren't worth pursuing.

(McAfee 2005: 82)

Nicholas Carr makes a broader objection to the web services vision, arguing that it

... reveals a common shortcoming in the thinking of technologists: their tendency to confuse business with information processing, to want to see companies as, in essence, computers. They overlook, or give short shrift to, the physical and human characteristics of commercial organizations – to all the things that can't be reduced to digital code, that can't be 'exposed' or 'made transparent' through networks.

(Carr 2004: 103)

The shortsightedness identified by Carr is indeed a besetting sin of technologists. How far Carr's point undermines the entire web services concept is open to question, though. Not everything in business can be reduced to digital code; but much can.

## FORMAL LANGUAGES AND BUSINESS INNOVATION

Whether the business logic will justify McAfee's negative conclusion about web services will depend in part on how solvable the technical problems are. But there is a question there also.

The software which, in *The Economist*'s words, 'describe[s] what the component inside is and what it does' must use an agreed language or languages capable of defining the nature of whatever services may be offered via the common directory. The existing Web Services Description Language concerns itself only with technical and contractual issues – points such as 'this is the form of request required from a would-be trading partner', 'this is the time-period for which my offer remains valid', and so forth. Initiatives like RosettaNet are endeavouring to develop formal languages to define the actual business content of web services, but these can only hope to cover offerings that are thoroughly 'commoditised'. One city-centre hotel room geared to overnight stays on business trips may be much like another – once a few basic features, such as travelling time from the airport, are specified, all the data needed in order to go ahead with a room booking is available. But new businesses commonly aim to fill 'gaps in the market', suggesting that they will often contain elements of novelty.

When businesses market novel products or services, it would presum-ably not be possible to define them adequately in a formal language created before the business innovation occurred. (Expecting to be able to do so would be rather like expecting classical Latin to have translations for 'diesel engine' or 'television'.) The dream of complex new business forms emerging like living species from a primaeval cyber-soup ignores the crucial role of human intellectual creativity in business advance.

## DISPOSABLE APPLICATIONS

Still, a great deal of business activity does involve commoditised goods and services, and in those cases there is no conceptual problem about replacing human-to-human or human-to-machine with machine-to-machine business interactions. How far, and in which ways, web services develop depends mainly on how well the technical issues are addressed and on the matters of business advantage discussed by McAfee. Within companies, web services are already becoming a reality. At the inter-company level, whether web services develop beyond relationships between known partners into the stranger-to-stranger scenario is at present an open question.

Certainly, companies by now believe that web services are the way of the future. A February 2007 report by the business analysts Forrester found that SOA is now European companies' third software-spending priority, behind only application-integration projects and security initiatives. Application integration allows data to move smoothly between particular pairs of applications, but web services offers the possibility of data flowing between *any* applications: according to the analyst Jon Collins, 'What everyone wants is to have web service interfaces to all packaged services.'[7] It is all taking much longer than anticipated – a September 2007 survey of technology professionals showed a high proportion who felt that their companies' benefits from SOA investment had to date fallen short of expectations – but the consensus remains enthusiastic for the long term.

Even the concept of a universal web-services register allowing component services to be assembled on the fly into one-time applications (which might have sounded like science fiction) is now being taken very seriously. According to the journalist Mark Samuels, in mid-2006 the analysts Gartner were

> ... predict[ing] that by 2010 more than 80 per cent of new applications will be composed of assembled service components, and suggest[ing] that the useful life of applications will continue to shrink to the 'seemingly absurd limits' of just-in time and disposable applications.[8]

If these predictions turn out to be even half correct, then the business computing environment in the near future will be very different from today.

---

[7] Quoted by William Knight, 'Communication cord', *Computing* 20 July 2006.
[8] Mark Samuels, 'Your new software: best before ...', *Computing* 3 August 2006.

# 13 The Open Source Movement

Since IT became crucial to business, software has standardly been treated like other business supplies. Just as a company needing to install a piece of apparatus or machinery will either purchase it from an outside manufacturer or get it built by its own technicians, so when software is needed the company will either buy a standard package from a software house or employ programmers to write it.

Software is an unusual kind of business supply, though. Champions of the open source movement believe that buying and selling software like capital equipment or consumable supplies is the wrong economic model: software is not that kind of thing at all. Society will get substantially less benefit from computer technology than it should, while people persist in this false perception of how software fits into the economic structure.

For many years, advocates of 'free software' were seen by the sober business community as naively impractical idealists. More recently, though, the case has been argued in hard-nosed terms that make sense to economists and businesspeople, and free software has been colonising economic niches that previously were occupied by paid-for systems developed by Microsoft and other orthodox players. A point of view that seemed naive if not plain silly is being taken seriously.

Some even see the open source movement as potentially world-changing. Eric Raymond's (2001) *The Cathedral and the Bazaar*, the leading statement of the open-source thesis, was described on its cover by the venture capitalist Guy Kawasaki as 'The most important book about technology today.' The political scientist Steven Weber (2004: 7) calls open source 'in some ways the first and certainly one of the most prominent indigenous political statements of the digital world'.

## A PARTING OF THE WAYS

Thirty years ago, the concept of software as a tradable commodity scarcely existed. Computer hardware was manufactured and sold; companies that wanted to computerise bought the hardware and employed programmers to make it do what they wanted (the tasks commonly being specific to the particular organisation). Hardware manufacturers such as IBM supplied operating-system software and languages bundled with their machines, but these were not treated as separate marketable packages – they were things you had to have to make the machine do anything. Individuals with access to computers through their work had fun writing hobby programs, which they swapped freely with other enthusiasts. Not until the early 1980s did it become normal to buy software applications separately from hardware.

The split between contrasting views of software as property is graphically described in Steven Levy's (1984) *Hackers*. 'Hackers' in the original sense were youngsters who became passionate about mastering the workings of computers, in days when tiny memories and lack of modern user interfaces meant that getting the machines to do anything interesting required a lot of abstruse technical know-how. (The alternative sense of hackers as people who intrude into other people's systems had not yet emerged – some writers reserve 'hacker' for the former sense and distinguish the bad guys as 'crackers'.)

Levy describes the communities of enthusiasts who coalesced at places such as MIT and Berkeley, California, as evolving a 'hacker ethic' whose axioms included 'Mistrust authority', 'Access to computing ... should be unlimited' and 'All information should be free'. Within that cultural background, when in 1975 a group of these youngsters who had purchased one of the earliest home computers (the Altair) went to a meeting that demonstrated a high-level language (Basic) running on it, it seemed unobjectionable to 'borrow' one of the paper tapes containing the code and duplicate it for club members' benefit.

The teenager who, with a friend, had coded Altair Basic and sold it to the manufacturer was a college dropout called Bill Gates. To him this was straightforward theft. He published an open letter in hacker newsletters:

> ... most of you steal your software... Who can afford to do professional work for nothing? What hobbyist can put three man-years into programming, finding all the bugs, documenting his product and distributing for free?

To an economist, Bill Gates's point here seems an obvious truism. The idea that software, or any other useful good that takes intense effort to produce, should be given away without charge might sound charming, but it cannot work. If those responsible for producing the good are not paid by those who consume it, then little will be produced. Hobbyists may generate a certain amount of software for the fun of it, just as a gardener might raise a few apple trees and give the fruit away to friends for the pleasure of interacting with nature – but there is no way that the total appetite of society for apples could be satisfied in that fashion: far fewer apples will be produced voluntarily than people would be glad to pay for. If software is not treated as property to be sold for money, then programmers will lose out, because they are not paid for their labour, but would-be users of software will lose out too, because software that ought to be written never will be. This is basic economics: 'there ain't no such thing as a free lunch'.

To most of the hacker community, on the other hand, Gates's letter was inflammatory. He received a storm of protest letters. A local computer club threatened to sue him for calling its members thieves.

## THE FREE SOFTWARE FOUNDATION

Gates and the hackers went their separate ways. No reader needs to be told that Gates made a good thing out of his proprietary approach to software. The hobbyists continued to work in the style that pleased them, and in due course they produced a champion for their approach: Richard Stallman.

Stallman developed an editor, Emacs, in 1975, which in a later version is probably still the most widely used editor in the scientific community. In the mid-1980s he produced a C compiler, gcc, which again remains a staple tool in academic computing. In 1984 he initiated the GNU Project, a collaborative hacker enterprise that aimed to emulate all the functions and facilities of the Unix operating system within free software. In 1985 Stallman formed the Free Software Foundation as a vehicle to manage this massive undertaking.

These were large achievements, but the most significant thing about Stallman is the ideology underpinning his work. For Stallman the concept of *free software* is not a convenience for hobbyists but a moral imperative. Stallman is an intense man – he has been described as an 'implacable Old Testament prophet' (Moody 2002: 29), living on a shoestring, wearing his hair down to his shoulders, and he believes passionately that in a modern society the hacker ethic is an essential component of political freedom.

This attitude, while perhaps admirable in the abstract, is not likely to impress the average businessperson. Until fairly recently the business world, if it even knew about open-source software or the GNU Project, took for granted that these were things that hobbyists and academics might have fun with but that could have little relevance to the world of industry and commerce. The name 'open source' was coined in 1998 for the movement that the hacker approach has morphed into, as a deliberate attempt to distance this movement from the anti-business connotations of Stallman's term 'free software'.

Nevertheless, developments in the present decade have begun to suggest that even in sober economic terms, leaving politics aside, the future may lie with Stallman and the hackers, more than with Bill Gates.

## 'OPEN SOURCE', 'PROPRIETARY', 'FREE'

Before examining Eric Raymond's arguments for the economic rationality of open source, let me define some terms. The opposition *open source* versus *proprietary* covers several separate distinctions. Software is open source if it is released as source code, which users can read, modify and adapt to their purposes, rather than as opaque compiled object code, which has to be used as is. Code is proprietary if its owners actively enforce their copyright in it to prevent people using it without payment. (GNU software, by contrast, is released under a form of licence – the General Public Licence, GPL – which actively requires any new software based on it to be freely available.) Stallman often insists that the phrase 'free software' relates to 'free as in freedom, not as in beer' – he did not himself give away products such as Emacs; but he sold them for nominal prices that covered modest individual living expenses without amounting to the foundation of a commercial empire.

In practice, it has made sense to contrast open source with proprietary, because most software has either been proprietary and distributed as object code for whatever price the market will bear, or else has been distributed as source code, freely or cheaply, unencumbered by copyright restrictions. If programs are distributed as source code that is easy to copy and modify, it is difficult to maintain copyright and hence to charge significant prices – though companies do sometimes choose to distribute software free of charge but in object-code form, as Microsoft does with its Explorer browser. The reader should bear in mind that open source *v.* proprietary is a broad rather than logically clear-cut contrast. In due course we shall see that it is blurring.

## TECHNICAL AND ECONOMIC ISSUES

Eric Raymond's *The Cathedral and the Bazaar*, first published as a series of essays on the web, argued for two surprising points of view: one technical, the other economic.

The technical claim (in the essay with the same title as the book) is that it is possible for large-scale, high-quality software to be produced by a loosely organised community of free agents – by the kind of social set-up that Raymond sees as typical of a bazaar. People previously supposed that a tightly knit, carefully coordinated organisation was crucial – as it is for building a cathedral, where intricate architectural structures composed of massive masonry make careful planning essential.

The economic claim (argued in a sister essay, 'The Magic Cauldron') is that the hacker-style approach provides the right structure of incentives for software development to be well matched with society's software needs.

## TECHNICAL FEASIBILITY

Raymond illustrated the technical argument largely by reference to *Linux*, the operating-system kernel whose development was initiated by the Swedish-Finn Linus Torvalds in 1991. (Linux is part of, and depends on other parts of, the GNU Project, and the complete operating system is properly known as 'GNU/Linux'. The term 'Linux' is commonly used as shorthand for the entire system; I shall follow that usage for convenience, without any wish to undervalue the non-Linux components of the whole.) Linux is by now a serious threat to the hegemony of Microsoft's Windows, but Linux was built in a very un-cathedral-like way:

> From nearly the beginning, it was rather casually hacked on by huge numbers of volunteers coordinating only through the Internet. Quality was maintained not by rigid standards or autocracy but by the naively simple strategy of releasing every week and getting feedback from hundreds of users within days, creating a sort of rapid Darwinian selection on the mutations introduced by developers. To the amazement of almost everyone, this worked quite well.
>
> (Raymond 2001: 16)

Raymond argues that the traditional approach to software development leads to a mistaken perception of software bugs:

> In the cathedral-builder view of programming, bugs and development problems are tricky, insidious, deep phenomena. It takes months of scrutiny by a dedicated few to develop confidence that you've winkled them all out. Thus the long release intervals, and the inevitable disappointment when long-awaited releases are not perfect.
>
> (Raymond 2001: 31)

The bazaar approach, on the other hand, leads one to see the bug problem in terms of what Raymond calls 'Linus's Law': 'given enough eyeballs, all bugs are shallow'. In the bazaar model,

> ... you release often in order to get more corrections [at one stage, Torvalds was releasing updated versions of Linux every few days], and as a beneficial side effect you have less to lose if an occasional botch gets out the door ...

– because you only need to wind back a short way to return to the last non-botched version.

## WHAT DOES PROPRIETARY BUY US?

If software as complex as an operating system can be produced in the bazaar style, Raymond said, then we have to ask ourselves

> ... what, if anything, the tremendous overhead of conventionally managed development is actually buying us.
>
> Whatever it is certainly doesn't include reliable execution by deadline, or on budget, or to all features of the specification; it's a rare managed project that meets even one of these goals, let alone all three. It also does not appear to be ability to adapt to changes in technology and economic context during the project lifetime, either; the open-source community has proven *far* more effective on that score ...
>
> (Raymond 2001: 56)

This last point coincides with points made by Larry McVoy (1993) in a famous document, the 'Sourceware White Paper', which predicted that turning Unix into a closed-source, proprietary product would lead to its stagnation:

> A great deal of the early development of Unix was done by researchers because of Unix's ready accessibility ...
>
> Almost every good feature in computer operating systems today, including most features in DOS, Windows, and Windows/NT, came from the mind of one hacker or another. Typically, the work was not commissioned by a company, it was done as a research project and then productized. Without these people, we make no forward progress.

Another advantage in buying from an established company, in the case of conventional products, is that it gives the customer a legal recourse if the products prove unsatisfactory. But that is not a reason to prefer proprietary software, because software licences standardly exclude virtually all responsibility for product quality (they have to, because of the impossibility of ensuring that software is bug-free).

Raymond identified various other reasons why a software purchaser might think it worth paying the costs of commercial project management. In each case he argued that they are illusory.

## MANUFACTURE OR SERVICE?

Technically, then, Raymond believes that the bazaar approach *can* produce software. But, economically, why *will* it? An economist would suppose that it will not, or at least not enough software will be developed: people need incentives to produce anything.

In discussing the economic issue, Raymond was careful to explain that he was not saying that closed-source software development is morally objectionable, that there ought not to be copyright in software, or that there is an obligation on programmers to share their output altruistically. He was not advocating the open-source approach on idealistic, hacker-ethic grounds. He believes that approach makes practical sense as a means of providing for society's software needs.

In the first place, Raymond argued, 'software is largely a service industry operating under the … delusion that it is a manufacturing industry' (Raymond 2001: 120). The great majority of all code written by professional programmers is written for in-house use rather than sale, and most of what programmers do is maintenance rather than creation of novel programs. What serious software consumers are willing to pay for a package relates to the expected value of future 'service' (in a broad sense, including consultancy and training, upgrades and so forth), more than to the intrinsic properties of the package itself: if you doubt that, look at the rock-bottom prices put on remaindered copies of discontinued software lines (which, physically, still work as well as when the line was new). One enterprise-software developer has put the point this way: 'software is like fish: if it stops swimming, it dies'.[1] Computer games are an exception that really should be classed as products, not services; but games are a special case.

If we accept that business software is really a service industry, then logically consumers should not pay mainly through an up-front purchase price but through payments that continue as the service continues, via subscriptions or fees for support and maintenance. Even if the vendor owns copyright in the software package, it could make commercial sense for it to give copies away, to encourage a market for its paid-for support services.

Writing in 1996, Raymond noted that this pattern was already visible with the largest-scale business software, such as ERP systems, where development costs are so massive that they could not realistically be recouped through one-off purchase fees; ERP system vendors derive their income chiefly from after-sales consultancy payments. Raymond predicted that as the software industry matured, most of it would move in that same direction. And broadly speaking this is how companies that distribute Linux, such as Red Hat, are operating. (Red Hat was formed in 1995, selling packages comprising a Linux distribution with some applications, documentation and initial support, for about $50. It is now a global company with a market capitalisation of about $4.5 billion.)

---

[1] Quoted from an unnamed source in 'Barbarians in the Valley', *The Economist* 28 June 2003.

## CONSEQUENCES OF MANUFACTURE DELUSION

As Raymond sees it, the pricing model encouraged by 'manufacture delusion' has serious negative effects. It encourages developers to produce *shelfware* – packages that can be marketed well enough to sell, but that deliver little value in practice – and to put less effort into after-sales support than users need. It encourages developers to discontinue good lines prematurely in order to reap profits from newer packages. And it makes it difficult for good second-place products to compete against market leaders, stimulating excellence in both.

Although Raymond believes that much of the software development industry is destined to move on to the open-source model, he also believes that there are cases that will always be more rationally treated as products for sale. Raymond lists a series of considerations that push a specific software project in one direction or the other. The open-source model is especially attractive in cases where correctness of design and implementation are hard to assess other than by independent peer review, or where the package serves a business-critical function for the consumer (so that the consumer does not want to be tied to a single commercial supplier). Raymond's example of a package that fails most of his tests was software for sawmills that calculates optimal cutting patterns for extracting the most valuable configuration of planks from a given log. It is straightforward to evaluate the performance of such a system objectively; and it is not business-critical – sawyers can do the task reasonably well manually, if they have to. But, according to Raymond, cases like this that should remain closed-source are exceptions, not the norm.

Where software *is* business-critical, Raymond believes, user companies will come to realise that closed source is simply not acceptable as a strategic business risk.

> The brutal truth is this: when your key business processes are executed by opaque blocks of bits that you can't even see inside (let alone modify), *you have lost control of your business.* You need your supplier more than your supplier needs you – and you will pay, and pay, and pay again for that power imbalance.
>
> (Raymond 2001: 152)

## PROGRAMMING FOR MONEY OR LOVE

Still this does not answer the incentive question: why will people devote time and effort to developing software packages if they are distributed for little or no money?

In some cases, Raymond said, the programmers will be employed by software houses as programmers are now, to create packages that the company can then earn its living by supporting, rather than selling. And in other cases companies may derive other kinds of benefit through employing people to develop software that is given away. Raymond cited a case where Cisco assigned two of its programmers to write a complex distributed print-spooling system, and made it open source in order to stimulate the growth of a community of outside users and co-developers who would between them ensure that maintenance was available into the future. If the system had been closed-source and the two programmers had left the company, it would have been hard for someone new coming to the code to learn enough to maintain it.

But other open-source software will continue to be produced by unpaid volunteers, according to Raymond, in the same way that Linux has been. The volunteers need not necessarily be motivated by the intrinsic pleasure of hacking, or by peer esteem. Hackers are people with software needs of their own, which they will often want to solve for themselves rather than waiting an indefinite time until someone else happens to do the job – and, when hackers produce code that meets a specific need, it pays them to document it and contribute it to the community, rather than keep it to themselves, because in that way the ongoing effort of maintaining the code is taken over by the community.

Still, Raymond made clear that he believes the pure joy of hacking is and will continue to be a main driving force behind production of useful software.

To a businessperson, this is a very strange idea. In an academic context, though, it should be easy to understand the idea that good work depends on self-motivation and peer esteem more than on an employer/employee relationship: this is essentially how academic research functions. The fact that we know as much as we do about every subject under the sun, from the structure of the atom to the structure of government under the Plantagenets, is because researchers have chosen for themselves topics to work on and pursued them in the gaps of time between teaching and other duties, motivated by a mixture of love of study and the admiration of their fellow specialists.

Pure academic research might sound a far cry from software development, but in fact there are strong analogies. In particular, the fact that a complex software system is virtually never perfect (the 'last bug' is never found) makes it similar to academic research, where the last word is never said on any subject and there is always room for reinterpretation and further discovery. If software were rejected for a single flaw, we would have to do without computers altogether; so a software system must be evaluated in broader terms. Because of the complexity of software, the people involved in developing it are far better placed to do this than users, even users who have a general background in IT – just as members of the public who take an interest in advances in human knowledge, for instance by watching science or history programmes on television, have to rely on the professionals to sieve the sensible ideas from the dross.

Some business writers have begun suggesting that the 'bazaar' approach to software development may be a valuable model for wider areas of industry. Evans and Wolf (2005) argue that the success of Toyota has a lot to do with the fact that the famous Toyota Production System has a family resemblance with the way Linux has been developed.[2] In 2007 the US, British and European patent offices collaborated in piloting a 'Peer to Patent' scheme, which uses bazaar techniques to address some of the difficulties with the patent system discussed on pp. 68–69.

## THE BREAKTHROUGH TO CREDIBILITY

When Eric Raymond was writing in the late 1990s, he was making a prediction: the economic logic of open source meant that it was bound in due course to spread through the business computing environment.

By now it is clear that Raymond's prediction is coming true. We cannot yet foresee where the boundaries will ultimately fall between functions where open source will predominate and functions that will remain the preserve of proprietary systems, but nobody any longer could see open-source software as an impractical phenomenon associated with unrealistic hacker culture. For Linux in particular, a breakthrough to 'real world' credibility occurred in about 2002–3. Michael Dell (chief executive of Dell Computers) argued in 2002 that Linux was now superior to Unix. A report from the investment bank Goldman Sachs in 2003 judged that Linux had 'evolved into an enterprise-class operating system'.

## OPPOSITION FROM MICROSOFT

The chief locus of active opposition to the open source movement has been Microsoft, which has campaigned against it in various ways. One example was a page posted on the Microsoft website in 2000 documenting a series of so-called 'Linux Myths'. (Since 2004 this has evolved into a large collection of online documentation, under the title 'Get the Facts'.) Microsoft claimed that much of the buzz that Linux was starting to attract represented hype rather than reality, arguing that Linux fell down relative to proprietary operating systems with respect to considerations such as reliability (e.g. preservation of data in cases of system failure) and security, as well as shortage of available applications. In 2001 Steve Ballmer, Microsoft chief executive, described the

---

[2] The Toyota Production System has legendary status in modern management theory. Studies of it such as Ohno (1988) were responsible for introducing various Japanese concepts into the vocabulary of Western management.

GNU General Public Licence (which forces any software built with the help of GNU systems itself to be released on open-source terms) as a 'cancer' spreading throughout the software industry and destroying healthy economic relationships.[3]

More recently, Microsoft has argued that the apparent cost-saving with open source is illusory, once consultancy and/or maintenance fees are taken into account, and that for industrial-strength computing infrastructures it is actually cheaper overall to license Microsoft solutions. Likewise Jonathan Schwartz of Sun: 'Linux is like a puppy – in the beginning it's great, but you also have to take care of it.'[4]

Third-party analyses of this 'total cost of ownership' (TCO) issue have yielded mixed results. Microsoft in 2004 was quoting a study by the business analysts Gartner that found that, on desktops, TCO for Windows XP was 15–20 per cent lower than Linux, together with Microsoft's own independently audited study showing that, as server platforms, Windows Server 2003 was more than 10 times cheaper than Linux. On the other hand, the British Educational Communication and Technology Agency (a government advisory body) conducted a three-year trial in 48 schools comparing TCO of open source and proprietary environments, and in 2005 came up with average annual figures of £740 for open source versus £1132 for proprietary. A February 2006 study by Enterprise Management Associates, based on data from hundreds of companies, found that the idea that Linux involves large ongoing maintenance costs is out of date, and that Linux is now cheaper than Windows in that respect also.

One can debate how fair the 'Linux Myths' arguments were at the time, or just how fully they have ceased to be fair subsequently. But any remaining inclination to see open source as just a hobbyist's plaything was decisively exploded in 2003 by David Stutz, who had until then led Microsoft's anti-open-source strategy. A few days after he retired, Stutz used his new freedom to announce publicly that Linux is now becoming a legitimate alternative to Windows, and that Microsoft would need to be more creative in developing new products if it hopes to maintain its market position. (Similar assessments had been made as early as 1998 in confidential internal Microsoft memoranda, which were leaked and became famous as the 'Hallowe'en Documents'.)

The second of Stutz's points chimes with Larry McVoy's 1993 comment about closed-source software leading to stagnation. *The Economist* suggested in 2002 that the Microsoft anti-trust trial may have been near-pointless, because the lack of innovation resulting from its closed-source business model ensured that the company would fall behind:

---

[3] T.C. Greene, 'Ballmer: "Linux is a cancer"', *The Register* 2 June 2001, LinuxCancer.notlong.com.
[4] Quoted in 'The ponytail versus the penguin', *The Economist* 24 May 2003.

> What is striking is how little innovation there has been in the bits of the market that Microsoft dominates, and how much where it has little influence. Operating systems, web browsers and word-processing software all look much as they did five years ago. But not many people are using five-year-old mobile phones, handheld computers or music-sharing software.[5]

## OPEN SOURCE IN GOVERNMENT COMPUTING

Perhaps surprisingly, many early indications that open source has become a realistic option came not from private-sector companies but from governments, which are the largest consumers of software of all.

This might seem unexpected, for two reasons. In the first place, one does not normally associate governments and civil servants with innovative, radical developments. Second, the cost of software is less of an issue for governments, which are financed through taxation, than it is for companies, which need to control costs in order to stay in profit.

But governments care deeply about retaining control over their domains. Eric Raymond's warning that closed-source software implies losing control of one's business would sound even more chilling to a mayor who translated it into losing control of his city, or to a prime minister who translated it into losing control of his country.

Furthermore, security against loss of confidentiality and against malicious hacker ('cracker') attacks is often even more vital for government departments than for business – and one aspect of Microsoft's 'Linux Myths' that has been very widely criticised is the suggestion that open-source software is inherently insecure. Many commentators believe that security flaws have a better chance of being detected and eliminated under the 'democratic' code-review process characteristic of open-source development. Paul Cormier, executive vice-president of engineering at Red Hat, has put it this way:

> There are all of these eyeballs ... who have no agenda other than doing the right thing. The closed[-source] community relies on a small group of developers, and most of their vulnerabilities are found by the bad guys.[6]

A supremely security-conscious application area is cryptography, whose whole purpose is to defeat attacks by crackers; the cryptography expert Bruce Schneier wrote in 1999 that 'In the cryptography world,

---

[5] 'Giving the invisible hand a helping hand', *The Economist* 9 November 2002.
[6] Quoted by Dennis Fisher, 'Red Hat profits from fear', *IT Week* 11 November 2002.

we consider open source necessary for good security; we have for decades.'[7]

One US local authority (Golden Grove, California) adopted Linux as early as the mid-1990s. That was unusual then, but it has since become a common move – and one that is increasingly often motivated by deeper considerations than cost-saving. Otto Schily, German interior minister, quoted worries about Microsoft's security record, and the wish to avoid dependence on a private foreign company, as leading motives when in 2002 he announced a plan for German federal and *Land* governments to switch from Windows to Linux – though the plan did also aim at cost reductions. By then, several governments in Europe and the Americas had adopted policies that formally discouraged use of proprietary software in public projects. In 2003, when the city of Munich considered switching to Linux, Steve Ballmer interrupted his holiday in order to lobby the mayor to stick with Windows, offering a deal under which Microsoft would drop its prices to match the low cost of Linux – but Munich went with Linux anyway. According to *The Economist*, 'City officials said the decision was a matter of principle: the municipality wanted to control its technological destiny.'[8] In April 2004 the governments of Japan, China and South Korea (not always the best of friends) signed an agreement to promote a common Linux-based system as an alternative to dependence on Microsoft.

(The British government has been relatively cautious. A 2002 Cabinet Office report urged government departments to consider open-source alternatives, and the Department of Work and Pensions launched the first major open-source-based government application in 2003; the Office of Government Commerce ran year-long trials in 2003–4, which concluded that, with reservations in the desktop area, open-source technology could now be recommended for public-sector use. So far, though, not much has happened in practice. In February 2007 a group of organisations including Birmingham City Council set up a 'National Open Centre' to try to change this situation; some of the experts who spoke at the launch event claimed that leading members of the UK government are hostile to open source.)

Meanwhile, in the USA, the government security body Cert advised users in 2004 to consider giving up Microsoft's Explorer browser, because of its vulnerability to cracker attacks – the obvious alternatives being the open-source Firefox or Opera. And in January 2006 the US government pledged to provide public funding to support the work of rooting out bugs from Linux and other heavily used open-source systems.

---

[7] Quoted by Moody (2002: 285).
[8] 'Microsoft at the power point', *The Economist* 13 September 2003.

## ADOPTION BY THE PRIVATE SECTOR

In the economically harsh opening years of the new century, private-sector businesses focused on cost-cutting before all else: the priority was simple survival rather than possibly advantageous but risky innovation. However, the low entry cost of open-source systems made them appealing from that point of view too – though partisans of open source would argue that cheapness ought not to be the main motive for switching. In about 2003, open source began spreading into the business world.

Unilever announced a plan that year to move its global IT infrastructure from Unix onto Linux – for an expected saving of £66 million over three years, but also in order to achieve infrastructure simplification. Also in 2003, Reuters released a version of its Market Data System software on Linux, claiming this as the first major example of open-source use in the area of financial services; Reuters said that the Linux-based version gave a large performance improvement over a Unix-based alternative. By 2004, numerous large companies – including IT companies such as Google and Yahoo!, but also others such as Lufthansa and Ericsson – had adopted the open-source MySQL relational database. (Already in 2002 the open-source scripting language PHP had been reported as overtaking Microsoft's counterpart.)

By October 2004 a survey of large North American companies by Forrester Research found that more than half were running mission-critical applications under Linux. European firms have become even more enthusiastic than American ones.

In some cases, companies outside the IT sector even came to accept the logic of encouraging 'many eyeballs' to scrutinise their in-house code. In 2002, the merchant bank Dresdner Kleinwort Wasserstein fostered an external developer community for the middleware it uses to link the firm's different systems.

One thing that has been happening is senior managers discovering that their subordinates have quietly been running open-source systems in specific areas for some time past. For instance, Apache web-server software became the dominant choice soon after its first release in 1995 – but few business managers would have had views of their own about what web-server software to rely on. The difference now is that the senior people are giving the use of open source their blessing, publicising it, and adopting explicit open source policies at division-wide or company-wide levels.

## PROPRIETARY SOFTWARE IS OPENED

As the business world warmed towards open source, major vendors began to distribute some of their own, conventionally produced systems in source-code form, in order to maintain their competitive positions.

Computer Associates 'open-sourced' its struggling database Ingres in May 2004, and announced that it would collaborate with open-source organisations to develop new open software products. Sun open-sourced its highly successful Solaris operating system in June 2005. Meanwhile, in 2003 Oracle began encouraging its database customers to use a Linux-based architecture; and major hardware suppliers started to support open source by packaging open software with their products – Hewlett-Packard announced that it would do this with MySQL in June 2004, and Dell did likewise with Linux in April 2007.

By 2005, even Microsoft seemed to accept that open source was here to stay and that Microsoft must live with it. Microsoft's chief lawyer, Brad Smith, said:

> In the world of software development, there is a broad panoply of development models... We're going to have to figure out how to build some bridges between the various parts of our industry.[9]

At the LinuxWorld conference in Boston in April 2006, Microsoft startled participants by announcing that it would begin providing technical support for Linux running in its Virtual Server environment; Microsoft's Zane Adam promised 'This will help customers safely consolidate their Linux-based applications on Virtual Server.'[10] In October 2006 Microsoft formed a partnership with an Israeli-American firm, Zend, to make the open-source scripting language PHP work better with Windows.

## THE OTHER POINT OF VIEW

From the discussion so far, readers may have concluded that open source versus proprietary is a one-sided debate. It was appropriate to give the arguments in favour of open source a very full hearing, because they are so counterintuitive in terms of ordinary economic assumptions – and there seems little doubt that Raymond was right to argue that some of the 'obvious' economic reasons why the open-source model 'cannot work' are far weaker than they seem at first.

One specific aspect of Raymond's argument, furthermore, is by now accepted so widely as to be scarcely controversial. It is generally agreed that the old model of buying enterprise software with a one-off up-front payment is on the way out, in favour of the ongoing-subscription model. A survey by the international market research firm IDC in 2004 found that

---

[9] Quoted by Darryl Taft, 'Microsoft alters stance towards open source', *IT Week* 9 May 2005.
[10] Quoted by William Eazel, 'Shock as Microsoft supports Linux', *Computing* 4 April 2006.

both vendors and customers wanted this. Amy Konary of IDC concluded that 'The current licensing model just does not work',[11] for either side.

Nevertheless, the debate has two sides. By 2008 it was looking as though reliance on the ongoing-subscription model makes it hard for a company to become profitable.[12] And there are real drawbacks to the open source strategy; we need to look at these.

## HOW GOOD A PRECEDENT IS LINUX?

The first issue is theoretical. We have seen that Raymond's case is partly technical – software *can* be produced through 'bazaar' methods – and partly economic – if it can be, sufficient software *will* be produced that way. Raymond's argument for the economic logic of open source is reasonably persuasive, but the technical case seems weaker.

The idea that successful, complex software can emerge from a disorganised 'bazaar' contradicts longstanding axioms about software engineering. Frederick Brooks's (1975) IT classic *The Mythical Man-Month* pointed out that the more programmers that are assigned to a project, the slower development becomes, because of the increasing possibilities of hidden inconsistencies between separate individuals' work. The discipline of software engineering has evolved to cope with this problem through strong coordinating and planning mechanisms – that is, by enforcing a cathedral-building rather than a bazaar-like working method. Glyn Moody (2002: 151) claimed that 'Linus's Law' offers a solution to the problem identified by Brooks; but what *is* the solution? On the face of it, Linus's Law merely denies that the problem is real.

Clearly, Linux demonstrates that some complex software can be produced by loose networks of free agents. But Linux is only one example of open source (though some people talk as though 'open source' and 'Linux' were virtually synonymous); and Linux may be a special case. Unix, the system Linux set out to emulate, is a rather unusual large-scale software system. It consists of numerous independent utilities, many of which are individually quite small, and which interact with one another in a standard way by exchanging text files. This minimises the danger that work on one part of the system might inadvertently interfere with the way another part operates, so it is an ideal case for the bazaar approach to development. But there is no way that (say) a word-processing program could be designed with a similar architecture.

As Stephen Marshall (a Glasgow University business development manager) sees it,

---

[11] Quoted by Gregg Keizer, 'Subscription licensing is on the rise', *Computing* 1 April 2004.
[12] See 'A question of demand', *The Economist* 5 January 2008.

> ... the legendary robustness of Linux actually owes more to the good design of Unix than it does to the OSS [open source software] development process.[13]

Possibly, the success of Linux in particular is being taken to mean more than it really does.

## SECURITY FLAWS EMERGE

The second point is practical. Many people have been persuaded by the argument that democratic, many-eyeballs software development yields code with fewer bugs and security vulnerabilities. Once open-source software was deployed more widely, experience began to call this into question – at least in the specific, and especially sensitive, case of security flaws. According to a 2002 report by the analysts Aberdeen Group, 'Open-source software ... is now the major source of elevated security vulnerabilities',[14] having overtaken Microsoft in that role.

Supporters of the rival systems held a year-long competition, under rules mutually agreed in advance, to compare Windows 2003 and Red Hat Enterprise Linux in terms of metrics such as number of reported security vulnerabilities, and elapsed time between public disclosure of a security problem and release of a fix. The results were reported at the RSA Conference in February 2005: Windows won under all headings – time between security problem report and problem solution for Windows was on average less than half the Linux figure.

Open-source claims may stand up better with respect to fewness of bugs. (Bugs and security vulnerabilities are different things: a bug is a coding error that prevents software running the way its writer expects it to run; a security flaw is commonly a case where software that runs as intended creates an unnoticed opportunity for bad people to interfere.) A study reported in June 2006 found that the Linux 2.6 kernel contained only about a fifth as many bugs as would be expected in a proprietary program of similar size.

## MATCHING EFFORT TO NEEDS

Even if the open-source approach does on balance yield higher-quality software, with a more satisfactory maintenance/support model, than the proprietary approach, it seems that nothing in the open-source approach

---

[13] Stephen Marshall, 'Open source has its own problems', *Computing* 4 August 2005.
[14] Quoted by Dennis Fisher and Madeline Bennett, 'Open-source flaws multiply', *IT Week* 2 December 2002.

can guarantee that the range of functions for which software is produced offers a good match to the functions that need to be served.

We saw in Chapter 5, for instance, that commercial websites in Europe are now required by law to be accessible to disabled users. Linux is behind Windows in developing the features needed to support this. One can surmise (so far as I know the issue has not been studied) that this may be a consequence of the interests and preferences of the open-source developer community. They are enthusiastic about coding packages that they might want to use themselves, but hackers tend to be able young people who surely suffer from proportionately fewer disabilities than the general population. In consequence it may be that they have little natural understanding of what the new law requires, and little spontaneous interest in providing it. A conventional software company, on the other hand, can simply assign a task to a group of employees because it is a commercial imperative.

The analogy with academic research is again relevant, but this time in a negative sense. Probably everyone agrees that the best way to get at the truth about a pure academic topic, whether scientific or humanistic, is through open, voluntary research and debate by members of a global academic community. But at the same time, governments and taxpayers often suggest nowadays that this system yields an imperfect distribution of effort across the different research areas. They may feel, for instance, that mediaeval history, or literary theory, get more attention than the public really requires, while some applied topics, which may be intellectually less exciting, but potentially highly relevant for the prosperity of UK plc, are relatively neglected. With open-source software it is not clear what mechanisms could possibly get the analogous distribution of efforts well matched to society's needs.

## LEADERSHIP AND ORGANISATION

There are also issues, which became visible only once the open source movement matured and its products were used in more 'serious' contexts, about leadership and organisational coherence.

The ideologists of open source sometimes portray the movement as if it were an example of successful anarchy, in which individuals come forward to do what is needed without being subordinate to any central control. But if anarchy implies lack of organisation, that is not how open-source production operates. Steven Weber (2004: 62) suggests that Raymond's term 'bazaar' is misleading in this respect. Weber describes a fairly complex hierarchical organisational structure controlling Linux development (and other well-defined organisational patterns behind other open-source projects); what is different from commercial operations is not the existence of organisation but the fact that individuals adopt roles in the hierarchy, and take on specific tasks, voluntarily, without contractual obligations or financial incentives.

However, that throws all the greater burden on the leadership role. In the case of Linux, writer after writer attests to the crucial role of Linus Torvalds in guiding its development through the force of his engaging personality. Linux does demonstrate that complex software can be developed without legal employer/employee relationships, but it does not demonstrate that the leadership role is redundant. Leaders who can persuade people to accept their guidance purely voluntarily may be even harder to find than managers who can lead successfully with the help of employment discipline to reinforce their personal charisma.

The current generation of open-source project leaders will not fill their current roles for ever. For Linux, Glyn Moody (2002: 322–3) claimed that this will not be a problem, because Torvalds has been so successful at creating a 'distributed-leadership' model that no single individual will be needed to succeed him. Clearly this is a large claim, which remains to be tested. But even Moody noted that Richard Stallman 'says despairingly, "I'm going to keep working on the free-software movement because I don't see who's going to replace me."'

## WILL THE 'BAZAAR' MODEL SURVIVE?

Whether one uses Raymond's term 'bazaar' or some other tag to encapsulate the distinctive open-source approach to the process of software development, there is a question about how far this distinctiveness will be maintained in the future.

Now that large commercial software vendors such as Sun are making their conventionally developed source code available, and companies such as Red Hat and IBM, which are not themselves internally motivated by the hacker ethic, are playing major roles in the future development of systems that originated from the 'bazaar' culture, the open-source development world may become more like the conventional 'cathedral-building' world of proprietary software development. Since Linux in particular has become a crucial technology, it is increasingly coming under the control of a formal organisation, the Open Source Development Labs (OSDL), which is a non-profit entity supported by a consortium of technology companies – Torvalds joined OSDL in 2003 (it has since merged into a larger Linux Foundation).

In 2003 Red Hat decided to cease supporting its off-the-shelf Red Hat Linux product, which appealed to individual users, in order to focus on its Enterprise Linux product for the corporate market. Discussing the open-source rival MySQL to Oracle as a proprietary relational-database system, Martin Butler (president of the IT consultancy Butler Group) argued in 2004:

> The fact that MySQL comes from an open-source background does not make it anything special... MySQL is a commercial database marketed on the back of interest in open source... The truth is open source has, to a large extent, been hijacked by commercial enterprises.[15]

(A takeover of MySQL by Sun was announced in January 2008.)

Many readers felt that Butler's comments were exaggerated, but they were a hint at the way the wind is blowing. A more specific sign of the times came in 2005, in relation to an open-source content-management application called Mambo, which was originally created by an Australian company, Miro. In order to coordinate the future development of Mambo by the open-source community, in 2005 Miro set up the Mambo Foundation; but instead of welcoming participation by any competent enthusiast, the Foundation allows a real say over the Mambo development path only to participants willing to pay a five-figure annual fee and to commit several full-time workers to the project – in other words, to large companies but not to individuals.

If moves like Miro's become normal, we could eventually arrive at a position where 'open source' describes only the fact that a system is distributed as source rather than object code, but does not indicate anything special about the way it was developed. Linux's 'bazaar' origin would be just an interesting piece of history, rather than a precedent with current relevance.

We are a long way off that yet. An EU report on open-source software published in January 2007 (Ghosh 2007) found that almost two-thirds of open-source software is still produced by individuals (and another 20 per cent by organisations other than commercial firms). But we cannot assume that this will always be the case. (If it ceases to be the case, then the business world might find that reassuring.)

## NOT WHETHER, BUT WHAT

There is little doubt that open-source software is here to stay. The question now is how wide a range of business-computing functions open source is destined to fill.

Early efforts were all at the systems rather than applications end of computing, with editors such as Emacs, MySQL as a database system, new languages such as Perl, language compilers such as gcc, and the Linux operating system kernel. It began to seem that open source might be good for systems programming but applications would remain proprietary.

---

[15] Martin Butler, 'Hidden costs of open source', *IT Week* 19 July 2004.

The fact that open source took off in the systems rather than the applications area could be little more than a consequence of the point, already made, that systems software is chosen by computing staff, who are relatively likely to be aware of open source and its advantages, while applications are the aspect of computing that non-techie business-people care about, and they would traditionally have been ignorant or sceptical about the open source concept. Ignorance is encouraged by business education. Paul Murphy surveyed IT textbooks standardly used in business schools[16] and found that they portrayed an extraordinary world in which 'computing' is virtually synonymous with Microsoft packages; one could not guess that the bulk of industrial-strength computing was running under Unix.

Open-source efforts did spread into the applications area after the turn of the century. The office-productivity suite OpenOffice evolved as a free spin-off from Sun's (open source, but proprietary and paid-for) StarOffice. (Sun donated its source code in 2000, one advantage to Sun being that the hackers who develop OpenOffice produced innovations that Sun could incorporate back into StarOffice, which is bought by customers who need the 24/7 support and training that the hacker community cannot provide.) A list on Wikipedia identifies dozens of open-source application packages in areas such as finance (e.g. bookkeeping programs), science, education and assistive technology.

We have seen that the largest-scale genre of enterprise software is ERP: the GNU Project is attempting to develop an open-source counterpart to the systems marketed by SAP or Oracle ('GNUe', GNU Enterprise – see Tiffin and Müller 2001), though from the GNUe website at June 2007 it appears that progress has been limited. In June 2005 the open source body Eclipse launched a BI system, Birt, which is not a full-scale competitor to the proprietary systems available from companies like Cognos, but may be a first step in that direction.

The SourceForge site was founded in 2000 as a central repository for open-source applications, many of which are business-oriented. By 2007 SourceForge was hosting over 150,000 projects, and the most popular of them (such as the peer-to-peer file storage and retrieval utility BitTorrent) are downloaded tens of thousands of times a day.

On the other hand, although some SourceForge applications are evidently heavily used, most are not. According to Clay Shirky (2007: 52),

> ... most projects have never broken a hundred downloads, and more than half are simply inactive: A project was proposed, but nothing happened.

---

[16] 'Eight IT textbooks, 4,031 pages, 17 mentions of Linux', *LinuxInsider* 2 April 2004.

Indeed, in direct contradiction to its comments in 2002 quoted on p. 225, by 2004 *The Economist* was arguing that open-source techniques might be incapable of fostering real innovation; the magazine pointed out that the open-source success stories are all cases of systems that use new code to imitate the same functionality found in existing proprietary systems.[17]

## MICROSOFT RETURNS TO THE FRAY

At the time of writing, a large new question about the future of open source has arisen, in the form of legal moves by Microsoft.

We have seen that, after years of fighting the open source movement, by the middle of the decade Microsoft had begun looking for means of peaceful co-existence. That did not mean that Microsoft was happy with the situation. When, in 2007, it brought out new versions of Windows – Vista – and of Microsoft Office, there was controversy about whether the digital rights management features built into Vista (ostensibly to enable media companies to protect their intellectual property), and new document formats in Office, might in practice function to lock the user community in to Microsoft or Microsoft-approved software products, so that Microsoft Office users would not be able to swap documents with users of OpenOffice or other open-source applications.

Whatever the truth of that, its significance is probably overshadowed by the potential impact of patent claims Microsoft has been advancing. Since 2003, Microsoft has been asserting that Linux, OpenOffice and other open-source software violates hundreds of Microsoft patents. (It has not identified the specific patents, perhaps to make it harder for the open-source community either to challenge them legally or code round them.) In November 2006, Microsoft reached an agreement with one of the leading Linux distributors, Novell, under which Novell effectively conceded the validity of Microsoft's claims about Linux in exchange for Microsoft paying royalties on Novell patents. Novell's concession strengthens Microsoft's position legally if it should now decide to claim royalties from open-source users. And conversely it creates uncertainty for organisations that use (or are thinking of using) open-source software.

Richard Stallman's Free Software Foundation has tried to fight back, by revising the terms of the General Public Licence in a way that is intended to achieve the consequence that if Microsoft continues to press its case in the way it is currently doing, after the new licence comes into effect in July 2007 it would automatically forfeit its right to enforce patent claims. On the other hand, Linus Torvalds's OSDL, to the surprise of many, has endorsed the Microsoft–Novell agreement.

---

[17] 'An open-source shot in the arm?', *The Economist* 12 June 2004.

The legal issues involved in all this are so tangled that it would be foolish for a lawyer, let alone a business writer, to predict what the outcome will be if it comes to a full-dress battle in court. One can doubt, too, whether Microsoft has any real intention of going down that route. We saw in Chapter 4 how shallow-rooted software patents are in law. In an environment where governments round the world are increasingly chary of being tied to proprietary software, one might suppose that too aggressive a stance by Microsoft could rebound, by encouraging governments to use their control over legislation to destroy the basis for Microsoft's patent claims.

In any case, even if Microsoft's claims were accepted, in principle that would not eliminate Linux or other open-source software. It would remain open source, but users would have to pay Microsoft for the right to use it. Many companies might not find that particularly objectionable. However, it is an idea so contrary to the 'hacker ethic' that it could have a chilling effect on future open-source development. Referring to firms that continue to buy their Linux from Novell and hence, indirectly, support Microsoft's position, Richard Stallman commented that:

> What the shortsighted corporate types didn't grasp was that without the little-guy developers there might not be any high-quality free and open-source software for them to use five years down the road.[18]

At best it might mean that open-source software development would complete its transition out of the hands of the individual hackers who put Linux together, morphing into a wholly corporate activity.

None of that may happen. I find it hard to believe that one commercial company, no matter how powerful, will in practice be allowed to stifle a technological development that has led to so much positive activity internationally and has attracted the support of governments as well as individual users. But the fact that such a large question is genuinely open at the time of writing – by the time this book is in the reader's hands, the future may be clearer, but so far as the author knows things really could go either way – makes this a very good illustration of the point made in Chapter 4, that purely technical and business considerations in IT are heavily dependent on the legal and social framework within which business operates.

---

[18] Reported by Roger Parloff in 'Microsoft takes on the free world', *Fortune* 28 May 2007; an acronym has been expanded here for clarity.

## A MIXED ECONOMY

Assuming that legal problems do not kill off the open source movement, then we return to the question of how far open source is destined to replace proprietary software in the overall business domain.

Unless, like Richard Stallman, one is ideologically driven, there is no reason to hold that proprietary software should, or can, be replaced in every application domain. But by now there is no longer room for doubt that open source will be a large factor in the future business IT environment.

We are moving into a mixed software economy. Open source will clearly be strongest at the systems end; proprietary may retain a large presence at the applications end. Where the boundary between them will eventually run is an issue to be settled gradually, case by case, by reference to experience and to detailed business considerations rather than to theoretical principles.

# 14 Into the Future

## A SPECULATIVE CONCLUSION

The preceding chapters have covered 'the story so far'. It seems right to round things off with a few speculations about where e-business will go next. Needless to say, this can be no more than rash guesswork; anything said here may turn out to look very silly in a few years' time. Considering how fast things have been changing since the turn of the century, readers will not hold me to any conjecture I offer about the future.

Nevertheless, with that proviso, some brief suggestions may be worth airing.

## MOBILE COMPUTING

A first prediction is negative. For quite a long time now, people have been saying that the 'next big thing' will be *mobile computing*. Not quite yet, but in a year or two's time, the technology that is enabling users to connect wirelessly to the internet, wherever they happen to be, is going to transform the e-business scene. As one year makes way for the next, 'a year or two's time' moves forward to keep pace, but (we are told) it will happen *soon*. Johan Hjelm (2000: 2) saw us 'facing a wireless revolution' comparable in significance to the internet revolution. Peter Keen and Ron Mackintosh (2001: 5) saw mobile computing as inaugurating 'a new era in business'. Ravi Kalakota wrote:

> As new technologies and trends slowly shift the center of gravity from tethered to untethered models, a change-wave is unfolding. The companies anticipating this change-wave are moving quickly to reinvent themselves.
>
> (Kalakota and Robinson 2002: 2)

Kalakota uses the term 'M-business' for the new version of e-business that will be enabled by mobile computing. I do not believe in M-business.

Certainly there are e-business activities that are already occurring and that could not occur without mobile computing. We have looked at some of them. The fact that CRM may allow company representatives to brief themselves in detail when arriving for a visit to a client firm is a significant, useful consequence of mobile technology. Advertising sent to mobile phones and tailored to individual subscribers' profiles, such as the service launched in Britain in September 2007 by Blyk, is seen by some as the next big thing in e-advertising. But things like these do not add up to an e-business 'revolution'.

When the visionaries discuss some of the specific possibilities that are on the way, I find them underwhelming. For instance, we are told that it will be easy to operate one's bank account while on the move – but how many people will want to? When I do something with my account that is less routine than paying in a cheque, I want to be sitting quietly with my files around me so that I can be sure I am getting it right. Someone in a strange town who would like to have dinner in an Italian restaurant will be able to get directions to the nearest one over a mobile phone or PDA. Yes, but it is usually obvious where the restaurant quarter in a town is, and if one is feeling choosy rather than just needing to refuel quickly then surely one wants to wander past a few and get a direct impression of their quality?

The goal of developing systems that automatically convert web pages into formats that are readable on small PDA or mobile-phone screens is an interesting technical challenge, to which much effort is being devoted. But even assuming that it is solved successfully, I question whether it will transform any aspect of business life. A small screen must necessarily be a second-best: it physically contains much less information.

Firms have been attracted by the idea that mobile computing can enable their staff to work when away from base; even before wireless internet connections, we have been used for some time to seeing people tapping away on laptops in airport departure lounges and on trains. But, although technology may be making it possible for employees to work during every waking hour, healthy human beings cannot work all the time. Managers soon began to realise that there is a risk of mobile technology linked to commercial pressures pushing people into an unsustainable lifestyle. Alan Thompson, head of Toshiba Information Systems, commented in 2003:

> When you're young you sleep when you collapse – as you get older, it's different. We don't want to push people over the edge into mental illness... We want to say that it's fine to be switched off and away from your work.[1]

In the same year, Microsoft UK found that its staff issued with mobile equipment felt seriously stressed by 'ambiguous expectations' about always-on working, and they had to issue formal guidelines about switching mobile phones off and disconnecting from the internet.

---

[1] Quoted in *IT Week* 3 February 2003.

Steve Harvey, its director of people and culture, explained 'We don't want to burn people out.'[2]

## THE HYPERMOBILITY MYTH

For a while I wondered whether my own scepticism about M-business simply showed that I am a dinosaur. If so, I am not alone. Geoffrey Moore expressed a point of view I share when he wrote:

> I do not carry a PalmPilot, preferring a pocket size notebook and a pen... In general, I hate 'being connected,' which I associate with being either interrupted or confused, not with being in touch ...
>
> (Moore 1999: 45)

By now it is becoming clear that our scepticism is solidly grounded. Swisscom (Switzerland's counterpart to BT) employs an anthropologist, Stefana Broadbent, to head its User Adoption Lab, which studies how human beings interact with technology. Broadbent and her team use the term *hypermobility myth* for the idea that people will find it useful to work while on the move.

After studying workers who spend more than half their time out of the office – salespeople, consultants, pilots, journalists and photographers – she found that they generally stick to communications while on the move, gathering information that they then work on when they get back to their desks. Hotel rooms and airports are, she says, 'not seen as an appropriate environment for substantive work' and are used mainly for e-mail.[3]

Chaffey (2007: 134) quotes a study that found that out of 41 million passengers a year using Schiphol Airport, Amsterdam, only about 12 a day use its Wi-Fi hotspots.

Keen and Mackintosh (2001) claimed 'it's impossible to over-hype the potential of M-commerce'. In reality, hype is what it is. Mobile computing will have a role in e-business, but not a revolutionary role.

## REGULATION OF THE PROFESSION

Something that I suspect is destined to be a large change, particularly from the point of view of young recruits to our profession, is state regulation of entry. In Chapter 5 we saw that in one particularly sensitive area there have already been government moves towards imposing statutory controls on who is allowed to practise. My prediction is that this will go much further.

---

[2] Quoted by Richard Tyler, 'When it's OK to switch off', *Daily Telegraph* 13 November 2003.
[3] 'Home truths about telecoms', *The Economist Technology Quarterly* 9 June 2007.

Just as it is already against the law (and has been for a long time) to take work as a civil engineer, an architect or a doctor (whether or not one is in fact competent) unless one's name is on a state-approved register of individuals entitled to practise, so I expect the day to come when it will be illegal to take a job in IT unless one is a registered IT practitioner.

And if that day does come, there will be more to getting on to the register than just gaining a qualification from some institution that teaches computer science. As in medicine or engineering now, the qualification will need to be accredited by some external state-recognised institution, there will perhaps be a requirement for a period of supervised practical experience in industry, and so forth; and standards will generally be tightened up.

In fact this is more than a vague surmise. Security is the only IT area where the British government has already made a concrete move towards entry regulation; but already in November 2005 the Cabinet Office eGovernment Unit made a decision in principle to turn public-sector IT into a clearly structured profession. Once that plan comes to fruition, extending statutory requirements into the private sector would be an obvious next step.

Note that I say nothing about whether this will be a good or a bad thing – merely that I believe it will happen. There is an argument that in an area as fast-moving as IT, state regulation of recruitment might interfere with the creative innovation process that British IT needs, if it is to continue flourishing when the more run-of-the-mill work is executed more cheaply in other parts of the world. However, now that the activities of our profession have such a massive impact on almost all aspects of life, I do not see that argument prevailing against the public-welfare argument that nobody should be let loose to practise our profession without a state-enforced guarantee of competence.

Readers may ask whether any paper qualification can really guarantee this. In truth it cannot. But then we know that duly qualified doctors, too, sometimes make dreadful mistakes; yet we do not hear a groundswell of opinion calling for state registration of doctors to be abolished as a waste of resources.

## UNSTRUCTURED DATA

Turning to technological developments: one area that looks set to become much more important in future than it has been to date is unstructured-data processing.

The term 'unstructured data' in this context essentially refers to information held electronically as documents in free-form English prose (or prose in another human language), as opposed to files consisting of known arrays of fields with predictable meanings containing values drawn from predictable ranges. Structured data files are organised so that specific information can easily be extracted automatically; but, broadly speaking, one has to be human in order to be able to read a document written in English.

(Graphics files might also be called 'unstructured data' – it takes a human being rather than a machine to interpret a picture. But in practice this is less of an issue, because electronic graphics files are normally associated with some written material.)

E-mails, letters, reports, manuals and so on add up to a large and growing proportion of the total information held electronically by an organisation (typically about 85 per cent, by one estimate). Furthermore, the unstructured material tends to include the most important data. If structured data on one day's sales were to go missing from a supermarket's data warehouse, that would be regrettable but not tragic – there are plenty of other days, whose overall sales patterns will not be so very different. On the other hand, if the organisation lost all record of a change of business strategy decided at a board meeting that may have lasted much less than a day, or of a contract that took only seconds to sign, it might be in real trouble. Admittedly these extreme possibilities are unrealistic: even if the electronic files containing meeting minutes were destroyed through some mischance, those who attended the meeting would have a memory of it; and a contract will exist on paper as well as in electronic form. That does not alter the point that the most crucial data held by a company tend to be unstructured data.

## THE NEED FOR BETTER TECHNIQUES

Techniques for computer processing of unstructured data are at present fairly primitive and unsatisfactory, and until recently business made little use of them. What is changing that is the imposition on business of new regulatory regimes. The e-discovery requirements discussed on p. 90 are an obvious example. If the laws that have been coming in as a response to Enron, WorldCom and similar scandals survive, rather than being revoked as impractical when memories of those scandals fade, then companies will be vulnerable unless they acquire the ability to find automatically whatever has been said somewhere within their mountains of unstructured data about given topics or issues. That will require much more than merely the ability to extract every document containing a particular keyword. Much research currently is being devoted to systems that process unstructured data in more sophisticated ways.

Here the present author should declare an interest. As it happens, much of my own career has been devoted to linguistics and computational natural-language processing, so a prediction that processing unstructured data is the coming thing may sound self-serving. But in fact the linguistically informed computational techniques with which I have been involved, while they lead to results that are very interesting for our understanding of language as an aspect of human behaviour, have turned out over the past 10 or 20 years to be over-refined in terms of delivering outputs that business can put to practical use. If the unstructured-data problem is solved in a way that is satisfactory from a business viewpoint, I do not expect the methods to be connected closely with my own research.

On the other hand, if such solutions are developed, they will not be relevant only for regulatory compliance. That may be the pressure that is currently driving this activity, but if firms come to have at their disposal good ways of processing unstructured data, they will undoubtedly apply them to many of their own business purposes, unconnected with regulatory demands.

A leading supplier of software for processing unstructured data is the Cambridge-based Autonomy, founded in 1996 and one of the very few world-class British IT companies. Recently, Autonomy has been talking about this area in terms of 'meaning-based computing' (MBC). Its chief executive, Mike Lynch, illustrated the idea in August 2006:

> ... with structured information the point of IT is to automate, so if you are a bank, the database with the account information spots if someone goes overdrawn and then sends them a letter, with no human being involved in the process at all. The aim of MBC is to enable companies to do a similar thing with unstructured information.[4]

Good unstructured data techniques will find many uses. 'Algorithmic share trading' is now a significant fraction of activity on stock markets: companies take and implement buy or sell decisions without human involvement, enabling them to take instant advantage of favourable opportunities before these have time to be reflected in the share price. Apart from the share prices themselves, another type of data feed that is just beginning to be used for algorithmic trading is newswires: if the trading computer can interpret the economic implications of a news item, that will often be very relevant to a buy or sell decision – but it depends on the ability to interpret automatically prose that is designed for human consumption.

We saw in Chapter 11 that automatic 'knowledge management' was for many years a dream that eventually was more or less given up as apparently unachievable. But the idea that what makes an organization more than just a jumble of disconnected people, buildings and equipment is the knowledge held within it in a diffusely distributed fashion remains a persuasive one. Successful techniques for processing unstructured data might go some way towards converting the knowledge-management vision into reality.

---

[4] Quoted by James Murray, 'What is meaning-based computing?', *IT Week* 21 August 2006.

## ENVOI

So much for peering into the future from the first decade of the new millennium. Many readers will discover at first hand how e-business actually develops over the decades to come. No doubt, with hindsight, they will find the foregoing paragraphs quaint.

I sincerely hope that they will nevertheless have found this book helpful, as they develop from onlookers into participants in the evolution of e-business. And I offer them my best wishes for enjoyable as well as remunerative careers.

# References

Abbreviations for frequently cited serial titles:

*CACM*: *Communications of the Association for Computing Machinery*
*HBR*: *Harvard Business Review*

Ammann, J., J.M. González-Barahona, and P. de las Heras Quirós, eds. (2001). *Free Software/Open Source: towards maturity*. Special issue of *Upgrade*, vol. 2, part 6.

Barnes, S. and B. Hunt, eds. (2001). *E-Commerce and V-Business: business models for global success*. Butterworth-Heinemann.

Battelle, J. (2005). *The Search: how Google and its rivals rewrote the rules of business and transformed our culture*. Nicholas Brealey.

Baye, M.R. and J. Morgan (2003). 'Red Queen pricing effects in e-retail markets'. BayeMorganRedQ.notlong.com.

Blackstaff, M. (2001). *Business and Finance for IT People*. Springer.

Boldrin, Michele and D.K. Levine (2006). 'Perfectly competitive innovation'. Federal Reserve Bank of Minneapolis Staff Report 303.

Bonabeau, E. (2004). 'The perils of the imitation age'. *HBR* Jun 2004, 45–54.

Brin, D. (1998). *The Transparent Society: will technology force us to choose between privacy and freedom?* Perseus Books.

Brooks, F.P. (1975). *The Mythical Man-Month: essays on software engineering*. Addison-Wesley.

Brynjolfsson, E., L.M. Hitt, and S. Yang (2002). 'Intangible assets: computers and organizational capital'. *Brookings Papers on Economic Activity* 2002.137–81.

Brynjolfsson, E., T.W. Malone, V. Gurbaxani, and A. Kambil (1994). 'Does information technology lead to smaller firms?' *Management Science* 40.1628–44.

Cairncross, Frances (2002). *The Company of the Future: how the communications revolution is changing management*. Harvard Business School Press.

Carr, D., A. Gray, E. Watkins, and G. Yang (2000). 'Amazon one-click shopping'. CGWY1click.notlong.com.

Carr, N.G. (2003). 'IT doesn't matter'. *HBR* May 2003, 41–9.

Carr, N.G. (2004). *Does IT Matter? Information technology and the corrosion of competitive advantage.* Harvard Business School Press.

Castronova, E. (2001). 'Virtual worlds: a first-hand account of market and society on the cyberian frontier'. CESifo Working Paper 618, University of Munich, December 2001.

Castronova, E. (2005a). *Synthetic Worlds: the business and culture of online games.* University of Chicago Press.

Castronova, E. (2005b). 'Real products in imaginary worlds'. *HBR* May 2005, 20–22.

Cellan-Jones, R. (2001). *Dot.bomb: the rise and fall of dot.com Britain.* Aurum Press.

Chaffey, D. (2007). *E-Business and E-Commerce Management: strategy, implementation and practice,* 3rd edn. Prentice Hall/Financial Times.

Chircu, Alina N. and R.J. Kauffman (2001). 'Digital intermediation in electronic commerce: the eBay model'. In Barnes and Hunt (2001).

Coase, R.H. (1937). 'The nature of the firm'. *Economica* n.s. 4.386–405; reprinted in R.H. Coase, *The Firm the Market and the Law,* University of Chicago Press, 1988, and in Williamson and Winter (1993).

Cooper, R. and W.B. Chew (1996). 'Control tomorrow's costs through today's designs'. *HBR* Jan–Feb 1996, 88–97.

Cotteleer, M., E. Inderrieden, and Felissa Lee (2006). 'Selling the sales force on automation'. *HBR* Jul–Aug 2006, 18–22.

Cringeley, R.X. (1996). *Accidental Empires: how the boys of Silicon Valley make their millions, battle foreign competition, and still can't get a date,* new edn. Penguin.

Davenport, T.H. (1998). 'Putting the enterprise into the enterprise system'. *HBR* Jul–Aug 1998, 121–31.

Davenport, T.H. (2000). *Mission Critical: realizing the promise of enterprise systems.* Harvard Business School Press.

Davenport, T.H. (2006). 'Competing on analytics'. *HBR* Jan 2006, 99–107.

Dhamija, R., J.D. Tygar, and M. Hearst (2006). 'Why phishing works'. In *Proceedings of the Conference on Human Factors in Computing Systems (CHI2006),* Montreal.

Dibbell, J. (2006). *Play Money: or, how I quit my day job and made millions trading virtual loot.* Basic Books.

Downes, L. (2004). 'First, empower all the lawyers'. *HBR* Dec 2004, 19.

Downes, L. and C. Mui (1998). *Unleashing the Killer App.* Harvard Business School Press.

Drucker, P.F. (1992). 'The new society of organizations'. *HBR* Sep–Oct 1992, 95–104; reprinted in P.F. Drucker, *On the Profession of Management*, Harvard Business School Press, 1998.

Easterly, W. and R. Levine (2003). 'Tropics, germs, and crops: how endowments influence economic development'. *Journal of Monetary Economics* 50.3–39.

Edelman, B. (2006). 'Adverse selection in online "trust" certifications'. EdelmanAdverse.notlong.com

Epstein, J.M. and R.L. Axtell (1996). *Growing Artificial Societies: social science from the bottom up.* MIT Press.

Evans, P. and R. Wolf (2005). 'Collaboration rules'. *HBR* Jul–Aug 2005, 96–104.

Farrell, Diana (2003). 'The *real* new economy'. *HBR* Oct 2003, 104–12.

Feld, C.S. and Donna B. Stoddard (2004). 'Getting IT right'. *HBR* Feb 2004, 72–9.

Ferry, Georgina (2003). *A Computer Called LEO: Lyons teashops and the world's first office computer.* Fourth Estate.

Fridensköld, Emilie (2004). 'VAT and the Internet: the application of consumption taxes to e-commerce transactions'. *Information and Communications Technology Law* 13.175–203.

Friedman, Batya, P.H. Kahn, and D.C. Howe (2000). 'Trust online'. *CACM* Dec 2000, 35–40.

Fukuyama, F. (1995). *Trust: the social virtues and the creation of prosperity.* Free Press.

Gelbord, B. (2000). 'Signing your 011001010'. *CACM* Dec 2000, 27–8.

Ghosh, R.A. (2007). *Economic Impact of Open Source Software on Innovation and the Competitiveness of the Information and Communication Technologies (ICT) Sector in the EU.* GhoshReport.notlong.com.

Glaeser, E.L., R. La Porta, F. Lopez-de-Silanes, and A. Shleifer (2004). 'Do institutions cause growth?' Working Paper 10568, National Bureau of Economic Research.

Gloor, P. (2000). *Making the e-Business Transformation.* Springer.

Goldfinger, C. (1997). 'Intangible economy and its implications for statistics and statisticians'. *International Statistical Review* 65.191–220.

Goolsbee, A. (2000). 'In a world without borders: the impact of taxes on Internet commerce'. *Quarterly Journal of Economics* 115.561–76.

Gordon, R.J. (2000). 'Does the new economy measure up to the great inventions of the past?' *Journal of Economic Perspectives* 4.49–74.

Gordon, R.J. (2004). 'Five puzzles in the behavior of productivity, investment, and innovation'. In A. Lopez-Claros and X. Sala-i-Martin, eds., *The Global Competitiveness Report 2003–04*, Oxford University Press.

Hagel, J. and A.G. Armstrong (1997). *Net Gain: expanding markets through virtual communities*. Harvard Business School Press.

Hagel, J. and J.S. Brown (2001). 'Your next IT strategy'. *HBR* Oct 2001, 105–13.

Hannemyr, G. (2003). 'The internet as hyperbole'. *The Information Society* 19.111–21.

Harford, T. (2006). 'Pop goes the econ'. *The Chronicle of Higher Education*, 10 Feb 2006, B15.

Harrison, R. (2007). 'SecondLife: revolutionary virtual market or Ponzi scheme?' *Capitalism 2.0*, 23 Jan 2007, Harrison07.notlong.com.

Harvey-Jones, J. (1988). *Making It Happen: reflections on leadership*. Fontana/Collins.

Hitt, L.M. (1999). 'Information technology and firm boundaries: evidence from panel data'. *Information Systems Research* 10.134–49.

Hjelm, J. (2000). *Designing Wireless Information Services*. Wiley.

Huang, H., Claudia Keser, J. Leland, and J. Shachat (2003). 'Trust, the Internet, and the digital divide'. *IBM System Journal* 42.507–18.

Humby, C. and T. Hunt (2007). *Scoring Points*, 2nd edn. Kogan Page.

Jewkes, J. (1977). 'Delusions of Dominance: a critique of the theory of large-scale industrial dominance and of the pretence of government to "restructure" British industry'. Hobart Paper 76. Institute of Economic Affairs.

Johnston, R.B., H.C. Mak, and Sherah Kurnia (2001). 'The contribution of Internet electronic commerce to advanced supply chain reform – a case study'. In Barnes and Hunt (2001).

Kalakota, R. and Marcia Robinson (2001). *E-Business 2.0: roadmap for success*. Addison-Wesley.

Kalakota, R. and Marcia Robinson (2002). *M-Business: the race to mobility*. McGraw-Hill.

Kannan, P.K., Ai-Mei Chang, and A.B. Whinston (2001). 'E-business and the intermediary role of virtual communities'. In Barnes and Hunt (2001).

Keen, A. (2007). *The Cult of the Amateur: how today's internet is killing our culture and assaulting our economy*. Nicholas Brealey.

Keen, P.G.W. and R. Mackintosh (2001). *The Freedom Economy: gaining the mcommerce edge in the era of the wireless internet*. Osborne/McGraw-Hill.

Landauer, T.K. (1995). *The Trouble with Computers: usefulness, usability, and productivity*. MIT Press.

Larose, D.T. (2005). *Discovering Knowledge in Data: an introduction to data mining*. Wiley.

Lee, H.L. (2004). 'The triple-A supply chain'. *HBR* Oct 2004, 102–12.

Lessig, L. (2002). *The Future of Ideas: the fate of the commons in a connected world*. Vintage Books.

Levine, R., C. Locke, D. Searls, and D. Weinberger (2000). *The Cluetrain Manifesto: the end of business as usual*. Perseus Books.

Levy, S. (1984). *Hackers: heroes of the computer revolution*. Dell.

Levy, S. (2000). *Crypto: secrecy and privacy in the new code war*. Allen Lane.

Liebowitz, S.J. (2002). *Re-Thinking the Network Economy: the true forces that drive the digital marketplace*. Amacom.

Lipnack, Jessica and J. Stamps (1998). 'Why virtual teams?' In P. Lloyd and Paula Boyle, eds., *Web-Weaving: intranets, extranets and strategic alliances*, Butterworth-Heinemann.

Lloyd, I.J. (2004). *Information Technology Law*, 4th edn. Oxford University Press.

McAfee, A. (2005). 'Will Web services *really* transform collaboration?' *MIT Sloan Management Review* Winter 2005, 78–84.

McGrath, Rita G. and Ian C. MacMillan (2005). 'Market busting: strategies for exceptional business growth'. *HBR* March 2005, 81–9.

McVoy, L. (1993). 'The sourceware operating system proposal: revision 1.8', milquerz.notlong.com.

Majchrzak, Ann, A. Malhotra, J. Stamps, and Jessica Lipnack (2004). 'Can absence make a team grow stronger?' *HBR* May 2004, 131–7.

Malone, T.W. (2004). 'Bringing the market inside'. *HBR* Apr 2004, 107–14.

Malone, T.W., Joanne Yates, and R.I. Benjamin (1987). 'Electronic markets and electronic hierarchies'. *CACM* Jun 1987, 484–97.

Manasian, D. (2003). 'Digital dilemmas: a survey of the internet society'. Supplement to *The Economist* 25 Jan 2003.

Marcus, J. (2004). *Amazonia*. The New Press.

Microsoft (2007). *Developing the Future 2007: a report on the challenges and opportunities facing the UK software development industry*. DevFuture2007.notlong.com.

Miers, D. (2005). 'BPM – too much BP, not enough of the M'. In Layna Fischer, ed., *Workflow Handbook 2005*, Future Strategies Inc.

Moody, G. (2002). *Rebel Code: Linux and the open source revolution*, new edn. Penguin.

Moore, G.A. (1999). *Crossing the Chasm: marketing and selling technology products to mainstream customers*, 2nd edn. Capstone.

Morville, P. and L. Rosenfeld (2006). *Information Architecture for the World Wide Web: designing large-scale Web sites*, 3rd edn. O'Reilly.

Mougayar, W. (1998). *Opening Digital Markets: battle plans and business strategies for internet commerce*, 2nd edn. McGraw-Hill.

Murphy, A. (2003). 'The Web, the grocer and the city: on the (in)visibility of grounded virtual retail capital'. Working Papers in Services, Space, Society no. 10, University of Birmingham.

Narayanan, V.G. and A. Raman (2004). 'Aligning incentives in supply chains'. *HBR* Nov 2004, 94–102.

Needle, D. (2004). *Business in Context: an introduction to business and its environment*, 4th edn. Thomson Learning.

Niederst Robbins, Jennifer (2006). *Web Design in a Nutshell: a desktop quick reference*, 3rd edn. O'Reilly.

Nohria, N., W. Joyce, and B. Roberson (2003). 'What really works'. *HBR* Jul 2003, 43–52.

Norris, G., J.R. Hurley, K.M. Hartley, J.R. Dunleavy, and J.D. Balls (2000). *E-Business and ERP: transforming the enterprise.* Wiley.

O'Neill, Onora (2002). *A Question of Trust: the BBC Reith Lectures 2002.* Cambridge University Press.

Odlyzko, A. (2004). 'Privacy, economics, and price discrimination on the internet'. In L. Jean Camp and S. Lewis, eds., *Economics of Information Security*, Kluwer.

Oellermann, W.L. (2001). *Architecting Web Services.* Apress.

Ohno T. (1988). *Toyota Production System: beyond large-scale production.* Productivity Press.

Packard, V.O. (1957). *The Hidden Persuaders.* Longmans, Green.

Perez, Carlota (2002). *Technological Revolutions and Financial Capital: the dynamics of bubbles and golden ages.* Edward Elgar.

Pfeffer, J. and R.I. Sutton (2006). 'Evidence-based management'. *HBR* Jan 2006, 63–74.

Rapaille, G.C. (2006). 'Leveraging the psychology of the salesperson'. *HBR* Jul–Aug 2006, 42–7.

Raymond, E.S. (2001). *The Cathedral and the Bazaar: musings on Linux and open source by an accidental revolutionary*, revised edn. O'Reilly. Online at catb.org/~esr/writings/

Rayport, J.F. and B.J. Jaworski (2004). 'Best face forward'. *HBR* Dec 2004, 47–58.

Resnick, P., R. Zeckhauser, E. Friedman, and K. Kuwabara (2000). 'Reputation systems'. *CACM* Dec 2000, 45–8.

Rheingold, H. (1993). *The Virtual Community: homesteading on the electronic frontier*. Addison-Wesley.

Rice, J.B. and R.M. Hoppe (2001). 'Supply chain vs. supply chain: the hype & the reality'. *Supply Chain Management Review* Sep–Oct 2001, 47–53.

Rigby, D.K. and Dianne Ledingham (2004). 'CRM done right'. *HBR* Nov 2004, 118–29.

Romer, P. (1994). 'New goods, old theory, and the welfare costs of trade restrictions'. *Journal of Development Economics* 43.5–38.

Sampson, G.R. (2003). 'The myth of diminishing firms'. *CACM* Nov 2003, 25–8.

Sampson, G.R. (2006). 'Economic and social implications of business-process automation strategies'. In *Frontiers of e-Business Research 2005, Proceedings of eBRF 2005*, Tampere (Finland), 2006.

Schoder, D., R. Strauss, and P. Welchering (1998). *Electronic Commerce Enquête 1997/98: survey on the business uses of electronic commerce for companies in the German speaking world*. Konradin-Verlag.

Schumpeter, J.A. (1943). *Capitalism, Socialism and Democracy*. Allen & Unwin. 5th edn, 1976.

Scoble, R. and S. Israel (2006). *Naked Conversations: how blogs are changing the way businesses talk with customers*. Wiley.

Seybold, Patricia B. (2006). *Outside Innovation: how your customers will co-design your company's future*. Collins.

Shirky, C. (2007). 'In defense of "ready, fire, aim"'. *HBR* Feb 2007, 52–4.

Siegel, D. (1997). *Creating Killer Web Sites*, 2nd edn. Macmillan.

Smith, A. (1776). *An Inquiry into the Nature and Causes of the Wealth of Nations*. Glasgow edition, ed. by R.H. Campbell and A.S. Skinner, 2 vols., Clarendon Press, 1976.

Smith, H. and P. Fingar (2003). *IT Doesn't Matter – Business Processes Do: a critical analysis of Nicholas Carr's I.T. article in the Harvard Business Review.* Meghan-Kiffer Press.

Spector, R. (2000). *Amazon.com: Get Big Fast: inside the revolutionary business model that changed the world.* Random House.

Stallman, R. (2001). 'Harm from the Hague'. In Ammann *et al.* (2001).

Sterne, J. (2001). *World Wide Web Marketing: integrating the Web into your marketing strategy,* 3rd edn. Wiley.

Stewart, T.A., ed. (2003). 'Does IT Matter? an HBR debate'. *Harvard Business Review Online,* Jun 2003.

Suarez, F. and G. Lanzolla (2005). 'The half-truth of first-mover advantage', *HBR* Apr 2005, 121–7.

Symonds, M. (2003). *Softwar: an intimate portrait of Larry Ellison and Oracle.* Simon & Schuster.

Tiffin, N. and R. Müller (2001). 'GNU enterprise application software'. In Ammann *et al.* (2001).

Trailer, B. and J. Dickie (2006). 'Understanding what your sales manager is up against'. *HBR* Jul–Aug 2006, 48–55.

Wallis, J.J. and D.C. North (1988). 'Measuring the transaction sector in the American economy'. In S. Engerman and R. Gallman, eds., *Long Term Factors in American Economic Growth,* University of Chicago Press.

Warsh, D. (2006). *Knowledge and the Wealth of Nations: a story of economic discovery.* W.W. Norton.

Weber, S. (2004). *The Success of Open Source.* Harvard University Press.

Weintraut, J.N. (1997). Introduction to R.H. Reid, *Architects of the Web: 1,000 days that built the future of business,* Wiley.

Whiteley, D. (2004). *Introduction to Information Systems: organisations, applications, technology and design.* Palgrave Macmillan.

Williamson, O.E. and S.G. Winter, eds. (1993). *The Nature of the Firm: origins, evolution, and development.* Oxford University Press, paperback edn.

Winter, S.G. (1993). 'On Coase, competence, and the corporation'. In Williamson and Winter (1993).

Wishart, A. and Regula Bochsler (2002). *Leaving Reality Behind: the battle for the soul of the internet.* Fourth Estate.

Zhang, Ivy X. (2005). 'Economic consequences of the Sarbanes–Oxley Act of 2002'. AEI-Brookings Joint Center for Regulatory Studies Related Publication 05-07, ZhangECSO.notlong.com.

# Index